Brigham Henry Roberts

The Gospel

An Exposition of its First Principles

Brigham Henry Roberts

The Gospel
An Exposition of its First Principles

ISBN/EAN: 9783337280659

Printed in Europe, USA, Canada, Australia, Japan

Cover: Foto ©Lupo / pixelio.de

More available books at **www.hansebooks.com**

THE GOSPEL.

AN

EXPOSITION OF ITS FIRST PRINCIPLES.

BY

ELDER B. H. ROBERTS,

Author of Life of John Taylor; Outlines of Ecclesiastical
History; New Witnesses, Etc.

Revised and Enlarged Edition.

PUBLISHED BY
GEORGE Q. CANNON & SONS CO.,
SALT LAKE CITY, UTAH.
1893.

"Religion, my honored friend, is surely a simple business, as it equally concerns the ignorant and the learned, the poor and the rich."—Burns.

COPYRIGHT 1893:—BY B. H. ROBERTS.

PREFACE TO THE FIRST EDITION.

THIS work has been written for the purpose of instructing the youth of Zion in the first principles of the gospel.

For the most part our parents have been converted to the gospel while living in the various States of this country, or in foreign lands, by the preaching of the servants of God sent forth of him to proclaim the ushering in of the Dispensation of the Fullness of Times, and to call mankind to repentance. They carefully and thoroughly examined every principle advanced by them; for notwithstanding the doctrines taught by the Elders were older than the earth, and in various dispensations have been expounded by prophets and apostles whose testimony is recorded in the Bible, yet something in the spirit by which they were proclaimed, and the manner in which they were combined, made them a new gospel—a new religion.

Not only did our parents hear the public discourses of the servants of God, but in the home circle—to which they invited the teachers of the seemingly New Faith—the gospel, the harmony and beauty of its principles, the consistent blending in it of justice and mercy, its sanctifying influence upon the human character, its spirit and powers, were all common topics of their conversation; until they not only intellectually assented to it as a grand system of truth, but also became imbued with its spirit, and felt and enjoyed its powers.

With the youth of Zion it has been different. Being removed from the errors of the sectarian world, it has been thought they would accept the gospel as a matter of course. It may be stated as a general truth, that too much in this respect has been taken for granted; and in too many instances our youth have not been instructed so thoroughly in the things of God as they ought to have been. Many have grown up in lamentable ignorance of even the First Principles of the gospel—which ignorance is often confounded with unbelief, or mistaken for infidelity.

To such the gospel has only to be presented intelligently, and in its native simplicity, to be accepted. "Whoever examined our religion," said one of the Fathers of the early Christian Church, "but what he accepted it?" So now: the Gospel has only to be understood to be admired and believed.

It is to place within their reach a thorough exposition of the First Principles of the gospel that this work has been prepared, and is now presented to the youth of Zion: and it is the earnest hope of the author that by a patient perusal of these pages those who now believe the gospel will find their faith strengthened and confirmed; and those who do not believe it, be convinced of its truth.

It is but fair to the writer to say that the work has been written amid the busy scenes of missionary life in a foreign land. Its preparation has been frequently interrupted by travel, and the performance of many other duties requiring the writer's attention. If this work, therefore, in point of excellence shall fall below what was desired by the General Superintendency of the Mutual Improvement Associations, at whose instigation it was written, it is hoped these circumstances will in some degree excuse it.

THE AUTHOR.

PREFACE TO THE SECOND EDITION.

I HAD determined in the second edition of this work to very much alter its general plan and enlarge it; but a number of friends who have used "The Gospel" as a text-book in our Church schools, in Improvement Associations and theological classes, persuaded me not to materially change or too much enlarge it. Their experience in using the little work as a text-book gives weight to their opinions, and I have so far yielded to their judgment that I have made but few changes, and those merely verbal, in this edition of the book.

I have, however, added as a supplement, a series of articles originally written for *The Contributor*, on "Man's Relationship to Deity." Those articles were intended in the first place to be supplemental to "The Gospel," and as the theme has a close relation to the subject of which the work treats, I thought it would increase the interest in the whole subject to publish them in this edition.

THE AUTHOR.

CONTENTS.

	Page.
CHAPTER I.—Introductory	9
CHAPTER II.—General Salvation	11
CHAPTER III.—General Salvation	18
CHAPTER IV.—General Salvation	23
CHAPTER V.—Individual Salvation	31
CHAPTER VI.—Principles and Ordinances	43
CHAPTER VII.—Faith	50
CHAPTER VIII.—Faith.—The Bible	57
CHAPTER IX.—Faith.—The Old Testament	69
CHAPTER X.—Faith.—The New Testament	76
CHAPTER XI.—Faith.—The New Testament	82
CHAPTER XII.—Faith.—The New Testament	94
CHAPTER XIII.—Faith.—Tradition	105
CHAPTER XIV.—Faith.—Revelation	112
CHAPTER XV.—Faith.—The Character of God	125
CHAPTER XVI.—Faith.—Course of Life	135
CHAPTER XVII.—Repentance	146
CHAPTER XVIII.—Repentance	151
CHAPTER XIX.—Repentance.—Historical Illustration	159
CHAPTER XX.—Repentance.—Historical Illustration	164
CHAPTER XXI.—Baptism	175
CHAPTER XXII.—Object of Baptism	187
CHAPTER XXIII.—The Subjects for Baptism	199
CHAPTER XXIV.—The Mode of Baptism	207
CHAPTER XXV.—The Holy Ghost	215
CHAPTER XXVI.—The Holy Ghost.—Who May Receive It	221
CHAPTER XXVII.—The Holy Ghost.—How Imparted	227
CHAPTER XXVIII.—The Holy Ghost.—Character and Source	237
CHAPTER XXIX.—The Holy Ghost.—Its Power	245
CHAPTER XXX.—Authority	252
CHAPTER XXXI.—Laws of Spiritual Development	261
CHAPTER XXXII.—History of the Gospel	265
CHAPTER XXXIII.—Salvation for the Dead	279
CONCLUSION	293
SUPPLEMENT.—Man's Relationship to Deity	295

THE GOSPEL.

CHAPTER I.

INTRODUCTORY.

IN the investigation of any subject, it is of first importance that the terms employed be thoroughly understood; hence, I begin the subject in hand by asking and answering the question, What is the Gospel? The definition to the term I shall derive from the scriptures; not from one passage alone, but from the consideration of a number of passages.

The Apostle Paul, in defining the Gospel, calls it: "The power of God unto salvation to every one that believeth."*

From other scriptures, to be considered presently, we shall see that Paul could not have meant a mere intellectual assent to the truth of the several principles composing the Gospel, but an active, living faith in them—a belief which accepts them, not in theory only, but in practice also—a belief which leads up to an implicit obedience to the ordinances and precepts of the Gospel. It is only such a belief that can make

---

* Rom i: 16.

the Gospel the power of God unto salvation. In proof of this I call attention to the following scriptures: "Not every one that saith unto me, Lord, Lord, shall enter into the kingdom of heaven; but he that doeth the will of my Father which is in heaven. * * * Therefore whosoever heareth these sayings of mine, and doeth them, I will liken him unto a wise man, which built his house upon a rock: and the rain descended, and the floods came, and the winds blew, and beat upon that house; and it fell not: for it was founded upon a rock. And every one that heareth these sayings of mine, and doeth them not, shall be likened unto a foolish man, which built his house upon the sand: and the rain descended, and the floods came, and the winds blew, and beat upon that house; and it fell: and great was the fall of it."*

"Wherefore lay apart all filthiness and superfluity of naughtiness, and receive with meekness the engrafted word, which is able to save your souls. But be ye doers of the word and not hearers only, deceiving your own selves."†

And now to come to a passage which must set at rest forever all controversy on the question. In speaking of Jesus, the writer of the book of Hebrews says: "Though he were a son, yet learned he obedience through the things which he suffered, and being made perfect, he became

---

* Matt. vii: 21, 24-27.   † James i: 21, 22.

the author of eternal salvation unto all them that obey him."* Not to those who do not obey him.

From these scriptures we deduce the following definition: The Gospel is the power of God unto salvation unto every one who believes and obeys it.

CHAPTER II.

GENERAL SALVATION.

HAVING defined what the Gospel is, it is my purpose now, for convenience, to separate the subject into two grand divisions. These I shall call respectively: General Salvation, and Individual Salvation.

By General Salvation, I mean a salvation that is as universal as the race of man; that will extend to the sinner as well as to the saint; to the unbeliever, as well as to him who believes; to the impenitent, as well as to the penitent; in short, a salvation that is secured to every son and daughter of Adam, irrespective of his or her belief or unbelief, obedience or disobedience.

By Individual Salvation, I mean a salvation from certain consequences that result from transgressing one or more of God's holy laws; a salvation secured by complying with certain condi-

---

* Heb. v: 8, 9.

tions specified in the Gospel of Jesus Christ, and which can only be secured to those who fulfill said conditions.

First, then, as to General Salvation: Whatever mystery may hang over man's existence, he is conscious of these two facts: first, that he does exist; and second, judging from all human experience, as well as by the decrees of God, the time will come when he will die. No matter how strong the body, how perfect the health, or how buoyant the spirit, man knows that sooner or later time will sap the vital forces, unbend the body's strength, and in a few years the all-beholding sun shall see him no more in all his course.

The experience of the race proves that man is dust, and to dust he must return. It is true that a few, for the time being, have escaped this fate, through being translated by the special providence of God; as in the case of Enoch and many of his people;* the prophet Elijah;† the three Nephite apostles,‡ and also John, the apostle.§ But even those who have attained this peculiar privilege, will doubtless yet have to pass through the mysterious change we call death, in order that the decrees of God may be fulfilled. This calamity of death, then, falls upon all mankind;

---

* Pearl of Great Price pp. 18, 19, 22.　† II. Kings, ii. Doc. and Cov. Sec. cx. 13.　‡ III. Nephi xxviii: 7-33.　§ St. John xxi: 21-25, Doc. and Cov. Sec. vii.

and it was brought into the world through no act of theirs.

Adam transgressed the commandments given to him by his God; and through that act, sowed the seeds of death, and became mortal, and his progeny inherited, as a legacy, that mortality, and so death passed upon all mankind. And since death was brought upon mankind through no act or fault of theirs, justice demands that they should receive full and complete redemption from that evil which falls upon them through the acts of another, over which they had no control.

Such redemption has been wrought out through the Atonement of Jesus Christ; and, in proof that that redemption from the consequences of Adam's transgression is universal, extending alike to the righteous and unrighteous, I cite the following scripture: "And many of them that sleep in the dust of the earth, shall awake, some to everlasting life, and some to shame and everlasting contempt."*

From this it appears that not only the righteous —those who are worthy of everlasting life—are to come forth from their graves, but also the wicked—those worthy only of shame and everlasting contempt. To this agrees the testimony of Jesus, "For as the Father hath life in himself; so hath he given to the Son, life in himself. * * * Marvel not at this; for the hour is coming, in

---

Dan. xii : 2.

the which all that are in their graves shall hear his voice, and shall come forth; they that have done good unto the resurrection of life, and they that have done evil unto the resurrection of damnation."* Or, as the last two clauses were given to the Prophet Joseph Smith, by inspiration: "They who have done good in the resurrection of the just, and they who have done evil in the resurrection of the unjust."†

This, too, is in harmony with Paul's teaching, pronounced on the occasion of his defense before Felix: "After the way which they call heresy, so worship I the God of my fathers, believing all things which are written in the law and in the prophets; and have hope towards God, which they themselves aslo allow, that there shall be a resurrection of the dead, both of the just and the unjust."‡

If it were necessary to add anything more to this array of testimony, it would be found in the words of John the Revelator. In the twentieth chapter of Revelations is given an account, first, of the resurrection of the just, and their reign of peace upon the earth for a thousand years; and then follows a description of the general resurrection, in which the writer says: "And I saw the dead, small and great, stand before God. * * * And the sea gave up the dead which were in it;

---

* John v: 26, 28, 29.   † Doc. and Cov. Sec. lxxv: 16, 17.   ‡ Acts xxiv: 14, 15.

and death and hell delivered up the dead which were in them, and they were judged every man according to his works."*

It is certain, then, that the resurrection of the dead is universal, extending alike to all classes and races of men. And thus there is a general salvation from the consequences of Adam's fall. "For as by the offense of one (Adam) judgment came upon all men to condemnation; even so by the righteousness of one (Christ) the free gift came upon all men to the justification of life."† And again, "Since by man came death, by man came also the resurrection of the dead. For as in Adam all die, even so in Christ shall *all* be made alive."‡

The reader will observe that the redemption is as universal as the fall. If it were possible, still more explicit is the testimony of the Book of Mormon on this subject of man's redemption, as will be seen from the following passages: "And he (Christ) shall come into the world to redeem his people; and he shall take upon him the transgressions of those who believe on his name; and these are they that shall have eternal life, and salvation cometh to none else; therefore the wicked remain as though there had been no redemption made, except it be the loosing of the bands of death; for behold, the day cometh that

---

* Rev. xx: 12, 13. † Rom. v: 18. ‡ I. Cor xv: 21, 22.

all shall rise from the dead and stand before God, and be judged according to their works."

"Now there is a death which is called a temporal death; and the death of Christ shall loose the bands of this temporal death, that all shall be raised from this temporal death: the spirit and the body shall be re-united again in its perfect form; both limb and joint shall be restored to its proper frame, even as we now are at this time; and we shall be brought to stand before God, knowing even as we know now, and have a bright recollection of all our guilt. Now, this restoration shall come to all, both old and young, both bond and free, both male and female, both the wicked and the righteous; and even there shall not so much as a hair of their heads be lost; but all things shall be restored to its perfect frame, as it is now, or in the body, and shall be brought and be arraigned before the bar of Christ the Son, and God the Father, and the Holy Spirit, which is one eternal God, to be judged according to their works, whether they be good or whether they be evil."*

"Behold I have given unto you my gospel, and this is the gospel which I have given unto you, that I came into the world to do the will of my Father, because my Father sent me; and my Father sent me that I might be lifted up upon the cross; and after that I had been lifted up

---

* Alma xi: 40, 41, 42, 43, 44.

upon the cross, that I might draw all men unto me; that as I have been lifted up by men, even so should men be lifted up by the Father, to stand before me, to be judged of their works, whether they be good or whether they be evil. And for this cause have I been lifted up; therefore, according to the power of the Father, I will draw all men unto me, that they may be judged according to their works."*

"Behold, he (Christ) created Adam, and by Adam came the fall of man. And because of the fall of man, came Jesus Christ, even the Father and the Son; and because of Jesus Christ, came the redemption of man. And because of the redemption of man, which came by Jesus Christ, they are brought back into the presence of the Lord; yea, this is wherein all men are redeemed, because the death of Christ bringeth to pass the resurrection, which bringeth to pass a redemption from an endless sleep, from which sleep all men shall be awoke by the power of God, when the trump shall sound; and they shall come forth, both small and great, and all shall stand before his bar, being redeemed and loosed from this eternal band of death, which death is a temporal death."†

Still, some of skeptical inclination, will refuse to admit that justice has its perfect development in this scheme of redemption through Christ's

---

*III Nephi xxvii: 13-15. †Moroni ix: 12, 13.

Atonement. They insist that the sin of Adam should not be visited upon his posterity even for a moment. Why should man die? How is it that through the sacrifice of one who is innocent, salvation may be purchased for those under the dominion of death?

CHAPTER III.

GENERAL SALVATION.

IN answer to the questions with which the last chapter closed, I may say that however difficult it may be to comprehend fully all things connected with man's fall, and God's plan for his redemption, we may be assured that the fall was not a blunder, nor was it an accident. The prophet Lehi bowed down under the weight of years, when giving his last testimony and instructions to his son Jacob, said: "Behold, all things have been done in the wisdom of him who knoweth all things. Adam fell that men might be; and men are, that they might have joy."*

All that has befallen man, we may rest assured, is essential to his eternal and perfect happiness. From our limited experience, we know that men learn to appreciate the joys of prosperity by

---

* II Nephi ii: 24, 25.

drinking deeply from the cup of adversity; they learn to prize the boon of health, by languishing upon the bed of affliction; they learn the value of wealth, by experiencing want and poverty; the sweets of life are rendered still more sweet by the draughts of bitterness we are compelled to drink; and the ever intermittent gleams of sunshine are made more bright by the renewing storms which darken the sky; and thus—

> " 'Tis sorrow builds the shining ladder up,
> Whose golden rounds are our calamities."

As it is with these things I have mentioned, so it is in respect to the greatest blessing Deity can bestow upon man—the gift of eternal life. How great that gift, it is difficult for us to understand. It is not to live merely three score years, nor a thousand years, nor ten thousand years, but ETERNALLY; and while

> "The stars shall fade away, the sun himself
> Grow dim with age, and nature sink in years;
> Man shall flourish in immortal youth,
> Unhurt amid the war of elements,
> The wreck of matter and the crash of worlds."—

But in order that his children might know how to prize the greatest of all his gifts, Deity has ordained that they should pass through the dark valley of death; and in the meantime, by passing through this probation we call life, they might have the opportunity of demonstrating before the heavens their integrity to principles of righteousness and truth; and by coming in contact with evil, they might forever prize that which is pure and good; that vice might ever be hideous to them, and virtue lovely—and thus the eternal happiness of man be made secure. Thus with death, as with many other things, that which at times we consider our greatest calamity, turns out to be our greatest good.

As to the second question*—How is it that through the sacrifice of one who is innocent salvation may be purchased for those under the dominion of death?—I will observe, in passing, that what should most concern us, is, not so much *how* it is that such is the case, but is it a *fact*. Is it true that God has etsablished such a scheme of redemption, is what should concern us most.

To that question the blood sprinkled upon a thousand Jewish altars, and the smoke that darkened the heavens for ages from burnt offerings, answers yes. For those sacrifices, and that sprinkled blood were but typical of the great sacrifice to be made by the Messiah.

Even the mythology of heathen nations retains the idea of an atonement that either has been, or is to be made for mankind. Fantastic, distorted, confused; buried under the rubbish of savage superstition it may be, but it nevertheless exists. So easily traced, so distinct is this feature of heathen mythology, that some writers have

---

* See Discourse of J. Taylor, J. of D. vol. 10, p. 114.

endeavored to prove that the gospel plan of redemption was derived from heathen mythology. Whereas the fact is that the Gospel was understood and extensively preached in the earliest ages;* men retained in their tradition a knowledge of those principles or parts of them, and however much they may have been distorted, traces of them may still be found in nearly all the mythologies of the world.

The prophets of the Jewish scriptures answer the foregoing question in the affirmative. The writers of the New Testament make Christ's Atonement the principal theme of their discourses and epistles. The Book of Mormon, speaking as the voice of an entire continent of people, whose prophets and righteous men sought and found God, testifies to the same great fact. The revelations of God as given through the Prophet Joseph Smith are replete with passages confirming this doctrine, and lastly, the Saints who have received this doctrine and walked in obedience to the laws of heaven, bear testimony that the Spirit of God has borne record to their spirits that the Atonement of Christ is a grand reality.

This evidence is more than sufficient, it seems to me, to establish the *fact* of the atonement

---

* See Pearl of Great Price, Writings of Moses, pp. 12 to 31. Gal. iii, 8. Heb iv, 2, in connection with latter part of chap iii. I Cor. x, 1–4. Mediation and Atonement by the late Prest. John Taylor —Appendix.

beyond the possibility of a doubt; and if there are some things in it not within the scope of our comprehension, still there is sufficient foundation for our glorious hope of eternal life through its power; for the evidence proving the fact of that Atonement is sufficient, wanting nothing, either in quality or quantity.

The Atonement is not the only fact which man accepts without being able to comprehend it. Such facts exist all about us. For example, here stands a row of trees; here is the plum tree, the peach, pear, apple, cherry and the apricot. They send their roots down into the same soil; their fibres become interlaced in it; and yet each tree has the mysterious power to draw from the same soil the substances which produce its own peculiar fruit. So it is throughout the vegetable kingdom. But *how* it is that the peach tree produces the peach, while the plum tree, from the same soil, produces the plum; or how one plant produces wheat, while another at its side produces barley, we cannot tell. But there is the fact; and how stupid would he be considered who rejected the fact, because, forsooth, he cannot understand the mysterious powers or forces which produce it!

As Bishop Watson remarks to Sir Edward Gibbon, in the letters which comprise his Apology for Christianity:—"In physics you cannot comprehend the primary cause of anything: not of the light by which you see; nor of the elasticity of the air by which you hear; nor of the fire by which you are warmed. In physiology you cannot tell what first gave motion to the heart, nor what continues it, nor why its motion is less voluntary than the lungs; nor why you are able to move your arms to the right or left by a simple volition; * * * nor comprehend the principle by which your body was at first formed, nor by which it is sustained, nor by which it will be reduced to earth." The list might be indefinitely extended, for the facts in nature which are incomprehensible are more numerous than those of revelation. And yet those who insist that all the facts connected with revelation should be of such a character that they are perfectly comprehended, refuse not to accept the facts in nature because they are incomprehensible. Why cannot they treat with equal fairness the facts of revelation, and leave it to time and further revelation to make that clear which is now obscure?

CHAPTER IV.

GENERAL SALVATION.

UNBELIEVERS delight to represent God, the great Law Giver, as unspeakably cruel in demanding such an Atonement as Christ made for the salvation of the children of men.

But let it be borne in mind that he who made the Atonement did so voluntarily. Testifying to his disciples respecting the matter he says: "Therefore doth my Father love me, because I lay down my life that I may take it up again. No man taketh it from me, but I lay it down of myself. I have power to lay it down and I have power to take it again. This commandment have I received of my Father."*

When his enemies gathered about him,—a former friend betraying him with a kiss,—and Peter prepared to defend him with the sword, he chided him for his rashness, commanding him to put up his sword, and added: "Thinkest thou that I cannot now pray to my Father, and he shall presently give me more than twelve legions of angels? But how then shall the scriptures be fulfilled, that thus it must be?"†

Thus down to the very last moment, it appears that Jesus could have been delivered from the sacrifice had he so willed it. But the principle which was the guiding-star of his life—"Father, not my will, but thy will be done" influenced him in this instance, and he drank of the cup given him of his Father, and wrung out the dregs in agony; but he did it voluntarily, and that, too, out of his great love for mankind.

Among men we sometimes see this willingness

---

* John x. 17, 18. † Matt. xxvi: 53, 54.

to suffer for others. Men there are who would lay down their lives for their friends. In the times when imprisonment for debt was customary in England, we often meet instances where out of pure love and kindness towards his fellows, a man under no obligation whatever to do so, has paid the debts of the unfortunate, satisfied the demands of the law, and set the captive free. It is related of Lord Byron that when he was a lad attending school, a companion of his fell under the displeasure of a cruel, overbearing bully, who unmercifully beat him. Byron happened to be present, but knowing the uselessness of undertaking a fight with the bully, he stepped up to him and asked him how much longer he intended to beat his friend. "What's that to you?" gruffly demanded the bully. "Because," replied young Byron, the tears standing in his eyes, "I will take the rest of the beating if you will let him go."

That partakes to some extent, at least enough so for illustration, of the spirit by which the Son of God was actuated when he offered himself a ransom for mankind, to redeem them from the power and dominion of death, from which they were powerless to free themselves.

There was something more, however, in the suffering of the Messiah than merely the ordinary pangs and terrors of personal death. As stated by the late President John Taylor, "The suffering of the Son of God was not simply the suffering of personal death; for in assuming the position that he did in making an atonement for the sins of the world, he bore the weight, the responsibilities and the burden of the sins of all men, which, to us, is incomprehensible. As stated, 'The Lord your Redeemer suffered death in the flesh; wherefore he suffereth the pains of all men.' And Isaiah says: 'Surely he hath borne our griefs and carried our sorrows;' also, 'The Lord hath laid on him the iniquity of us all;' and again, 'he hath poured out his soul unto death, and he was numbered with the transgressors, and he bear the sins of many;' or, as it is written in the second book of Nephi, 'For behold, he suffereth the pains all men, yea the pains of every living creature, both men, women and children, who belong to the family of Adam;' whilst in Mosiah it is declared, 'he shall suffer temptations and pains of body, hunger, thirst and fatigue, even more than man can suffer, except it be unto death; for behold, blood cometh from every pore so great shall be his anguish for the wickedness and abominations of his people.'"*

By this Atonement of Messiah's there is especially one fact thrown out into bold relief, that is, the great love of God and Christ for mankind. When you come to think of the unspeakable agony, of the anguish of heart, of the pains that racked the body and distressed the mind of the

---

* Mediation and Atonement ch. xxi.

Savior at the time of his betrayal, and during his trial and crucifixion, you may begin to see how great the love of the Father for mankind must be, when he would consent for his only begotten Son to pass through this great humiliation and affliction, in order to redeem mankind from the bonds of death. On such contemplation increased emphasis will be given to the passage —"In this was manifested the love of God towards us, because that God sent his only begotten Son into the world that we might live through him."* And also to this—"For God so loved the world, that he gave his only begotten Son, that whosoever believeth in him should not perish, but have everlasting life. For God sent not his Son into the world to condemn the world, but that the world through him might be saved."†

Then what shall we say for the greatness of the love of the Son of God, who of his own free will volunteered to take upon himself the task of man's redemption! Not only of redeeming him from death, but from the consequences of all sins, that is, on certain conditions, as we shall see further on!

I have often thought that the love of a son for his mother must ever be made stronger, and become more sanctified, through bringing to mind the sufferings which brought her to the very gates of death, to give him life; her subsequent

---
* I. John iv: 9.
† John iii. 16, 17.

devotion, anxiety, toil and watchfulness in the years of his childhood and youth, making her a being "enskyed and sainted," to him. So it is with Christ. The recollection of the love he bears for us as manifested in the sufferings he endured in our stead, for upon him was laid the iniquity of us all, and by his stripes are we to be healed—the recollection, I say, of his excruciating agony in Gethsemane, where he sweat great drops of blood, in the council chamber of the Jews, in the streets of Jerusalem at the hands of the rabble, and finally upon Calvary, in order to satisfy the inexorable claims of justice, must seal and make perfect the bond of love which connects us with him; and bears witness to the world how great, how infinite the love of Christ for us, how great the price paid for our ransom. Well may the Apostle say—"Ye are not your own, for ye are bought with a price."*

In the Atonement made for man, there is a nice balancing of the relative claims of Justice and Mercy. The law given to man being transgressed, Jusice demanded the payment of the penalty, which was death. And as Adam had no power to liberate himself from the captivity thereof, his sleep in the grave must have been eternal; so also with all his posterity to whom his mortality was bequeathed as an evil legacy, had not Mercy put in her claims and prevented Justice from

---

* I Cor. vi. 19, 20.

being cruel. The Son of God having it given him to have life in himself,* and being capable of making an infinite atonement, he stood forth as the great friend of man and offered himself as a sacrifice to satisfy the claims of Justice. That offering was accepted by the great Law Giver, and upon the demands of Justice being satisfied, —the law having no further claim upon him, the captive is set free from the dominion of death.

Mercy is not permitted to rob Justice, but she claims her own. Justice is not permitted to be cruel, but he retains his dignity—his demands are satisfied. As the late President Taylor very beautifully and very truthfully said: "Is justice dishonored? No; it is satisfied; the debt is paid. Is righteousness departed from? No; there is a righteous act. All requirements are met. Is judgment violated? No; its demands are fulfilled. Is mercy triumphant? No; she simply claims her own. Justice, judgment, mercy and truth all harmonize as the attributes of Deity. Justice and truth have met together, righteousness and peace have kissed each other, justice and judgment triumphant as well as mercy and peace; all the attributes of Deity harmonize in this great, grand, momentous, just, equitable, merciful and meritorious act."†

---

* John v: 26.

† Mediation and Atonement, ch. xxiv. To the reader who would make a more thorough investigation of this subject than these pages afford, I refer him to the following passages and works. Book of

Through this Atonement, made by Messiah, a full and complete redemption from the consequences of Adam's transgression is brought about; that is, a victory over the grave is secured; and that, too, through the merits of Jesus Christ. And while the law transgressed by Adam has been vindicated, the posterity of Adam, who became subject to death through his disobedience, are redeemed from the grave without anything being required of them. For as their agency was not concerned in bringing about the mischief, neither is anything demanded of them in order to obtain redemption from it.

So far salvation is free, universal, and unconditional; extending to every man, woman and child who has ever breathed the breath of life. And hence the Prophet Joseph Smith wrote as one of the articles of our faith—"We believe that men will be punished for their own sins, and not for Adam's transgression."

This is what I mean, then, by General Salvation: Free redemption for all mankind through the resurrection from death, which was the great penalty affixed to the law that Adam transgressed. This is what the Atonement of Christ accomplished for man, but this is not all it did, as we

---

Mormon, II Nephi, Chap. ii. Mosiah xv, 18—27. Alma xxxiv, 7—17. Alma xlii, 1—26. Doc. and Cov. Sec. lxxvi, and especially the "Mediation and Atonement" by the late Prest. John Taylor Also Watson's Apology for Christianity, Letter vi. Jenyn's Internal Evidences of the Christian Religion, the concluding chapter.

shall see when we come to speak of Individual Salvation.

Meantime, through the fall, comes our present state of probation; our opportunities for gaining an experience in this life; of coming in contact with good and evil; learning to love the one and despise the other, by seeing them placed in contrast with each other, working out their respective results, to the production of happiness on the one hand, and misery on the other. From which experience we shall learn on what basis rests the eternal felicity of intelligences, and how to perpetuate it throughout the ages yet unborn.

CHAPTER V.

INDIVIDUAL SALVATION.

HAVING dealt with what I called General Salvation, I now turn to Individual Salvation. You have seen that man is redeemed from the evils brought upon him through Adam's sin, without any act of belief or obedience being required of him. This is because his agency or will was not exercised in breaking the law given to Adam. The calamity overtakes him through no fault of his; and consequently his deliverance, so far, comes without his seeking—in fact, it comes independent of him. In this matter, man is passive, being acted upon by the relative claims of Justice and Mercy.

But apart from the transgressions of our first parents, there is a vast amount of sin, crime and corruption in the world. Envy, hatred, malice, contention, evil-speaking, jealousy, and covetousness abound; to say nothing of the greater evils of lying, drunkenness, stealing, fornication, adultery, and debauchery of every description, which would be improper even to name.

Selfishness is the starting point of the present system of industrialism; chicanery and fraud enter into all the avenues of trade; dishonesty walks the streets without shame; licentiousness revels in its own wantonness; whoredoms are poisoning the life's blood of the nations; prostitution flaunts its shame upon the streets, and takes up its abode in the very shadow of the church, where men meet to worship God. Instead of beautifying the earth, man is but making many portions of it sink-holes of iniquity; where poverty, misery, degradation, drunkenness, crime and sin lie festering in their filthiness under the sunlight of heaven, until the very earth is defiled under the inhabitants thereof.

Now, who is responsible for all these evils, this seething mass of iniquity, which blights like a hell-sent plague this fair creation of ours—the earth? I answer that every man and every woman and every child, who has arrived at the years of accountability—who understands the difference between good and evil—is responsible for it, so far, and to that extent that his or her individual acts contribute to the grand aggregate of crime in this sin-stained world.

In the commission of these individual sins, too, man's agency becomes a factor. He sins knowingly, willfully, and sometimes wantonly. He transgresses the laws of God and of nature in spite of the protests of his conscience, the convictions of his reason and the promptings of his judgment. He becomes desperately wicked and so depraved that he actually seeks evil and loves it. He hugs it to his bosom and cries, "Evil, be thou my good; sin, be thou my refuge!"

For the transgression of that law which brought death into the world, Justice had no claims upon the posterity of Adam, because their agency was not concerned in it, hence a free redemption was provided from the calamity that overtakes them. But in the case of these individual sins, where the agency of every person is exercised, justice demands that the penalties affixed to the violated laws be satisfied, and the transgressors punished. But here again the principle of mercy is active. As I have before stated, the victory over death is not the only benefit arising from the Atonement of the Messiah; but by the sacrifice which he made he purchased mankind as an inheritance for himself, and they became of right under his dominion, for he ransomed them from an endless sleep in the grave. Nor is that all, but as the scripture saith: "He hath borne our griefs and carried our sorrows. * * * He was wounded for our transgressions, he was bruised for our iniquities; the chastisement of our peace was upon him; and with his stripes we are healed. * * * The Lord hath laid on him the iniquity of us all."* So that his Atonement not only broke the bonds of death, but also atoned for the individual sins of men on condition of their obedience—their loyalty to Christ, who by virtue of his Atonement redeemed them from endless death, and therefore of right became their law-giver, and had power given him to dictate the terms upon which the full benefits of his Atonement should be applied to individuals, in order to release them from the penalties which follow as a consequence of their personal violations of the principles of righteousness.

First, however, let us settle it in our minds from authority that the Atonement of Christ has this two-fold force that I have ascribed to it, viz.: that it redeems all mankind from death; and also redeems them from the consequences of personal sins, through obedience to Christ.

The first part of the proposition has already been discussed and proven in those chapters devoted to the consideration of General Salvation, and those arguments need not be repeated here.

That the second part is true is evident from

---

* Isaiah liii: 5, 6.

such scripture as: "He that believeth and is baptized shall be saved, and he that believeth not shall be damned;* and, "Being made perfect, he became the author of eternal salvation unto all them that obey him."† But while you are under the necessity of sustaining the proposition, so far as the Jewish Scriptures are concerned, by inference, by conclusions drawn from the consideration of numerous passages, in the Book of Mormon we have passages which at once sustain the doctrine: "And also his blood atoneth for the sins of those who have fallen by the transgression of Adam, who have died not knowing the will of God concerning them, or who have ignorantly sinned. But woe, woe unto him who knoweth that he rebelleth against God; *for salvation cometh to none such, except it be through repentance and faith in the Lord Jesus Christ.*‡

Alma, in answering a question asked him by the lawyer Zeezrom, said of Jesus:—"And he shall come into the world to redeem his people; and he shall take upon him the transgressions of those who believe on his name; and these are they that shall have eternal life, and salvation cometh to none else; therefore the wicked remain as though there had been no redemption made, except it be the loosing of the bonds of death; for behold the day cometh that all shall rise from

---

* Mark xvi. 16. † Heb. v: 16. ‡ Mosiah iii: 11, 12.

the dead and stand before God and be judged according to their works."*

Still more plain in relation to the effect that Messiah's Atonement has upon the personal sins of men, is the word of the Lord through the Prophet Joseph Smith to Martin Harris, warning him to repent lest his sufferings be sore—how sore, how exquisite, how hard to bear he knew not: "For behold, I God, have suffered these things for all that they might not suffer if they would repent, but if they would not repent, they must suffer even as I, which suffering caused myself, even God, the greatest of all, to tremble because of pain, and to bleed at every pore, and to suffer both body and spirit; and would that I might not drink the bitter cup and shrink—nevertheless, glory be to the Father, I partook and finished my preparations unto the children of men."†

These passages to my mind prove the dual character of Messiah's Atonement—the redemption from the consequences of Adam's transgression, from death; and redemption from personal sins on condition of implicit obedience to the laws of Christ—to the gospel, which we have already seen is the power of God unto salvation to everyone who believes and obeys it.

It will doubtless be observed by the attentive

---

* Alma xi: 40, 41. † Doc. and Cov. Sec. xix, 16–18. See also Mosiah iii, 20, 21.

reader that upon this showing those who die before they are capable of knowing good or evil, before they arrive at the years of accountability and who, therefore, are pure and innocent, are saved by the merits of Jesus Christ alone. Being redeemed from the death brought upon them by the fall of Adam, by the Atonement made by Christ, and having committed no personal sins —dying in the days of their innocence—they have nothing to repent of. Having broken no law, Justice has no claim upon them; they fall into the arms of Mercy alone, and there they are secure. Well might Jesus exclaim—"Suffer little children to come unto me, for of such is the kingdom of heaven!" But those who interpret that scripture to mean that little children have to be baptized or perform or have performed for them any other ordinance, in order that they might come unto Christ, or to save them in the kingdom of God, are woefully ignorant of the gospel, and fail to grasp the grandeur, the consistency the perfection there is in it.

It was doubtless these considerations which caused Mormon to say, in writing to his son Moroni: "Listen to the words of Christ your Redeemer, your Lord and your God. Behold I came into the world not to call the righteous but sinners to repentance: the whole need no physician, but they that are sick; wherefore little children are whole for they are not capable of committing sin, wherefore the curse of Adam is taken from them in me, that it hath no power over them; * * * and after this manner did the Holy Ghost manifest the word of God unto me, wherefore my beloved son, I know that it is solemn mockery before God that ye should baptize little children. Behold I say unto you that this thing shall ye teach, repentance and baptism unto those who are accountable and capable of committing sin; yea, teach parents that they must repent and be baptized and humble themselves as their little children, and they shall all be saved with their little children. And their little children need no repentance, neither baptism. * * * Little children are alive in Christ, even from the foundation of the world."*

No less implicit is the word of the Lord through the Prophet Joseph Smith: "But behold I say unto you, that little children are redeemed from the foundation of the world through mine Only Begotten. Wherefore they cannot sin, for power is not given unto Satan to tempt little children, until they begin to become accountable before me."†

Moreover, it appears that Mercy has special claims upon those men and women, and also upon nations and races who know not the laws of God, or have never heard the gospel. The first Nephi in speaking of the Atonement of

---

* Moroni viii, 8-12. † Doc. and Cov. Sec. xxix, 46, 47.

Christ and its effects where proclaimed and rejected, says: "Wherefore he has given a law; and where there is no law given there is no punishment; and where there is no punishment, there is no condemnation; and where there is no condemnation, the mercies of the Holy One of Israel have claim upon them because of the Atonement; for they are delivered by the power of him (Christ); for the Atonement satisfieth the demands of his justice upon all those who have not the law given to them, that they are delivered from that awful monster, death and hell and the devil, and the lake of fire and brimstone (see Alma xii, 17),* which is endless torment; and they are restored to that God who gave them breath, which is the Holy One of Israel."†

And so Moroni: "For the power of redemption cometh on all they that have no law; wherefore he that is not condemned, or he that is under no condemnation cannot repent; and unto such baptism availeth nothing."‡

---

* The torments of the ungodly sinners are likened unto a lake of fire and brimstone by this writer, Nephi—not that sinners are plunged into a lake of fire and brimstone as so-called orthodox Christians teach. Indeed, in the above passages there is a definition of what the lake of fire is—it is "endless torment," which ever exists for the punishment of impenitent sinners—each one partaking of it to such a degree and for such time as is necessary to satisfy the demands of justice. In the very chapter above quoted Nephi says of the wicked: "And their torment is *as* a lake of fire and brimstone, whose flames ascendeth up for ever and ever, and have no end."

† II. Nephi ix, 25, 26. ‡ Moroni viii, 22.

To this also agrees the teachings of Paul: "For as many as have sinned without law shall also perish without law;* and as many as have sinned in the law, shall be judged by the law."†

So also the word of the Lord to Joseph Smith: "And again I say unto you, that whosoever having knowledge, have I not commanded to repent? And he that hath no understanding it remaineth in me to do as it is written."‡

Hence it is that the heathen nations who have had no law given to them, and have died without law, will have part in the first resurrection.§

Still, those who have died without law are placed at this disadvantage; that if they are not under the condemnation of the law, through not having had it delivered to them, neither are they sanctified by the law, and consequently their development in spiritual knowledge and experience is not such as may warrant us in expecting that they are prepared to inherit the same degree of glory with those who have received the law of the gospel, faithfully observed all its requirements, and through their obedience have become sanctified by it, and inherit the celestial glory, the highest of all. Therefore, it is written of those who die without the law: "These are they

---

* I venture the suggestion, basing it on the sense of the whole passage, that it should read: "Shall also be *judged* without the law."

† Rom ii, 12. ‡ Doc. and Cov. Sec. xxix, 49, 50. § Doc. and Cov. Sec. xlv, 54. See also Mosiah xv, 24, 25.

who are of the terrestrial [world], whose glory differs from that of the church of the First Born, who have received the fullness of the Father, even as the moon differs from the sun in the firmament. Behold *these are they who died without law.*"*

I know of nothing that is written, however, which prevents us from believing that they may, eventually, enter the celestial kingdom. Of one thing at least we may rest assured, and that is, that they will receive all the glory, all the exaltation, that their capacity can comprehend and enjoy, and they will be satisfied with the mercy and justice of God.†

But now to return to those to whom the gospel is preached, and who can only hope for salvation from the penalties affixed to sin, by obeying the precepts and ordinances thereof. How far is their obedience taxed? What principles are they to accept, what precepts practice, what ordinances observe?

To the first question I make answer: That since Christ ransomed mankind by his own death and suffering, from an endless sleep in the grave, in order to attain the additional grace of an immunity from the consequences of our personal violations of the laws of righteousness—a forgiveness of sins—man's obedience to him must be implicit and absolute. It is the duty of man

---

* Doc. and Cov. Sec. lxxvi, 71, 72.
† See chapter on Salvation for the Dead.

to obey the whole Gospel, all precepts, all ordinances, as far as they are made known unto him—in short, it is binding on him to live by every word which proceedeth from the mouth of God. In proof of this, I have only to add that when Jesus commanded his appostles to go into the world and preach the Gospel he said: "Go ye therefore and teach all nations, baptizing them in the name of the Father, and of the Son, and of the Holy Ghost: Teaching them to observe *all* things whatsoever I have commanded you"*

There is no one single thing, however great, that man can do and then be under no further obligations to continue to observe the laws of righteousness. The reply of Jesus to the young man who came running to him saying, "Good Master, what good thing shall I do, that I may have eternal life?" was—"If you will enter into life, keep the commandments." The young man asked, "which;" that is, which of the commandments must he keep. And here I will say that by reading a little between the lines it is not difficult to see that the young man had an idea that there was some great thing he could do, and by that one act secure eternal life. But the answer of Jesus dispelled that illusion, for he said:—"Thou shalt do no murder, thou shalt not commit adultery, thou shalt not steal, thou shalt not bear false witness; honor thy father and thy

---

* Matt. xxviii, 19, 20.

mother; and thou shalt love thy neighbor as thyself. The young man sayeth, all these things have I kept from my youth up; what lack I yet? Jesus said unto him, if thou wilt be perfect, go and sell all thou hast and give it to the poor, * * * and come and follow me."*

It will be observed from the foregoing that it was not enough that the young man keep the commandments in the law of Moses, not enough that he sell all that he had and give it to the poor, but he must then come and follow his Master. How much that means! But I shall not particularize, I shall sum up the matter by saying that this case, together with the observations in the preceding chapters, plainly proves that if man would be perfect, if he would obtain the full benefits of Messiah's atonement, complete absolution from his personal violation of holy, righteous laws, as well as deliverance from the grave, his obedience to the laws of Christ—the Gospel, must be implicit, absolute.

CHAPTER VI.

PRINCIPLES AND ORDINANCES.

IN this chapter I shall deal briefly and collectively with those principles that must be accepted, the ordinances that must be observed,

---

* Matt. xix: 16-22.

the precepts that must be followed and the kind of a life that must be led in order to secure a forgiveness of individual sins, and obtain and grow in the favor of heaven—in short, what laws and ordinances man is required to obey in the Gospel of Jesus Christ.

I shall enter into no analysis of the respective principles spoken of, but shall merely point them out, and enter into a more particular consideration of them further on in the work.

Certain it is that faith enters into and forms a part of the Gospel. Men are required to believe in God, and in Jesus Christ: and by that I mean, not merely an assent to their existence, but an acceptance of the whole system of truth revealed by them for man's salvation. Faith of necessity is a factor in the Gospel, because it is the incentive to all action; for unless men believe in God's existence, and in the revelations and commandments which he has given them, they will consider themselves under no obligations to obey him; and hence will neglect the things which concern their salvation. It was the knowledge of this fact, doubtless, which led Paul to say: "He that cometh to God must believe that he is (i.e. exists), and that he is a rewarder of them that diligently seek him."* And Jesus, too, when he said: "If ye believe not that I am he

---

*Heb. xi: 6.

(the Redeemer, the Son of God), ye shall die in your sins."*—had the same thing in his mind.

Hence, I say, faith is of necessity a part of the Gospel, a fundamental principle of it; and therefore much importance is given to it by the writers of Scripture. How great that importance is may be learned from the fact that Jesus said, on the one hand, "He that heareth my word, and believeth on Him that sent me, hath everlasting life, and shall not come into condemnation; but is passed from death unto life":† while on the other hand He said, "He that believeth not shall be damned."‡

Belief in God and in Jesus Christ—in the sense I have described in the foregoing—when once fixed in the mind and heart, leads men to obedience to God's laws. It leads them to repentance and every other good work.

Repentance is made particularly prominent in the scheme of man's salvation. It was taught by John the Baptist in the wilderness of Judea; the main feature of his mission seemed to have been to call men to repentance. It was taught, too, by Messiah himself. On the occasion of some telling him of certain Galileans whose blood Pilate had mingled with their sacrifices, he said: "Suppose ye that these Galileans were sinners above all Galileans, because they suffered these

---

* John viii: 24. † John v: 25. ‡ Mark xvi: 16.

things? I tell you nay; but except ye repent, ye shall all likewise perish."*

Going to the time when the Apostles began to fulfill the mission given to them to preach the Gospel, it will be found that this same principle, in connection with others, is urged upon the acceptance of the people. On that occasion Peter preached a discourse in which he proved from the old Scriptures that Jesus was the Messiah, and in answer to the cries of the people, "Men and brethren, what shall we do?" he answered, "Repent and be baptized every one of you, in the name of Jesus Christ for the remission of sins, and ye shall receive the gift of the Holy Ghost."†

Following this case is another, also recorded in the Acts of the Apostles, in which the Gospel was taught and obeyed by the people of Samaria, under the teachings of one Philip and the apostles Peter and John. In this latter case there is a development of the same principles that were taught on the day of Pentecost. I can do no better than quote the passage which gives the history of the circumstance: " Then Philip went down to the city of Samaria and preached Christ unto them. And the people with one accord gave heed unto those things which Philip spake, hearing and seeing the miracles which he did. For unclean spirits, crying with loud voices,

---

* Luke xiii : 1, 3.   † Acts ii : 38.

came out of many that were possessed with them; and many taken with palsies, and that were lame, were healed. And there was great joy in that city: * * * [and] when they believed Philip preaching the things concerning the kingdom of God, and the name of Jesus Christ, they were baptized, both men and women. * * * Now when the apostles which were at Jerusalem heard that Samaria had received the word of God, they sent unto them Peter and John: who, when they were come down, prayed for them, that they might receive the Holy Ghost (for as yet he was fallen upon none of them; only they were baptized in the name of the Lord Jesus). Then laid they their hands on them, and they received the Holy Ghost."*

The same principles that are here taught—the same ordinances that were observed by the people of Samaria—are enumerated in another scripture, as the "principles of the doctrine of Christ." The language is: "Therefore not†

---

* Acts viii: 5-8, 12, 14-17.

† I quote the passage here as it stands in the inspired translation of the Bible—or, rather, what should be called the inspired revision of the Bible—by the Prophet Joseph, that is, "*not* leaving the principles," etc.; and it seems to me that all must agree that that is right. For, admitting that faith, for instance, is a principle of the doctrine of Christ—and it is enumerated as one in this very passage—how can that principle be left and we go on unto perfection? It is a principle that enters into religious life, no matter how far advanced in all that is excellent the individual may be. It is a principle that underlies the actions of the Gods, and enters into

leaving the principles of the doctrines of Christ, let us go on unto perfection; not laying again the foundation of repentance from dead works, and of faith towards God, of the doctrines of baptisms, and of the laying on of hands, and of resurrection of the dead, and of eternal judgment, and this will we do if God permit."*

It is scarcely necessary for me to say that these doctrines must be accepted, and the ordinances observed by those who would obtain favor with God, and the remission of their sins; for I have already pointed out the fact, that implicit obedience to the law of Christ—the Gospel—is the only means of salvation for man. And furthermore it is written: "Whosoever transgresseth, and abideth not in the doctrine of Christ, hath not God. He that abideth in the doctrine of Christ, he hath both the Father and the Son."†

It would seem, then, that it is binding upon man to receive the whole Gospel, with all its prin-

---

their life and work—" by faith the worlds were made." We might as well admonish the mathematician to leave the fundamental principles of his science and expect him to go on unto perfection. But he cannot do it. The simple principle of addition, subtraction, multiplication and division, enter into his calculations, whatever his advancement in the science of numbers; and in like manner the e fundamental principles of the gospel are connected with our spiritual advancement, and we cannot leave them, and go on to perfection—hence Joseph Smith's rendering must be correct.

* Heb vi: 1-3.   † II. John ix.

ciples, precepts, ordinances and sacraments. And not only are they to be received but the candidate for eternal life should continue therein. He must not be content with being born of the water and of the spirit into the kingdom; he should not forever remain in his childhood in spiritual things: but as the natural child gradually obtains control over the limbs, and makes them obey his will, either to stand erect, walk, or run; and so continues until he develops into the skillful workman whose hand is able to execute whatever his brain conceives—so in spiritual things—those born into the kingdom of God should grow in grace and in the knowledge of the truth. The injunction placed upon those who accept the faith of the Gospel* is that they add to their "faith, virtue; and to virtue, knowledge; and to knowledge, temperance; and to temperance, patience; and to patience, godliness; and to godliness brotherly kindness; and to brotherly kindness, charity. For if these things be in you, and abound, they make you that ye shall neither be barren nor unfruitful in the knowledge of our Lord Jesus Christ."†

Such, in brief, is the Gospel of Jesus Christ as

---

* The reader will observe that the words of Peter which I quote in the above are addressed by him "to them that have obtained like precious faith" with himself—to the Saints (see 1st verse of the chapter quoted), hence I say the injunction is to those who have accepted the Gospel—to the children of the Kingdom.

† II. Peter i: 5-8.

taught by the Messiah and his apostles in Palestine. The same was taught by the prophets and apostles among the Nephites on the western hemisphere. The same is restored to the earth in our day through the revelations of God and the inspired teachings of Joseph Smith, and other men whom the Lord has raised up in this generation. Such are the principles which in the aggregate constitute the power of God unto salvation to those who believe and obey them.

CHAPTER VII.

FAITH.

IT is now my purpose to enter into a more particular consideration of the respective principles and ordinances which constitute the Gospel, or plan of man's salvation.

First in order, both from necessity and because of its importance, is the principle of faith. And following the same method of investigation I adopted at the commencement of this inquiry, *viz*: defining as clearly as I am able, the meaning of the words and terms used, I come to the question, What is faith? And in answer say that it is an assurance in the mind of the existence and reality of things which one has not seen, or which to him have not been demonstrated. It may be an assurance in the mind of the existence of some Being whom we have not seen, but whose works are visible, and who has been seen by others; or it may be of the transpiring of some event at which we were not present, but of which others bear witness; or it may be an assurance of the correctness of certain deductions based upon scientific calculations, though the principles of the science, and the method of dealing with them, by which the conclusions are reached, we neither understand nor are able to follow; in whatever it may be, that assurance of the mind which accepts as truth those things which one has not seen, and does not know for a certainty from his own experience to be absolutely true, is faith. For example, to bring to our aid the assistance of illustration, few, perhaps none of my readers have ever seen the Lord Jesus Christ; yet the writers of the New Testament bear testimony to the reality of his existence, and relate the circumstances which make up his eventful career. The writers of the Book of Mormon do the same in relation to his labors on the western hemisphere; Joseph Smith testifies that, in vision, he saw both Jesus and his Father, in the spring of 1820.* Joseph Smith and Sidney Rigdon bear record that they saw him in February, 1832;† and Oliver Cowdery and Joseph Smith say they

---

* Pearl of Great Price, p. 59.   † Doc. and Cov., sec. 76.

saw him in the Kirtland Temple, in April, 1836.*
These evidences establish an assurance, or faith, in the mind, concerning the existence of Jesus, the Lord.

Again, none of us, and perhaps no one living, was at the battle of Waterloo; yet the fact of that battle taking place is testified to by many historians; no one doubts it, and the evidence in the case is so certain, that one may say he has perfect faith or assurance, approaching almost within the lines of absolute knowledge, that the event transpired—that assurance in the mind is faith.

Still another illustration: Mathematicians claim that they can weigh the earth, and measure the distance between our planet and the sun. One may not be acquainted with the methods of their calculations, or the principles involved in them, yet such is the character and learning of the thoughtful men who make the claim, that we accept their statements and conclusions as true, though we may not be able ourselves to comprehend the science which reveals to them, perhaps to the certainty of demonstration, these facts:—this confidence in their statements—this assurance of the mind, is faith.

Other elements enter into this principle, but at this stage of our investigation, I desire to

---

* Doc. and Cov., sec. 110.

present the subject in its simple rather than in its complex character.

A step further in the investigation of this principle brings us to the consideration of the facts upon which faith rests, or from which it springs. I think a careful reading of the remarks already made in this chapter will lead the reader to see that faith is based upon evidence, upon testimony. It is the evidence we have in the testimonies of the writers of our Scripture, and the prophets of God to which I have alluded, supported to some extent also by the glorious works of nature, that creates in the mind faith in the existence of God. That Paul held these views, that is, that faith is based upon evidence, is clearly seen in this passage: "For whosoever shall call upon the name of the Lord shall be saved. How, then, shall they call on him in whom they have not believed? And how shall they believe in him of whom they have not heard? And how shall they hear without a preacher? And how shall they preach except they be sent? So then faith cometh by hearing, and hearing by the word of God;"* or, in plainer terms—"faith cometh by hearing the word of God."†

Faith is based upon evidence, then, and here I would remark, that the faith will be true or false

---

* Rom. x: 13-17.

† I understand that such is the rendering of this passage—Rom. x: 17—by the Prophet Joseph.

according as the evidence or testimony is truthful or untruthful. Evidence is to faith what the fountain is to the stream; and as an impure fountain cannot send forth pure streams, so incorrect evidence cannot establish a true or profitable faith.

By way of illustration I borrow the following from the Works of Orson Pratt:

"When Europeans first began their explorations in the New World, the Indians whom they met were much amazed at the power and explosive properties of gun-powder, and asked many questions respecting the manner in which it was produced. The Europeans, taking advantage of the ignorance of the savages, and seeing an opportunity to increase their wealth by the deception, told the Indians that it was the seed of a plant which grew in the lands they had come from, and doubtless it would thrive in their land also. The Indians, of course, believed this statement, and purchased the supposed seed, giving in exchange for it large quantities of gold. In implicit faith they carefully planted the supposed seed, and anxiously watched for its sprouting and the appearance of the plant; but it never came. They had faith in the statements made to them by the Europeans, but as these statements were false, and therefore the evidence on which the Indians based their belief untrue, their faith was vain."

Thus must it ever be. Only correct evidence, only truthful testimony can produce fruitful, profitable faith. No matter how sincere one's belief may be in an error, that will not transform the error into truth. The sincere faith of the Indians in what the Europeans had said about the "gun-powder seed" did not make that substance produce a plant yielding gun-powder. And so faith in false doctrines, founded upon false testimony, cannot savor of salvation.

It is also worthy of note, in passing, that the character and intensity of the faith depends largely upon the quality and quantity of the evidence. If a credible witness testifies to any matter of fact, however strange or unusual the fact may be, one would have some degree of faith in it; but if another witness to the fact, equally credible with the first, also testifies to the same thing, one's faith would be greatly increased; and so as the evidence was multiplied the faith would grow, until at last faith would become so perfect that it would pass almost into the domain of knowledge.

So much for faith in general. Now to consider it as a principle of revealed religion. Here it occupies a prominent place. It is the foundation on which religion rests, and the source of all righteousness. In religion, it is in God that faith centers; it is to him that religious faith directs the eyes of man, and bids him hope through Christ to obtain eternal life. And as this is the primary principle in religion, it is my purpose to show from the Scriptures that there is an abundance of evidence which, if carefully considered, will not fail to produce faith in the mind of him who is desirous to know the truth as to the existence of God, the divinity of Christ's mission and the truth of the Gospel.

Before I proceed with that investigation from the Scriptures, however, I think it will be profitable to inquire briefly into the authenticity and credibility of the Scriptures themselves; that is, as to the Jewish Scriptures; for I consider such an inquiry respecting our other Scriptures, the Book of Mormon, Doctrine and Covenants and the revelations contained in the Pearl of Great Price, as altogether unnecessary here.

The reason that I undertake to devote several chapters to this inquiry, is because some have supposed that the testimony of the Bible respecting God is so far imperfect that it is scarcely reliable. And to the extent of my ability, I desire to check a growing skepticism in relation to the Bible, and therefore will endeavor to prove that not only are the revelations contained in the Bible sufficient to lay a sure foundation for an intelligent belief in God, but that the Bible itself is both authentic and credible. I must ask my readers to remember, however, that this of itself is a subject for a volume, and I can but devote a few pages to it; and therefore ask that too much be not expected.

CHAPTER VIII.

FAITH.—THE BIBLE.

A WORD, in passing, on the Bible as a whole. I am of the opinion that a very great many people look upon the Bible as simply one book, one testimony—one witness for God; when in fact it is not *one* book, but a collection of books; not one witness for God, but the collected testimony of many witnesses for him.

The word does not come, I am assured on very good authority, from the word *biblos*, as many have supposed; nor does it signify *the book* by way of eminence—the Book of books, but it is a word derived from the Greek *biblia*, meaning *the books*, and is a term first applied by Chrysostom to denote the collection of small books which constitute the Old and New Testaments; and this term with the prefix "Holy," soon came into general use. This is how the Jewish Scriptures came to be called the Holy Bible; meaning, really, the holy or sacred books. The Bible is made up of sixty-six distinct books, bound together in one volume, and written by about forty different authors. And if each book is not a separate and independent witness for God, it cannot be denied that each author is.

The first of the sacred writers is Moses, whom

Bacon calls "God's first pen;" the last is the Apostle John. These two writers, the first and the last, are separated by a period of some two thousand years; and the men who wrote as they were moved upon by the Holy Ghost, in that lapse of time, and whose works have been preserved to us in the Bible, occupied various positions in life, ranging from the grand old war king of Israel, David, and the wise king Solomon, down to the humble shepherd Amos, the despised tax collector Matthew, and Peter, the unlearned fisherman. But whatever the condition of life occupied by these men, or whatever the nature of their respective writings, whether histories, biographies, poems, prophecies, or only didactic discourses on morals or religion, they all, in some way or other, bear witness to the existence of God, and give us some information respecting his character and attributes.

It is now our task to inquire briefly into the authenticity and integrity of these writings. For convenience I shall take up the two Testaments, the Old and the New, separately:

First, then, the Old Testament: It is maintained by the best biblical scholars, that the books which now constitute the Old Testament, were collected as we have them, immediately after the return of the Jews from the captivity in Babylon; that would be about the middle of the fifth century, B. C. The work is ascribed to Ezra, Nehemiah, and the men of the great synagogue. In proof of this they point to the testimony of the son of Sirach, who flourished between the years 310-370, B. C.;* and who speaks of the canon—with its three divisions—as finally made up.† By the "three divisions," I mean those divisions made by the Jews in their scriptures, and which are supposed to be contemporary with the completion of the canon. Those divisions are (1) the Pentateuch, or Law;‡ (2) the Prophets; and (3) the Hagiographa.§ It is of these divisions that the son of Sirach speaks.

Josephus in his first book against Apion (section viii) enumerates twenty-two books, "Which contain the record of all the past times; which are justly believed to be divine; and of them, five belong to Moses, which contain his laws, and the traditions of the origin of mankind till his death. This interval of time was little short of three thousand years; but as to the time from the death of Moses till the reign of Artaxerxes, king of Persia [5th cent. B. C.], the prophets, which were after Moses, wrote down what was done in

---

* *Vide* Kitto.

† See the prologue to the Book of Ecclesiasticus, in the Apocrypha.

‡ The five books of Moses—Genesis, Exodus, Leviticus, Numbers, and Deuteronomy.

§ This is a Greek term for the sacred writings not included in the other two divisions. The Talmud places the following books in this division: Ruth, Psalms, Job, Proverbs, Ecclesiastes, Canticles, Lamentations, Daniel, Esther, Ezra and Chronicles. The books not included in this list, nor in the Pentateuch, of course, constitute the division called the Prophets.

their time in thirteen books, the remaining four books* contain hymns to God and precepts for the conduct of human life. It is true our history hath been written since Artaxerxes, very particularly, but hath not been esteemed of the like authority with the former by our forefathers, because there has not been an exact succession of prophets since that time."

This testimony settles the question back to the commencement of the fifth century B. C., that is, for a period of about twenty-four hundred years the authorship of the respective books of the Old Testament has been ascribed to the men who today are regarded as their authors. The rabbins say: "The wise men have left us the Law, the Prophets, and the Hagiographa, combined into one whole;" and then they specify the authors of the sacred books. That specification ascribes the respective books to the men now regarded as the author of them. The Talmud says: "Moses received the law at Sinai, and transmitted it to Joshua; Joshua to the Elders; the Elders to the Prophets; the Prophets to the men of the Great Synagogue," and, as we have seen, it was Ezra, Nehemiah, and the men of the Great Synagogue

---

*Our thirty-nine books of the Old Testament were so grouped by the Hebrews as to make but twenty-two, which accorded with the twenty-two letters of the Hebrew alphabet. What are generally known as the minor prophets, twelve in number, are connected as one book. The Book of Ruth was coupled with Judges; Ezra with Nehemiah; Lamentations with Jeremiah; while the two books of Samuel, Kings and Chronicles were counted but one each.

who made up our present collection of books known as the Old Testament. Josephus in speaking of those who wrote the scriptures says—"Every one is not permitted of his own accord to be a writer, nor is there any disagreement in what is written; they being only prophets that have written the original and earliest accounts of things as they learned them of God himself by inspiration; and others have written what hath happened in their own times, and that in a very distinct manner also."*

From the books of the Old Testament something may be learned as to the manner in which the original parchments of the sacred books were preserved previous to the days of Ezra, extending as far back even as to Moses himself—1451 B. C. and some of the passages that I shall notice—belonging to a subsequent period to Moses, yet previous to the days of Ezra—refer to a collection of sacred books that leave small doubt that the books of Moses and other sacred writings were the ones to which allusion is made.

We are told that after Moses wrote the Law, he delivered it to the priests, the sons of Levi, with a commandment to put it in the side of the Ark of the Covenant,† that it might be there for a witness against Israel, whom Moses by the spirit of prophecy, foresaw would turn away from God.

---

* Josephus against Apion, Book I, Sec. 8.
† Deut. xxxi: 9, 24, 25, 26.

In laying down the duties of the future King of Israel, Moses says: "And it shall be when he sitteth upon the throne of his kingdom, that he shall write him a copy of this law in a book out of that which is before the priests, the Levites"*—showing that it was the intention of Moses to have the Law always preserved by the priests. When Joshua had completed the book that bears his name, it is said: "And Joshua wrote these words in the book of the Law of God;† which was doubtless the book which Moses had placed in the Ark of the Covenant in care of the priests.

When the form of government of Israel was changed into a monarchy, Samuel explained the character of the new kingdom to the people, "and wrote it in a book and laid it up before the Lord."‡ This was three hundred and fifty years after Moses, and yet the practice of laying up these important records before the Lord, as Moses had done with his books, still prevailed; and I doubt not were placed side by side with the books of Moses and Joshua, if not attached to them.

Four centuries and a half later than Samuel, bringing us to about 640 B. C., in the reign of good king Josiah, Hilkiah, the high priest, when the temple was undergoing some repairs, found the Book of the Law in the house of the Lord,§

---

*Deut xvii: 18. †Joshua xxiv, 26. ‡ I. Sam. x : 25. § II. Kings xxii—see the whole chapter.

and sent it to the king, who read it; and when he saw how far Israel had departed from the observance of it, and the judgments pronounced against them on condition of their forsaking the law, he sought to lead his people to repentance.

Isaiah, some seventy years before this, when wishing to confirm some of his own prophecies, recommended the people to seek out the Book of the Lord and read it.* The value of this passage is, that it gives us the testimony of Isaiah that such a book as "the Book of the Lord" was known to the people, that they had access to it, that it was a recognized authority on questions about which there might arise doubts. And there can scarcely be two opinions as to this book, alluded to by Isaiah, being either the original or an authorized copy of the writings placed in the keeping of the priests, and found by Hilkiah.

We have traced this matter down to 640 B. C.; there is one more step to take, to reach Ezra, in whose days the books of the Old Testament were collected, some one hundred and eighty-five years after the date above noted.

What became of the sacred records of the Jews at the time Jerusalem was laid waste by Nebuchadnezzar, about 588 B. C.,† is difficult to learn. But the document granting permission to Ezra and the priests to go and rebuild the temple at

---

* Isaiah xxxiv: 16.
† This is the Hebrew Chronology, according to Usher.

Jerusalem is addressed to him thus: "Artaxerxes, king of kings, unto Ezra, the priest, a scribe of the law of the God of heaven, perfect peace." Then follows permission for all the people of Israel in his realm to go to Jerusalem with Ezra. He then continues: "Forasmuch as thou art sent of the king * * * to inquire concerning Judah and Jerusalem, *according to the law of thy God which is in thy hand.*"* From this it appears that during the captivity the priests were permitted to retain possession of the sacred records. At any rate Ezra had them when he departed from Babylon for Jerusalem, so that they had been preserved, and that, doubtless, by the priests. This brings us to the period when the books of the Bible were collected as we have them today. And from that time, more than two thousand years ago, until the present, the Old Testament has been what it is now; the multiplication of copies and of translations, as well as the subsequent controversies between Jews and Christians, combined to secure the sacred writings against alterations.

No one will contend that the Old Testament contains all the writings of the Jews, perhaps not all the sacred or inspired writings; for there are a number of books and writings of prophets referred to in these very books of the Old Testa-

---

* Ezra vii: 12-14.

ment, which are not to be found in the collection. But that fact does not destroy the value of these we have, or refute the testimony they bear for God. That very care which may have excluded from the sacred collection some books which were really inspired, has also prevented many worthless and uninspired books from becoming connected with the word of God.

What is set down so far in this chapter relates to the Hebrew version of the Scriptures alone; but about three hundred years B. C., by some set down at 285 B. C., an event occurred which did much to preserve the integrity of the Hebrew Scriptures; by that I mean the probability of alterations being made in them was lessened, and they the more likely to be brought down to us just as they were written originally.

At the date above given, Ptolemy Philadelphus, King of Egypt, was gathering up the books which constituted the splendid Alexandrian Library, and being informed by his librarian, Demetrius Phalerius, concerning the Hebrew Scriptures, he at once set himself at work to procure a Greek translation of them. The better to secure this object he set at liberty many Jews in his kingdom, and sent word to the high priest at Jerusalem, Eleazar, his desire, asking that six Elders from each tribe of Israel, such as were skilled in the law, should be sent to him to translate their Scriptures for him. This was done, and it is said that the work was completed in seventy-two days.*

This translation is called the *Septuagint*, meaning the seventy, often represented by the Roman numerals LXX; but whether it is so called because it was translated by about seventy Elders, or for the reason that the translation occupied about seventy days is not clear. At any rate copies of this translation were multiplied, and in the days of Messiah's personal ministering in Judea was the version most in use, and the one he and his Apostles usually referred to, when sustaining their teachings by that which aforetime had been written by inspiration.

That this is true is evident from the following facts: There are in the New Testament 225 quotations from the Old;† and of these over one half, that is 120, agree *verbatim* with the Septuagint. "That these quotations," says an able writer, "must have been taken from the Septuagint is plain from the *copia verborum*, the remarkable fertility of expression, in the Greek language, which forbids us to believe that, had the quotations been from the Hebrew, the Greek rendering would have agreed *verbatim* with the passages in the Septuagint version. Of any Old Testament

---

*For a full account of this matter see Antiquities of the Jews by Josephus, Book xii, chapter ii

†The only books in the Old Testament not quoted in the New are Ruth, I. and II. Chronicles, Ezra, Nehemiah, Esther, Ecclesiastes, Song of Solomon, Lamentations, Obadiah, Nahum and Zephaniah.

passage made up of only ten words, there are not fewer than thirty modes of translating it into Greek; and such indeed are the possible varieties, that if thirty different persons were translating into Greek a Hebrew sentence of *three lines,* none of them, though all were to give a perfectly correct rendering, would be found exactly agreeing in the Greek words employed, or in the collection of these."

Again, of the one hundred and five remaining quotations in the New Testament, from the Old, thirty-nine agree *verbatim* with the Septuagint, except that a synonymous word occurs once in two or three lines. There are next, twenty-two quotations agreeing *verbatim,* or nearly so, with the Septuagint, but even in sense differing from the Hebrew text. Hence out of the two hundred and twenty-five quotations in the New Testament from the Old, we may say that not fewer than one hundred and ninety must have been taken from the Septuagint version.

From about three centuries B. C., then, the Old Testament has existed at least in two languages, and this has contributed much, as I before said, to prevent the corruption of the text and preserve the integrity of the Scriptures; for if changes were made in the Hebrew, it would be discovered from the LXX.; and if alterations were made in the LXX., it could be detected from the Hebrew. There were other translations made of the Scriptures into still other languages, but as my space is limited, I cannot give an account of them here.

We have now seen how the books of the Old Testament, as we have them at the present day, were collected by Ezra, some 2400 years ago; we then went to the last book written by Moses—Deuteronomy—and from it learned that his writings were deposited in the ark of the covenant in charge of the priests and Levites; how Joshua and Samuel also laid up their writings before the Lord; and how Isaiah referred the Jews to these sacred writings in confirmation of his own prophecies; how when in 640 B. C. the temple was undergoing some repairs the high priest found in it an ancient copy of the law; and how Ezra in Babylon had the sacred writings in his possession, so that he at that time would have no difficulty in fixing upon the authorship of the sacred books then before him.

I shall further examine this question of the authenticity of the Old Testament in my next chapter, but the testimony I shall there consider will also have a bearing upon its integrity, and will likewise tend to confirm the claims as to its containing the revelations of God to the Jews; and to this latter consideration I especially invite the attention of the reader.

CHAPTER IX.

FAITH.—THE OLD TESTAMENT.

CERTAIN it is that the Hebrew Scriptures, the Old Testament, the same collection of books that we now have, was recognized by the Lord Jesus Christ and the prophets and apostles of that dispensation as the word of God, and was referred to by them as "the law and the prophets." This is evident from the fact of their frequently appealing to those scriptures to sustain their own doctrine and teachings. Nearly every book of the Old Testament is quoted in the New, and therefore all the evidence which may be amassed in support of the divinity of Christ and the inspiration of the New Testament, sustains also the authenticity and inspiration of the Old; for the inspired writers of the former appeal to the latter as an unquestioned authority in matters relating to God. Hence, whatever evidence sustains the New Testament, supports also the Old. I trust the reader will bear this in mind, and when I have considered and proved, as I hope to do, the authenticity and credibility of the New Testament, remember that it is a witness for the Old Testament, an important, I might say an infallible one, since it is inspired; it comes as from God.

In our day the evidences which support the authenticity of the Jewish Scriptures have accumulated in a most remarkable manner. In 1835 the two rolls of papyrus, one filled with the writings of Joseph, who was sold into Egypt, and the other with those of Abraham, came into the hands of Joseph Smith. The roll containing the writings of Abraham was translated by the prophet, at least in part, and is published in the Pearl of Great Price under the title of the Book of Abraham. The manner in which these rolls of papyrus came into Joseph Smith's possession was as follows:

In 1831 the celebrated French traveler, Antonio Sebolo, penetrated Egypt as far as the ancient city of Thebes, under a license procured from Mehemet Ali—then viceroy of Egypt—through the influence of Chevalier Drovetti, the French consul. Sebolo employed 433 men for four months and two days; and entering the catacombs near ancient Thebes on the 7th of June, 1831, they procured eleven mummies. These were shipped to Alexandria, and from thence the great traveler started with his treasures for Paris. But *en route* for the French capital, Sebolo put in at Trieste, where he was taken sick, and after an illness of ten days died. This was in 1832. Previous to his death he willed his Egyptian treasures to his nephew, Michael H. Chandler, who was then living in Philadelphia, Pennsylvania, but whom Sebolo believed to be in Dublin, to which city he ordered the mummies shipped.

Mr. Chandler ordered the mummies forwarded to New York, where he took possession of them. There the coffins for the first time were opened, and in them were found two rolls of papyrus covered with engravings. While still in the custom house, Mr. C. was informed by a gentleman, a stranger to him, that no one in the city could translate the characters, but was referred to Joseph Smith, who, the stranger informed him, possessed some kind of gift or power by which he had previously translated similar characters.

Joseph Smith was then unknown to Mr. C. The mummies were shipped to Philadelphia, and from there Mr. C. traveled through the country, exhibiting them and the rolls of papyrus. He finally passed through Kirtland, where Joseph Smith was residing. Joseph, seeing the rolls of papyrus and the record upon them, had the Saints purchase them, and they were translated as before stated.*

This Book of Abraham, while it has no direct reference to the works of Moses, gives an account of the creation of this earth, which, substantially, is the same account as that given by Moses;†

---

*The above I have condensed from the account given of this matter by the Prophet Joseph in his history.

† Pearl of Great Price, pp. 41-45.

and is, at least, a strong collateral evidence to the correctness of the account in Genesis.

In the year 1830, the visions of Moses, through which he was enabled to write the account of the creation in Genesis, and the history of the world down to the time of the Flood, were revealed to Joseph Smith. This part of the world's history, as given to the Prophet Joseph, is substantially the same as that in Genesis, only more full and perfect than that; the Lord pointing out here and there where the record of Moses, as we now have it in the Bible, has been marred because of changes made by wicked men. Still, as I say, the accounts substantially agree, and in the revelations to which I have called attention the Lord says over and over again that these things he revealed to Moses, and that Moses bore record of them.*

This is testimony of the most direct character as to the authenticity of the books in our Bible giving this history. All ancient tradition says Moses wrote Genesis, and now in this day, a revelation is given from God to Joseph Smith, saying that an account substantially the same as that in Genesis was revealed to Moses, and that he recorded it.

I come now to the strongest witness of all for the authenticity, and also the divinity of the Jewish Scriptures; I mean the Book of Mormon.

---

*Pearl of Great Price, pp. from 1 to 31.

In the first place let me say that the Book of Mormon itself, as an inspired book, rests on so sure a basis, that however much men may be disposed to doubt the authenticity, credibility, and inspiration of the Jewish Scriptures, they cannot, if they investigate the claims of the Book of Mormon, doubt its truth.* And in these Nephite Scriptures is contained the most direct and positive proofs relative to the authenticity of the Bible.

According to the Book of Mormon, Lehi and his family left Jerusalem in the first year of the reign of Zedekiah, about 600 B. C. Soon after leaving Jerusalem, from his camp in the wilderness Lehi sent his sons back to that city to obtain the genealogies of his fathers, and a record of the Jews. In this mission his sons were successful, returning to their father's encampment in the wilderness with a set of brass plates on which the record and the genealogies were written.

The return of the sons of Lehi to their father was celebrated with great rejoicing. Nephi in his account of it says: "And after they had given thanks unto the God of Israel, my father, Lehi, took the records which were engraved upon the

---

*Those who desire to prosecute an investigation of this subject will do well to read the "Divine Authenticity of the Book of Mormon," by O. Pratt; and "A New Witness for God," by the author of this work.

plates of brass, and he did search them from the beginning. And he beheld that they did contain the five books of Moses, which gave an account of the creation of the world, and also of Adam and Eve, who were our first parents; and also a record of the Jews from the beginning, even down to the commencement of the reign of Zedekiah, king of Judah, and also the prophecies of the holy prophets, from the beginning, even down to the commencement of the reign of Zedekiah; and also many prophecies which have been spoken by the mouth of Jeremiah."*

Here is a direct reference to the Jewish Scriptures, in which five books are accredited to Moses —the same number as in our present Bible—and the prophecies of Jeremiah are also mentioned.

Then in a vision, in which the future was unfolded to Nephi, he saw that a book would go from the Jews to the Gentiles, and that it would be like the record upon the brass plates. This is the passage: "The angel said unto me, Knowest thou the meaning of the book? And I said unto him, I know not. And he said, Behold it proceedeth out of the mouth of a Jew; and I, Nephi, beheld; and he said unto me, the book that thou beholdest is a record of the Jews, which contains the covenants of the Lord which he hath made unto the house of Israel; and it also containeth many of the prophecies of the

---

* I. Nephi v: 10-13.

holy prophets; and it is a record like unto the engravings which are upon the plates of brass, save there are not so many; nevertheless they contain the covenants of the Lord, which he hath made unto the house of Israel; wherefore, they are of great worth unto the Gentiles."*

Nephi further informs us that it was his practice to read frequently to his people from these brass plates, that they might be informed concerning the dealings of God with their forefathers; and all through the Nephite Scriptures these brass plates are referred to. Moreover, whole chapters, and sometimes several chapters together, especially from the writings of Isaiah,† are transcribed from the brass plates to the record made by Nephi; and comparing these transcribed portions of the Old Testament found in the Book of Mormon with the parts which correspond to them in our present English version of the Jewish Scriptures, it will be seen that the difference is but slight; substantially they agree. The circumstance not only proves the authenticity of the Scriptures, but it is also a strong proof of the integrity of our present version of them.

It is true the Book of Mormon informs us that many plain and precious parts of this book, which proceeds from the mouth of the Jew, are taken away and others corrupted, but that does

---

* I. Nephi xiii: 21-23.   † See I. Nephi, chapters xx, xxi; II. Nephi vii, viii; also II. Nephi, from the xii to xxiv.

not affect the statement I make that the substantial agreement between these passages in the Book of Mormon and Bible, proves, in the main, the integrity as well as the authenticity of the Jewish Scriptures. Here, so far as the authenticity of the Old Testament is concerned, I shall, for the present, rest my case; and proceed with a like inquiry as to the New.

CHAPTER X.

FAITH.—THE NEW TESTAMENT.

THERE is an impression existing, and it is one encouraged by infidel writers, that the acceptance of the books now comprising the New Testament, was the arbitrary action of a council of bishops three or four hundred years A. D. This I believe to be a wrong impression. I do not think the list of books that now constitute the New Testament was made up in an arbitrary manner, at one time, or by any single council. It can be shown that the books and epistles now in the collection known as the New Testament, were accepted as inspired writings by the Christian churches, before the councils of the church undertook any discussion of the subject; and even when this question was before those councils, they merely decided what books before-time had been regarded by the churches as inspired.

The first council which undertook to pronounce a decision on the subject was that of Laodicea in the year 363 A. D. "Probably the decree of this council," as Archdeacon Paley remarks, "rather declared than regulated the public judgment, or, more properly speaking, the judgment of some neighboring churches, the council itself consisting of no more than thirty or forty bishops of Lydia and the adjoining countries;" and after this council the question, "What books were entitled to be received as Scripture?" was discussed with great freedom, and without any reference to the declaration made by the council of Laodicea.*

The list of inspired books of the New Testament, as we have them now, was accepted by the council of Hippo, held 393 A. D. The third council of Carthage, 397 A. D., and also the sixth of Carthage, 419 A. D., confirmed the decisions of the first. Thus, from that early date, the authorship and inspiration of the books of the New Testament may be said to have been fixed.

True, certain early Christian writers doubted the inspiration and authenticity of some of the books now in the New Testament; II Peter, the Epistle to the Hebrews, the Epistle of James and the Apocalypse† being among those whose inspiration and authenticity were questioned;

---

* Paley's Evidences, Part I, ch. ix.   † Revelations of St. John.

and some Bible scholars since those days have held the same doubts; but the preponderance of evidence is in favor of the inspiration of all the books of the New Testament, and of their being the productions of the men accredited in those early days, and by the councils named, with having written them.

It is quite evident, however, that the New Testament does not contain all the inspired writings of the apostles and disciples, since there are references in the books of the New Testament to other books written by the same authors, which would certainly be equally inspired with those we now have in the collection. Such, for instance, as another epistle to the Corinthians,* also a second epistle to the Colossians,† and another book of Jude.‡ Still, because some inspired books were lost, and others rejected by these councils, that does not affect those that remain as to their authenticity or inspiration; though had we those inspired books that were lost or rejected, many passages in the books that have been preserved to us might be made more plain.

Could it be proven even, that some of the books now retained in the New Testament collection were uninspired, and not written by those now accredited with being their authors, that would not affect these books about whose authenticity

---

* I. Cor. v.   † Col. iv : 16.   ‡ Jude 3.

and inspiration there has never been a question. Suppose all those books I have named as having had their authenticity questioned, should turn out to be forgeries, we would still have the four Gospels, the Acts, the thirteen Epistles of Paul that stand unquestioned; and as long as even one of these books remains unshaken as to its authenticity and inspiration, you have a witness for God and Christ in it—an exposition, to some extent, at least, of the character and attributes of Deity. For the New Testament, like the Old, is not one book, but a collection of books; each independent of the other. It is not one witness for God and Christ, but a collection of the testimonies of a number of witnesses. And if it could be proven (but I do not think it can be) that some of these books were of such doubtful origin that they are unworthy a place in the collection, it does not follow that the other books of the New Testament are also of doubtful origin and unworthy of confidence.

Furthermore, if it be admitted (and I am willing to admit it) that some of the texts in the books comprising the New Testament have been corrupted or changed, and portions thereof taken away, while these things tend to, and do weaken the testimony of the witnesses, and make many parts obscure, and even contradictory, still, after making all these concessions, enough remains uncorrupted and unimpaired, to give us in those books strong and reliable witnesses—whose testimony cannot be impeached—for God. And while some parts have been corrupted, and thus rendered imperfect, yet the narrative of the life of Christ, the Gospel he advocated, the moral precepts he inculcated in his system of truth, together with the revelations contained in those Scriptures respecting the character and attributes of Deity, are all substantially correct.

I refer again to the manner in which the list of books now composing the New Testament was decided upon. I have already stated that I do not think it was by the arbitrary decision of any one council at any one time, that the selection of this list of books was made and all others rejected. On the contrary it was most probably the work of years. "The most plausible supposition," says an unquestioned authority, "is that each of the most influential churches founded by the Apostles in person, made for its own use a collection of all the writings duly ascertained to be apostolic and inspired. The epistles sent to the different churches were soon, doubtless, communicated to the sister associations for the strengthening of each other's faith, hope and virtue." Indeed the Apostle Paul, in one instance at least, commands an interchange of apostolic writings. In his epistle to the Colossian saints he says: "And when this epistle is read among you, cause that it be read in the church of the Laodiceans, and that ye likewise read the epistle from Laodicea."* Doubtless, as stated by Chambers, "The brotherly love which was a notable feature of primitive Christianity, led Christians everywhere to make common property of the local messages from apostles, as valuable to them all alike. Nor did they ever dream of withholding from their brethren copies of such inspired writings as had come into their own hands. No general order from the apostles was needed to prompt individual Christians or congregations that had been favored with an inspired communication to make it equally well known to every neighbor. There must have been the most cordial reciprocity of communication in this matter, an unreserved sharing of new Scripture with each other; the fair and full interchange of apostolic oracles leading to such a multiplication, that each church possessed, for the benefit of its members, a copy of all inspired writings previously issued by the Apostles."† And here let me add, that in the multiplication of copies, it is not to be wondered at if the originals were soon lost sight of, or worn out by constant use.

---

*Col. iv: 16.   †Information for the People, Vol. II .Art. Bible.

CHAPTER XI.

FAITH.—THE NEW TESTAMENT.

THE earliest reference we have to any writings or collection of writings now in the New Testament, and in which they are recognized as authoritative scripture, is in the second Epistle of Peter. That apostle, writing about the year 65 A. D., says: "Account that the long suffering of our Lord is salvation; even as our beloved brother Paul also according to the wisdom given unto him hath written unto you; as also in all his epistles, speaking in them of these things; in which are some things hard to be understood, which they that are unlearned and unstable wrest as they do *the other scriptures*, unto their own destruction."*

It will be observed that the reference to the Epistles of Paul is of such a character that it leads us to infer that those Epistles were well and generally known by the church at large; for this Epistle of Peter's which we quote, is written to no particular branch of the church, but "to them that have obtained like precious faith with us through the righteousness of God and our Savior Jesus Christ;"† in other words, to the

---
* II. Peter iii: 15, 16.   † II. Peter i: 1.

church universal; and it can scarcely be doubted that some of the larger branches of the church, even in that early day, had the Epistles of Paul in a collected form. It will also be observed that Peter places these Epistles of Paul on equal authority with Scripture by saying, that the unlearned and unstable wrest them, "*as they do also the other scripture,* unto their own destruction."

There is a tradition that the apostle John, on his return from his banishment to Patmos—96 A. D.—made a collection of what he considered the inspired writings of the apostles and disciples of Christ; but the tradition seems not to be well founded. It is generally admitted, however, that he must have had before him the three other gospels when he wrote the one which bears his name, because his book called "The Gospel according to St. John," is supplemental in its character, and in it he gives prominence to those incidents in the life of his Master and the doctrines he taught, about which the other writers are either silent or have said but little. This peculiarity is accounted for by the supposition that John had before him the other three narratives of his Master's life and mission, and that he sought to make prominent what they had omitted or treated but briefly, that the church—in the four books—might have a complete history of Messiah's life, and labors and doctrines.

In his admirable work on the "Evidences of

copies carefully collated, and versions of them made in different languages.

VII. That they were received by Christians of different sects, by many heretics as well as Catholics, and usually appealed to by both sides in the controversies which arose in those days.

VIII. That the four Gospels, the Acts of the Apostles, thirteen Epistles of St. Paul, the first Epistle of John and the first of Peter, were received, without doubt by those who doubted concerning the other books which are included in our present canon—[authorized list].

IX. That the Gospels were attacked by the early adversaries of Christianity, as books containing the accounts upon which the religion was founded.

X. That formal catalogues of authentic scriptures were published, in all of which our present sacred histories were included.

XI. That these propositions cannot be affirmed of any other books claiming to be books of scripture; by which are meant those books which are commonly called apochryphal books of the New Testament.*

---

* Evidences of Christianity, part I. ch. ix. I would also recommend my readers to carefully study Dr. Lardner's Credibility of the New Testament, from which Dr. Paley obtains much, I may say nearly all of the material for his own admirable work. There is also a fine article on the subject, in Chamber's Information for the People, entitled *History of the Bible*; and another in Dr. Kitto's Biblical Lirerature, under the heading, *Canon of Scripture*.

Christianity," Archdeacon Paley maintains the following allegations respecting the comprising the New Testament are capab proof; in fact, to my mind, the learned deacon does prove them, and places them be the power of successful contradiction:

I. That the historical books of the Testament, meaning thereby the four Gos and the Acts of the Apostles, are quoted, alluded to, by a series of Christian writ beginning with those who were contempor with the apostles, or who immediately follow them, and proceeding in close and regular s cession from their time to the present.

II. That when they are quoted, or alluded they are quoted or alluded to with pecul respect, as book *sui generis*;* as possessing authority which belonged to no other books, a as conclusive in all questions and controversi amongst Christians.

III. That they were, in very early time collected into a distinct volume.

IV. That they were distinguished by appro priate names and titles of respect.

V. That they were publicly read and expounded in the religious assemblies of the Christians.

VI. That commentaries were written upon them, harmonies formed out of them, different

---

*That is, of its own kind.

Out of these eleven propositions I shall deal with but two, viz.: the first and tenth; referring my readers to Dr. Paley's work, for information as to the other propositions. And what is said here of these propositions, I shall select or condense from Paley's work, sometimes using his language as well as his facts, without troubling myself to indicate the quotations.

Well, then, as to his first allegation, viz.: that there are a series of Christian writers, beginning with those contemporary with the apostles, and extending on down to the present, who have quoted the chief books of the New Testament. To begin with, there is an epistle ascribed to Barnabas,* the companion of Paul, in some of his missionary tours. It is quoted as an Epistle of Barnabas, by Clement of Alexandria, A. D. 194; by Origen, A. D. 230; by Eusebius, A. D. 315, and more frequently by writers after that time, and is referred to by the writers above named, as an ancient work in their time, and as well known and read among Christians, though not accounted a part of scripture. It purports to be written soon after the destruction of Jerusalem under Titus.

In this epistle appears the following remarkable

---

* There is a manuscript copy of this epistle in connection with a copy of the New Testament entire, dating back to the fourth century, now in the St. Petersburg Library. It was found by Tischendorf in the convent of St. Catherine on Mount Sinai, in 1859, and is known as the Sinaitic Manuscript—the oldest one in existence.

passage: "Let us, therefore, beware lest it come upon us, *as it is written;* There are many called, few chosen." From the expression, "as it is written," we infer, with certainty, that at the time when the author of this epistle lived, there was a book extant well known to Christians, and of authority among them, containing the words "many are called, few chosen." Such a book is our present Gospel of St. Matthew, in which this text is twice found,* and found in no other book which existed in those days; therefore Barnabas must have referred his readers to Matthew's Gospel. Furthermore, the writer of the epistle was a Jew. The phrase, "It is written," was the very form in which the Jews quoted their scriptures. Hence, it follows that he would not have used this phrase, and without qualification, of any books but what had acquired scriptural authority. So that while the quotation "many are called, few chosen," confirms the existence of Matthew's Gospel; the expression "It is written," gives to it the authority or dignity of scripture.

There are other passages in the epistle which are the same in sentiment as some of the passages in Matthew,† some in which we recognize the same words. For example, "Give to every one that asketh thee;" and he says that Christ chose as his apostles men who were great sinners

---

*Matt xx: 16; xxii: 14.   † Matt. v: 42; ix: 13.

88   THE GOSPEL.

that he might show that he came, "not to call the righteous, but sinners to repentance."

There is also extant an epistle of Clement, bishop of Rome, whom the ancient writers without doubt or scruple assert to have been the Clement whom Paul mentions in Phil. iv, 3.* This epistle is spoken of by the early Christian writers as an epistle acknowledged by all. Of it Irenæus says (writing in the second century) it was "written by Clement, who had seen the blessed apostles, and conversed with them, who had the preaching of the apostles still sounding in his ears, and their traditions before his eyes." Dionysius, bishop of Corinth (the epistle is addressed to the Church of Christ) says, about the year 170 A. D., that the epistle of Clement "had been wont to be read in that church from ancient times."†

In the said epistle are found the following passages, evidently taken from our New Testament scriptures: "Especially remembering the words of the Lord Jesus which he spake, teaching gentleness and long suffering, for thus he said: "Be ye merciful, that ye may obtain

---

* "With Cl ment also, and with other my fellow-laborers whose names are written in the book of life."

† A copy of this epistle dating back to the fifth century, is connected with the Alexandrian manuscript of the New Testament now in the British Museum. The manuscript was given to Charles the I. in 1628 by Cyril Lucas, Patriarch of Constantinople.

mercy;* forgive that it may be forgiven unto you;† as you do so shall it be done unto you; as ye judge so shall ye be judged; as ye show kindness, so shall kindness be shown unto you; (with what measure ye mete, with the same shall it be measured to you.'"‡

In another place he says: "Remember the words of the Lord Jesus, for he said: "Woe to that man by whom offenses come; it were better for him that he had not been born, than that he should offend one of my elect; it were better for him that a millstone should be tied about his neck, and that he should be drowned in the sea than that he should offend one of my little ones."§

The reference in the foregoing to the passages I have indicated is too palpable to leave any room for doubt.

Connected with the Sinaitic manuscript copy of the New Testament, now in the St. Petersburg Library, to which I have already called attention in a foot note, is a manuscript copy of the "Shepherd" or "Pastor" of Hermas, dating from the fifth century; but that copies of it existed at a still earlier date is evident from the fact that it is quoted by Irenæus, A. D. 178; by Clement of Alexandria, A. D. 194; by Tertullian, A. D. 200; Origen, A. D. 230. In this ancient

---

* Matt v: 7.   † Luke vi: 37, 38.   ‡ Matt. vii: 1, 2.   § Matt. xviii.

work are many allusions to and some direct quotations from the Gospels of Matthew, Luke and John. Of the allusions may be cited, the confessing and denying of Christ;* the parable of the seed sown;† and the comparison of Christ's disciples to little children. Of the more direct quotations I mention the following: "He that putteth away his wife and marrieth another, committeth adultery;"‡ the singular expression, "having received all power from his Father," is undoubted allusion to Matthew xxviii, 18; and Christ being the "Gate," or only way of coming "to God," in plain allusion to John xiv, 6, and x, 7, 9.

I now come to Ignatius, who became bishop of Antioch about thirty-seven years after the ascension of Messiah; and therefore, from his time and station, it is probable that he had known and conversed with many of the apostles. Some of the epistles of this bishop are referred to by Polycarp, his contemporary, the bishop of Smyrna; and some are quoted by Irenæus, A. D. 178; and by Origen, A. D. 230. In these epistles are plain and undoubted allusions to the Gospels of Matthew and John, of which the following are but specimens: "Christ was baptized of John that all righteousness might be fulfilled by him."§ "Be ye wise as serpents in all things and harm-

---

*Matt. x: 32, 33. Luke xii: 8, 9.   †Matt. xiii: 3.   Luke viii: 5.   ‡Luke xvi: 18.   §Matt. iii: 15.

less as a dove."* "Yet the Spirit is not deceived, being from God, for it knows whence it comes and whither it goes."†

I now pass over several writers in whose works are similar quotations from the scriptures to those already noted; among them Polycarp, a convert to Christianity through the teachings of the Apostle John; as also Papias, his companion; Justin Martyr, separated from the last named by but twenty years; and also Hegesippus, who came about thirty years after Justin. This brings us to the year 170 A. D. At this time the churches of Lyons and Vienna in France, sent a relation of the sufferings of their martyrs to the churches of Asia and Phrygia. This epistle is found entire in the works of Eusebius [315 A. D.], and in it are direct allusions to the Gospels of Luke, John and the Acts of the Apostles. The one to John is, "Thus was fulfilled that which was spoken by the Lord, that whosoever killeth you, will think that he doeth God's service."‡

At that time these churches in France had for their bishop Pothinus, then about ninety years old, whose time, therefore, must have joined on to the times of the apostles.

"The evidence now," says Dr. Paley, "opens upon us full and clear." Irenæus succeeded Pothinus as bishop of Lyons. In his youth he

---

* Matthew x: 16.   † John iii: 18.   ‡ John xvi: 2.

had been a disciple of Polycarp, who was a disciple of John. * * * He asserts of himself and his contemporaries, that they were able to reckon up in all the principal churches the succession of bishops from the first. * * * The testimony which this writer affords to the historical books of the New Testament, to their authority, and to the titles which they bear, is expressive and positive. One principal passage runs as follows:

"We have not received the knowledge of the way of our salvation by any others than those by whom the Gospel has been brought to us. Which Gospel they first preached, and afterward by the will of God, committed to writing, that it might be for time to come the foundation and pillar of our faith. For after that the Lord rose from the dead, and they [the apostles] were endowed from above with the power of the Holy Ghost coming down upon them, they received a perfect knowledge of all things. They went forth to all the ends of the earth, declaring to men the blessings of heavenly peace, having all of them, and every one alike, the Gospel of God. Matthew then, among the Jews, wrote a Gospel in their own language, while Peter and Paul were preaching the Gospel at Rome, and founding a church there; and after their exit, Mark also, the disciple and interpreter of Peter, delivered to us in writing the things which had been preached by Peter; and Luke, the companion of Paul, put.

down in a book the Gospel preached by him (Paul). Afterward John, the disciple of the Lord, who also leaned upon his breast, he likewise published a Gospel while he dwelt at Ephesus, in Asia."

Nor is this writer less explicit respecting the book of the Acts of the Apostles.

The force of the testimony we have considered will be strengthened by remembering that it is the testimony, and the concurring testimony of writers who lived in countries remote from each other. Clement flourished at Rome; Ignatius at Antioch, and Irenæus in France.

I deem it unnecessary to pursue this inquiry further, and shall close by remarking that Clement of Alexandria, one of the most voluminous of Christian writers, follows Irenæus at a distance of but sixteen years. In the works of Clement which remain, the four gospels are repeatedly quoted by the names of their authors, and the Acts of the Apostles is expressly ascribed to Luke. This brings us to the year 194 A. D. Tertullian joins on to Clement, and is no less explicit in his reference to the New Testament than the writers who preceded him. Then follow numerous writers, among them Origen, A. D. 230; Eusebius, 315; and Jerome, A. D. 392.

So numerous are the references to scripture, in the writings of these men, that were our books of scripture lost, some aver, that they could be reproduced from the works of these writers alone.

From the date last given, there can be no question as to the existence of our New Testament or of its acceptance by the whole of Christendom, as containing the account of those events on which Christianity was founded.

CHAPTER XII.

FAITH—THE NEW TESTAMENT.

I NOW come to the tenth allegation of Dr. Paley, *viz.:* "Formal catalogues of authentic scriptures were published, in all of which our present sacred histories were included."

In the writings of Origen which remain, and in some extracts preserved by Eusebius, from works of his which are now lost, there are enumerations of the books of scripture, in which the four Gospels and the Acts of the Apostles are distinctly and honorably specified, and in which are no books beside what are now received. The date of Origen's works is 230 A. D.

Athanasius, about a century afterwards (330 A. D.), delivered a formal catalogue of the books of the New Testament, containing our scriptures and no others; of which he says, "In these alone the doctrine of religion is taught; let no man add to them, or take anything from them."

About twenty years after Athanasius (350 A.

D.), Cyril, bishop of Jerusalem, sent forth a catalogue of the books of scripture, publicly read at that time in the Church of Jerusalem, exactly the same as ours, except that the book of Revelation is omitted.

Fifteen years after Cyril (365 A. D.), the council of Laodicea delivered an authoritative catalogue of Canonical Scripture, like Cyril's, the same as ours, with the omission of Revelation.*

About thirty years later, that is, in 393 A. D., followed the council of Hippo, which delivered a catalogue of the books of the New Testament, which agrees with that now in our common English version. This was followed by the third council of Carthage, in 397 A. D., and by the sixth of Carthage 415 A. D., both of which confirmed the list of sacred books made out by the council of Hippo.

It seems to me that proving these two propositions selected from Dr. Paley's list, is sufficient to make out a case for the authenticity of the books of the New Testament; but when the reader remembers that the nine other allegations we quoted in chapter eleven can also be sustained by undeniable proofs, the case is made out so clearly that there can be no room for doubt.

Then the Book of Mormon comes in also as a witness for the New Testament as well as for the

---

* I have taken the preceding paragraphs of this chapter entire from Paley's Evidences of Christianity Part I., chap. ix, sec. 10

Old. Not so much a witness for the authenticity of the books composing it, however, as for the correctness of what is contained in them.

The writers in the Book of Mormon who bear a direct testimony as to what the New Testament scriptures contain, and in that way indirectly establish their authenticity and credibility, may be divided into two classes, prophetic and historical. By the former, I mean those who by the inspiration of heaven foresaw the birth and mission of Jesus Christ as it all, afterwards came to pass; by the latter, I mean those who lived at the time and were witnesses to the personal ministrations of Messiah, on the western hemisphere, and made a record of those things they saw and heard.

Of the first class, the prophetic, the first Nephi stands out most prominently; for he gives such a vivid description of the leading outlines of Messiah's life and labors on the earth, that it makes one feel in very deed that "prophecy is but history reversed," for had he lived and written in the first century of the Christian are instead of the fifth century preceding it, I feel sure that he could not have been more vivid or exact in writing the life, mission and doctrines of the Son of God;* and all that he predicts is

---

* For the remarkable prophecies which foretell the events here alluded to, I refer my readers to the xi, xii, xiii and xvi chapters of I. Nephi, Book of Mormon.

in strict accord with what is contained in the New Testament.

Next to Nephi we may place King Benjamin, whose testimony is found in the book of Mosiah, chapter iii, and next to him, Abinadi, whose prophecies in relation to the coming and mission of Jesus, are contained in the thirteenth, fourteenth, fifteenth and sixteenth chapters of Mosiah; and, lastly, Samuel, the Lamanite prophet, whose testimony is in the fourteenth chapter of Helaman.

All these prophets give the outlines of the life and mission of Jesus Christ, and, as before stated, what they say is in strict accord with what is written in the New Testament, by those who witnessed the events that these prophets of the Western hemisphere foretold.

On the other side of the line, that is, of the historical witnesses, they who lived at the time Jesus visited the western hemisphere and wrote an account of what took place, the III Nephi, the one whom the Lord made the chief of the apostles, is most conspicuous. He records the fact of Messiah's visit to the Nephites, after his resurrection and departure from his disciples in Judea; and gives a most particular account of the several visits of Jesus to his people, and of his organizing a church, after the pattern of the one organized in Jerusalem; also of the doctrines and moral precepts which he taught; in all of which there is a substantial agreement with what is recorded in the New Testament.*

Thus the Book of Mormon, is an additional witness for Jesus, testifying as well as the New Testament, that he is both Lord and Christ. It also sustains the New Testament, that is, if it does not directly prove the authenticity of the various books composing it, it does prove the correctness of what is contained in them, by testifying that the same person who was crucified by the Jews is the Son of God, the Savior of the world, and that he taught the same doctrines, ordinances, and precepts, and organized his church on the Western hemisphere after the pattern of that described in the New Testament; and all this, I take it, is very strong proof of the correctness of what is recorded in the New Testament scriptures—it is, in fact, the testimony of a mighty and numerous people, speaking from the silence of past ages, bearing witness of the truth as contained in the Jewish scriptures; and, withal, is such an evidence of their authenticity, and, likewise of their integrity, in the main—speaking now of both the Old Testament and the New—and of the correctness of the matter they contain, that before this new witness for God unbelief must hide its head; atheism must stand rebuked; the scorner is reproved;

---

*The reader is recommended to read carefully the whole Book of III Nephi, and compare it with the teachings of the New Testament.

they that watch for iniquity are cut off; the terrible ones are brought to naught; they that erred in spirit come to understanding; they that murmured learn doctrine; the meek increase their joy in the Lord and the poor among men rejoice.*

I have been led thus far into an investigation of the authenticity of the Jewish scriptures touching, too, here and there, the question of the integrity and truthfulness of them, by a desire to fix in the mind of the reader the fact that our principal volume of scripture is worthy of all confidence so far as the question of authenticity is concerned.

I am aware, however, that after treating of the question of authenticity, there still stands the question of credibility. After proving the authenticity of a book, I believe the further questions may be asked, and usually with great propriety—"Is it worthy of belief? *Can* it be believed? Is it credible?" To this rule I make one exception, and in the case in hand it is important. That exception is this: If it can be proven that God is the author of the book, or, what would be equivalent, if those who wrote it were inspired by his Holy Spirit, then if you prove such an authenticity as that, you prove at the same time the credibility of the book. For, let it be proven clearly that the book emanates from God directly or indirectly, then who could

---

Isaiah xxix: 18-24.

doubt its truth, its wisdom, or the events, however wonderful, it relates? Or who could question the mercy and justice of the acts of God as represented in that book or books that are the fruits of inspiration?

It matters not how at variance their contents may seem to be with our supposed knowledge of the laws of nature; our knowledge of those laws are so limited; our understanding of the mechanism of the universe so imperfect; our acquaintance with the universe and the forces that operate in it so insignificant, that let it be clearly proven that a revelation from God contradicted our supposed facts, and I believe the wisest, and best among the children of men, with becoming humility that would but add to their dignity, would bow in submission to the revelation.

Neither does it matter how much the conduct of Deity, as represented in such books, may violate what we understand to be the relative claims of stern Justice and sweet Mercy; our knowledge of the operation of those qualities, and their effect upon men in time and in eternity, and under varied conditions, is so uncertain and imperfect that we are liable to confound good with evil, and that which is indeed an infinite mercy, we may condemn as a piece of barbaric cruelty. In this matter we would bow also, and say, "Thy will, O Lord, be done," righteous must be all thy judgments, merciful are thy ways! Shall not the God of the whole earth do right?

In connection with these observations, I would remark, that throughout the Jewish scriptures, that is, in their composition, in their diction as well as in the excellence of their matter, whether in the historical, legislative, poetic, or prophetic books of the Old Testament; or in the gospel histories, the epistles or prophetic books of the New, everywhere may be traced the inspiration of Heaven; and the style and matter of the whole volume proclaims that the Spirit which prompted the writers and brought those books into existence, is divine.

Then again, if the prophecies contained in the volume of scripture be studied, and their fulfillment traced out in the history of the rise and fall of nations, cities and peoples; in the calamities that have overtaken the Jews* and their country; in the coming of Messiah and the work he performed, all of which was foretold by those holy men of God who spake as they were moved upon by the Holy Ghost—if all these prophecies and their fulfillment be considered, it seems to

---

* "You may question, if you will," says Bishop Lightfoot in the *Quarterly Review* for April, 1888, "every single prophecy in the Old Testament, but the whole history of the Jews is one continuous prophecy more distinct and articulate than all. You may deny, if you will, every successive miracle which is recorded therein; but again, the history of the Jews is from first to last one stupendous miracle, more wonderful and convincing than all."

me that there is an accumulation of evidence to the divinity of the Jewish scriptures, that must break down all the petty objections that unbelief can array against them. And indeed, I may say, that such has been the effect of these considerations on the human understanding that the noblest and brightest intellects of all ages have been so impressed with them, that they have yielded a ready assent to their divine inspiration, and worshiped the God whose character and attributes are unfolded in the revelations contained in them.*

Now, if to these evidences, which have been sufficient to convince men of powerful intellect, as well as of the masses of Christendom, be added the further fulfillment of prophecy in respect to taking the Gospel from the earth and then restoring it in the last days, much of which—pertaining to the restoration of the Gospel—has been fulfilled in our day; and then to this be added the testimony contained in the Book of Mormon to the divinity and general truth of the Bible; and to this the testimony in the Book of Abraham and the visions of Moses, as revealed

---

* In making this observation I do not close my eyes to the fact that there are exceptions to this general assertion; nor will I be so unjust as to claim that among unbelievers there are none who are honest in that unbelief. There have been men in all ages, or nearly so, who have doubted the truth of the Jewish scriptures, and some of them have been most brilliant in intellect, and not a few most upright in their manner of life, but these are the exceptions, not the rule; and the remark on this point in the text holds good.

to Joseph Smith and now contained in the Pearl of Great Price—pray tell me, youth of Israel, where is there room for unbelief on your part? Or where is there excuse for infidelity?

Let me remind my readers, that the Bible is a record of man's crimes and vices, as well as of his righteousness and virtues. It as faithfully ecords the former as the latter. But because it thus faithfully records the evils that men did as well as the good, it must not therefore be concluded that God sanctioned or condoned those evils. It was the doing of those very evils that brought down the displeasure of God upon those guilty of them. And what is true of individuals in this respect, is also true of peoples and nations.

Then again, as to the Old Testament, let it be remembered that when the Lord took the children of Israel from the land of Egypt to make of them a people for himself, he presented them first with the Gospel of Christ, with all its mercy and inspiring love and gentleness; but they would not live in accordance with its high moral precepts, nor reflect in their lives its spiritual excellence. Accordingly, a less perfect law was given to Israel; a law which in the New Testament is everywhere called "the law of carnal commandments;" a law more in keeping with their moral development; a law which breathed less of mercy, forgiveness and love and more of exacting, relentless justice; demanding an eye for an eye, and a tooth for a tooth—and this was to be their schoolmaster, to prepare them for the more excellent law of the Gospel of Christ.* Many things in that law of the Old Testament are imperfect, and must not be taken as reflecting the full glory and excellence of the divine wisdom or goodness. On the contrary it is plainly stated, and that too by the voice of inspiration, in the New Testament, that it was a law carnal and imperfect, yet withal containing more excellence than the people seemed able in those days to attain unto.

Add these considerations to the fact that in some of its details and in its translation the Bible has been marred by the hand of man; a number of sacred books lost, and some plain and precious parts taken away from those we have, and it is not surprising that men find imperfections in it, and some things difficult to harmonize with our ideas of the mercy and justice of God.

Yet, with all its imperfections, in the main it is true, and may be relied upon as a witness for God; that is, as to his existence, his character and attributes; and also to the existence, character and mission of his Son, Jesus Christ,

---

* In proof that the Gospel was first offered to ancient Israel, and then because of transgression the law of carnal commandments, I invite the reader's attention to the following scriptures: Heb., latter part of chap. iii, in connection with Heb. iv: 1, 2; I Cor. x: 1-4; and Gal. iii; also Doc. and Cov., sec. 84; see also the chapter on History of the Gospel in this work.

the Redeemer of the world, and of the plan of salvation—the Gospel. What it says of those, and topics associated with them, may be relied upon as God's truth; for the evidences of its authenticity and credibility are so numerous, I may say so overwhelming, that for my part, I see not how intelligence can disbelieve it.

CHAPTER XIII.

FAITH—TRADITION.

HAVING now concluded our inquiry as to the authenticity and credibility of our principal volume of scripture—the Bible; having proven, as I hope, to the satisfaction of my readers, that the Bible is authentic, and worthy of their confidence in what it says of God, of Christ and the Gospel, I have only to remark that the evidence it contains—especially when considered in connection with that found in the other scriptures, the Book of Mormon, Doctrine and Covenants and Pearl of Great Price—is sufficient to plant in the mind an intelligent belief in God, in Christ and in the Gospel as the plan of man's redemption. And now, after so long a digression, I return to the subject of faith in God.

I have already remarked* that faith is the first

---

* Chapter vii.

principle of religion, and that religious faith centers in God, to whom men look for salvation. I have also remarked that it is absolutely necessary for those who come to God to believe that he exists, for unless that fact is firmly fixed in their minds, men will consider themselves under no obligations to obey him.

The first evidence men have of the existence of God comes from tradition, from the testiomny of their fathers; and this has been the case from that event known as the Fall, until the present. Nor is this evidence unworthy our serious attention; it rests upon a surer foundation than is usually accorded it. Suppose we go back to its beginning, to its first introduction into the world, and observe how well founded it is.

According to the account given by Moses in Genesis, previous to the Fall, Adam associated with God; conversed with him respecting the works of creation, and gave names to the cattle, and all living things upon the earth. How long continued, or how intimate that association was, we are not informed in Genesis; but, at all events, it was long enough continued, and sufficiently intimate to fix definitely in the mind of Adam the fact of God's existence. Then when Adam and his wife transgressed God's law, their recollection of his existence did not vanish, but they tried to hide from his presence; and were afterwards visited of the Lord, who reproved them for their sin and pronounced the penalty which would overtake them for their transgression.

All I wish to call attention to in this is the fact that they knew positively of the Lord's existence before their transgression, and they did not forget it after that event; but on the contrary had a lively recollection of what they had seen and heard before they fell, and related it to their children, who, in turn, transmitted it to their children, and so from generation to generation the tradition of God's existence has been handed down until the present time.

But other considerations are yet to be noticed in respect to this tradition. It will be remembered that Adam and all the patriarchs previous to the Flood lived to a very great age. Adam lived nine hundred and thirty years, and during that time Seth, Enos, Cainan, Mahalaleel, Jared, Enoch, Methuselah and Lamech, the father of Noah, were born. Indeed the last named was fifty-six years old* when Adam died; so that for a number of years he must have had the pleasure of Adam's acquaintance; while the patriarchs between Adam and Lamech all associated with him for hundreds of years, and would learn well the story that the grand patriarch of our race would have to tell respecting Eden before the Fall.

Then again, we are told in Genesis† that when

---

* See Doc. and Cov. II Lecture on Faith, verse 30. †Gen. v: 28, 29.

Lamech was one hundred and eighty-two years old he begat Noah; and since Lamech was fifty-six years old when Adam died, Adam had been dead but one hundred and twenty-six years when Noah was born. After the birth of Noah, Lamech lived five hundred and ninety-five years, so that Noah associated with his father, who had seen Adam, for more than five hundred years; and also with a number of the other patriarchs—with Enos, the grandson of Adam, and son of Seth—with Cainan, Mahalaleel, Jared and Methuselah.* Then, the sons of Noah, Shem, Ham and Japheth, all of whom were born before the Flood, would likewise be acquainted with a number of these worthies who had lived with Adam and heard his testimony of God's existence.

Again, Noah lived three hundred and fifty years after the Flood; that would give him ample time and opportunity to teach his posterity for several generations the tradition respecting God, which he had received from a number of patriarchs, who lived previous to the Flood, and thus the said tradition became firmly fixed in the minds of men.

Traces of that tradition, and of these patriarchs connected with it, may be found in nearly all, and so far as I know, in all the mythologies of the world, as well in ancient as in modern times;

---

* Those desiring a more minute account of these points are referred to the Doc. and Cov., II Lecture on Faith.

as well in the mythology of the civilized Greeks and Romans, as in that of India, China, Egypt, and that of the American Indians. The tradition has evidently been corrupted, added to and twisted into fantastic shapes by the idle fancies of corrupt minds, but despite all the changes made in it, traces of this tradition are discoverable in the mythology of all lands.

I believe, too, with Crabb, "That the fictions of mythology were not invented [always] in ignorance of divine truth, but with a willful intention to pervert it; not made only by men of profligate lives and daring impiety, who preferred darkness to light, because their deeds were evil, but by men of refinement and cultivation, from the opposition of science, falsely so-called; not made, as some are pleased to think, by priests only, for interested purposes, but by poets and philosophers among the laity, who, careless of truth or falsehood, were pleased with nothing but their own corrupt imaginations and vain conceits."*

Thus the tradition of the patriarchs was, in time, degraded, by some branches of their posterity, to mythology—a muddy, troubled pool, which, like a mirror shattered into a thousand fragments, reflects while it distorts into fantastic shapes the objects on its banks. Still, under all the rubbish of human invention may be found

---

Crabb's Mythology of all Nations, pp. 174-5.

the leading idea—God's existence, and that fact alone, however mis-shapen it may be, proves how firmly fixed in the human mind is the tradition of the fathers; while the universality of that tradition goes very far towards proving its truth.

When once the idea of the existence of a God is suggested to the mind of man by the testimony of the fathers, and represented as he is by that tradition, as the Creator of the heavens and the earth, and also as the great governing power throughout the universe,—very much is discovered in the marvelous works of nature to strengthen and confirm, almost to a certainty, the truth of that tradition.

Man is conscious of his own existence, and that existence is a stupendous miracle of itself; he is conscious, too, of other facts. He looks out into space in the stillness of night, and sees the deep vault of heaven inlaid with planetary systems, all moving in exact order and harmony, in such regularity that he cannot doubt that intelligence brought them into being, and now sustains and directs the forces that preserve them. Thus the heavens declare the existence of God as well as his glory. This thought is in harmony with the tradition of his fathers, and he recognizes the identity between the intelligence that he knows must control the universe, and the God of which his fathers testify.

Nor is this all: but in the mysterious changes which take place on our own planet, in the gentle

Spring, luxuriant Summer, fruitful Autumn and blighting Winter, with its storms and frosts—the "mysterious round" which brings us our seed time and harvest, and clothes the earth with vegetation and flowers, perpetuating that wonderful power we call life, the strangest fact in all the works of nature—in these mighty changes, so essential and beneficent, man recognizes the wisdom and power of God of whom his fathers bear record.

As the heavens declare his existence and glory, so, likewise, do these changes and a thousand other things, connected with our earth, until lost in wonder and admiration, one exclaims with Paul, "The invisible things of him from the creation of the world are clearly seen, being understood by the things that are made, even his eternal power and godhead."* Or else he calls to mind another scripture, still more sublime—"The earth rolls upon her wings, and the sun giveth his light by day, and the stars also giveth their light, as they roll upon their wings in their glory, in the midst of the power of God. * * * Behold, all these are kingdoms, and any man who hath seen any or the least of these, hath seen God moving in his majesty and power."†

> "But wandering oft, with brute unconscious gaze,
> Man marks not Thee; marks not the mighty hand,
> That, ever busy, wheels the silent spheres!"

---

*Rom. i: 20. † Doc. and Cov. Sec. 88: 45-47.

This much we may say, in conclusion, the tradition of the fathers, confirmed by the power of God as manifested in the works of nature, lays a broad foundation for an intelligent belief in God's existence.

CHAPTER XIV.

FAITH.—REVELATION.

THE evidence of tradition, confirmed by the works of nature, created the assurance or faith in the minds of men that God existed; and that faith led them to the performance of works of righteousness that they might win his approbation; for doubtless, side by side with the tradition of his existence, came also the idea that he loved righteousness and truth, and those who wrought them. In other words, it is but reasonable to suppose that Adam brought from the period of his life on the other side of the Fall, some recollection of God's character and attributes, as well as of his being: And so well pleased was the Lord with the faith and works of some of these men, that he revealed himself to them, made them acquainted with his laws, purposes and designs, and conferred upon them authority to act in his name, as his messengers to the children of men who had not sufficient faith to seek for and enter into his presence.

Such men have lived in various ages of the world, and have ever been (or would have been, had the people only received them) a blessing unto their generation.

Such a character was Enoch, whom we are told walked with God,* and received a revelation from the Lord in which was made known to him events to take place even down to the glorious coming of the Son of God to execute judgment on the wicked.†

Noah also, the tenth from Adam, received a revelation from God, and was made a messenger to the people of his generation, but they refused to receive his testimony, and perished in their sins.

After Noah comes Abraham. He received special revelations from God, being visited by him in the plains of Mamre as the patriarch dwelt in a tent. It was at that time he received the promise of a son, and was told of the intention of the Lord to destroy the wicked cities of the plain, Sodom and Gomorrah; whereupon Abraham pleaded for the righteous that might be in the cities.‡ The Lord also gave him other revelations concerning the organization of the heavens and the laws by which they are

---

* Gen. v: 24.

† Jude, 14, 15. For a more detailed account of the revelations of God to Enoch, and the mighty work which that patriarch did, the reader is referred to the Pearl of Great Price, pp. 18 to 29 inclusive.

‡ Gen. xviii.

governed; the order which was followed in the creation of this earth, and some things pertaining to the redemption of man.*

The Lord also appeared unto Jacob in dreams and visions, and sent angels unto him, and to his son Joseph also, but we pass by these and come to the prophet Moses.

The first revelation the Lord gave to Moses, that we have any account of, was at the burning bush, in Mount Horeb. There the Lord said to him: "I am the God of thy father, the God of Abraham, the God of Isaac, and the God of Jacob. And Moses hid his face, for he was afraid to look upon God."† Then and there the Lord commissioned him to go and deliver Israel, in the performance of which labor he received many manifestations that God was with him.

In Exodus‡ we have an account of God's glorious descent upon Sinai in the presence of all Israel, and the revelations that he gave to them by his own voice: "And God spake all these words, saying, I am the Lord thy God, which have brought thee out of the land of Egypt, out of the house of bondage. Thou shalt have no other Gods before me."§ Then follow nine other commandments: "And all the people saw the thunderings, and the lightnings, and the noise of the trumpet, and the mountain smoking: And

---

* Pearl of Great Price—Book of Abraham, pp. 33-47. † Exodus iii: 6. ‡ Exodus xix, xx. § Exodus xx: 1-3.

when the people saw it, they removed and stood afar off. And they said unto Moses, speak thou with us, and we will hear; but let not God speak with us lest we die. * * * And the Lord said unto Moses, thus thou shalt say unto the children of Israel, ye have seen that I have talked with you from heaven."*

Subsequently to this there was another grand revelation which the Lord gave to a number of the leading Elders of Israel. Moses thus records it: "Then went up Moses and Aaron, Nadab, and Abihu, and seventy of the Elders of Israel: and they saw the God of Israel: and there was under his feet as it were a paved work of a sapphire stone, and as it were the body of heaven in its clearness, and upon the nobles of the children of Israel, he laid not his hand: also they saw God, and did eat and drink."†

Moses after this left the other Elders and went into the mount, where he received the law of the Lord written by the hand of God on tables of stone, and also was instructed how to build a tabernacle and the ark of the covenant. Indeed, throughout the lifetime of Moses the manifestations of God's power, and the revelations of his existence were frequent, and came in so direct a manner that there is left no room for doubt; for the Lord knew Moses face to face, so also knew Moses the Lord, and left his testimony on record.

---

* Exodus xx: 18, 19-22.   † Exodus xxiv: 9-11.

Time would fail me to tell of the revelations which God gave of himself to Joshua, and the judges whom he raised up to rule in Israel; to Samuel, and Daivd and Solomon, and the prophets Isaiah, Jeremiah, Ezekiel, Daniel and the rest. I pass by all these and come to the dispensation opened by the preaching of John the Baptist.

The first direct revelation of God's existence after the opening of that dispensation was at the baptism of Jesus, the Son of God. Matthew's testimony respecting this revelation is as follows: "And Jesus, when he was baptized, went up straightway out of the water: and, lo, the heavens were opened unto him, and he [John]* saw the Spirit of God descending like a dove and lighting upon Him; and lo, a voice from heaven, saying, this is my beloved Son in whom I am well pleased."† With this also agrees the testimony of both Mark and John.

---

*I supposed that John the Baptist was the only one who was a witness of the Holy Ghost resting upon Jesus in the form of a dove. In all the accounts given of this event, except by Luke, the pronoun "he" referring to John, as in Matthew, is used. While in Luke it is not said that anyone else saw it, but the fact is merely stated that "the Holy Ghost descended in bodily shape like a dove and rested upon him." John's own testimony is as follows: And John bore record saying, I saw the Spirit descending from heaven like a dove, and it abode upon him. And I knew him not; but he that sent me to baptize with water, the same said unto me, upon whom thou shalt see the Spirit descending and remaining on him, the same is he which baptizeth with the Holy Ghost." (John i: 32, 33.) †Matt. iii: 16, 17.

Then next in order, that is the next direct revelation, is on the occasion of the transfiguration of Christ on the Mount, thus related by Matthew: "After six days he taketh Peter, James and John, his brother, and bringeth them up unto the high mountain apart, and was transfigured before them: And his face did shine as the sun, and his raiment was white as the light. And behold there appeared unto them Moses and Elias, talking with him. Then answered Peter, and said unto Jesus, it is good for us to be here, if thou wilt, let us build three tabernacles; one for thee, one for Moses and one for Elias. While he yet spake a bright cloud overshadowed them: and behold a voice out of the cloud, which said: This is my beloved son in whom I am well pleased; hear ye him."* This same circumstance is also related by Mark and Luke.

The New Testament is replete with testimonies of the existence of God, both direct and indirect, but I shall here notice but one more; it will be found recorded in the Acts of the Apostles.† It is given at the martyrdom of Stephen. The Jews were so stung by Stephen's reproofs for their hardness of heart, that they rushed upon him, "But he, being full of the Holy Ghost, looked steadfastly into heaven, and saw the glory of God, and Jesus standing on the right hand of God, and said, Behold I see the heavens opened,

---

* Matt. xvii : 1-5.   † Chapter vii.

and the Son of Man standing on the right hand of God."

As before stated, the testimonies in the New Testament to the existence of God and his Son Jesus Christ are numerous. Indeed, I may say it is the one grand truth which the writers in that volume of revelation testify to; and around this primary fact, and dependent upon it for their existence and importance, are arranged all the other facts pertaining to man's redemption and future existence.

But I wish to turn from the witnesses in the Jewish scriptures to others; for, numerous as those witnesses for God and Christ are among the Jews, they are not the only ones.

In the Book of Mormon is an abridgment of the record of Ether, called the Book of Ether. It gives a brief account of a colony which the Lord led from the tower of Babel, where he confounded the language of the people, to the Western hemisphere. The prophet who, under God's direction, led this people in their journey, was the brother of one Jared. At the command of God he had built eight barges or vessels in which his company was to cross the mighty deep; and the brother of Jared prayed to the Lord that he would provide a means whereby they might have light in the barges, and he presented to the Lord sixteen small stones and asked that he would touch them with his finger and make them luminous, that they might give them light. And as the Lord, in answer to the earnest prayer of his servant stretched forth his hand to touch the stones, the brother of Jared saw the finger of the Lord, and he was struck with fear. Yet receiving encouragement from God, he asked the Lord to show himself to him, a petition which the Lord, in consequence of the great faith of the man, granted him, and testified to the redemption that he was yet to work out for the salvation of man. The testimony of the brother of Jared was placed upon record and was abridged by Moroni, and now comes to us in the sacred pages of the Book of Mormon* as a witness for God.

In the account given in the Book of Mormon of that colony which was led from Jerusalem, about six hundred B. C., by Lehi; and in the history of the nations that grew out of that colony, and flourished on the Western hemisphere, are many testimonies as to the existence of God; too many, in fact, to be enumerated here. All I can say is, that their prophets were visited by angels from heaven, and they were instructed by dreams and visions, in which were shown to them, in remarkable plainness, the coming and mission of Messiah; the object to be attained by, and the power of the Gospel of Christ. In all these things they were taught by the inspiration of heaven, accompanied by

---

*See Book of Ether in Book of Mormon, ch. iii.

wonderful demonstrations of the presence and power of the Lord.

Then, in III Nephi, in the Book of Mormon, is an account of two visits of the risen Redeemer to the Nephites (descendants of the aforementioned Lehi), and of his labors among that people. Here, as in Jerusalem, Jesus announced himself as the Son of God, and bore testimony to the existence of his Father. The multitude, to whom he first revealed himself, had the satisfaction of beholding the wounds in his hands and in his feet and in his side; and this, that they might know in very deed, that he was the one who had been slain in Jerusalem by the Jews, for the sins of the world—that he was the one of whom their prophets from the beginning had testified.

In the Book of Mormon, then, as in the Bible, is found a volume of testimony of God's existence; indeed, I may say the accumulated testimony of all the prophets of the Western hemisphere.

I now turn to the testimony of the prophet of our own day.

Joseph Smith, in giving an account of how he came to seek the Lord, informs us that he read that passage in James which says: "If any of you lack wisdom let him ask of God that giveth to all men liberally and upbraideth not; and it shall be given him."* In obedience to that

---
*James i: 5.

injunction, he retired to the woods to call upon the Lord, to learn from him which of all the religious sects he should join, for their division and contentions had perplexed his mind. For what occurred on that occasion I quote his own words:

"After I had retired to the place where I had previously designed to go, having looked around me and finding myself alone, I kneeled down and began to offer up the desires of my heart to God. I had scarcely done so, when immediately I was seized upon by some power which entirely overcame me, and had such astonishing influence over me as to bind my tongue so that I could not speak. Thick darkness gathered round me, and it seemed to me for a time as if I were doomed to sudden destruction. But, exerting all my powers to call upon God to deliver me out of the power of this enemy, which had seized upon me, and at the very moment when I was ready to sink into despair and abandon myself to destruction, not to an imaginary ruin, but to the power of some actual being from the unseen world, who had such a marvelous power as I had never before felt in any being—just at this moment of great alarm, I saw a pillar of light exactly over my head, above the brightness of the sun, which descended gradually until it fell upon me. It no sooner appeared than I found myself delivered from the enemy which held me bound. When the light rested upon me, I saw two personages, whose brightness and glory defy all description, standing above me in the air. One of them spake unto me, calling me by my name and said (pointing to the other), *this is my beloved son, hear him.*"*

Such is the testimony that Joseph Smith bears to the existence of God and his Son Jesus Christ; but there are other testimonies to follow.

In a revelation called "A Vision,"† is found the testimony of both Joseph Smith and Sidney Rigdon, from which I make the following extract:

"We, Joseph Smith, Jun., and Sidney Rigdon, being in the Spirit on the sixteenth of February in the year of the Lord 1832, by the power of the Spirit our eyes were opened and our understandings were enlightened, so as to see and understand the things of God—even those things which were from the beginning before the world was, which were ordained of the Father, through his Only Begotten Son, who was in the bosom of the Father, even from the beginning, of whom we bear record, and the record which we bear is the fullness of the Gospel of Jesus Christ, who is the Son, whom we saw, and with whom we conversed in the heavenly vision. * * * And while we meditated upon these things, the Lord touched the eyes of our understandings and they were opened, and the glory of God shone round

---

*Pearl of Great Price, pp. 87, 88. † Doc. and Cov., sec. lxxvi.

about; and we beheld the glory of the Son, on the right hand of the Father, and received of his fullness; and saw the holy angels, and they who are sanctified before his throne, worshiping God and the Lamb, who worship him forever and ever. And now, after the many testimonies which have been given of him, this is the testimony last of all which we give of him, that he lives; for we saw him, even on the right hand of God, and we heard the voice bearing record that he is the Only Begotten of the Father—that by him and through him, and of him the worlds are and were created, and the inhabitants thereof begotten sons and daughters unto God."

Surely their testimony lacks nothing to be desired either as to directness or plainness.

In the Kirtland Temple, on the third of April, 1836, another revelation of the existence of the Son of God was given, and another witness was added to the list of those who in this dispensation have beheld the Lord—this was Oliver Cowdery. I quote the following from the revelation:

"The vail was taken from our [the prophet Joseph's and Oliver's] minds and the eyes of our understanding were opened. We saw the Lord standing upon the breastwork of the pulpit, before us, and under his feet was a paved work of pure gold, in color like amber. His eyes were as a flame of fire, the hair of his head was white like the pure snow, his countenance shone above the brightness of the sun, and his voice was as the sound of the rushing of great waters, even the voice of Jehovah, saying—I am the first and the last, I am he who liveth, I am he who was slain, I am your advocate with the Father. Behold, your sins are forgiven you, you are clean before me, therefore lift up your heads and rejoice; let the hearts of your brethren rejoice, and let the hearts of all my people rejoice, who have, with their might, built this house* to my name, for behold I have accepted this house, and my name shall be here, and I will manifest myself to my people in mercy in this house."†

Such, in brief, are some of the direct testimonies we have from the Jewish and Nephite scriptures, and from the writings of inspired men in our own day concerning the existence of God and his Son Jesus Christ. And surely if human testimony can establish anything—any matter of fact, then the fact of God's existence is so established. The testimony comes from such a variety of sources, is delivered in so many different ages, from the first to the present, yet all blending so harmoniously, that it leaves nothing to be desired in point of consistency or harmony, quality or quantity.

Let me here observe, in concluding this chapter, that God is no respecter of persons; but they who will approach him in faith, as these

---

*The Kirtland Temple.   † Doc. and Cov., sec. cx, 1-7.

characters did, whose testimonies we have been examining, may have a knowledge of his existence also. But—adapting to my purpose the language of the Doctrine and Covenants*—after any portion of the human family are made acquainted—either through tradition, or the testimony of those who have sought and found him—with the important fact that there is a God who has created and does uphold all things, the extent of their personal knowledge respecting his character and glory, will depend upon their diligence and faithfulness in seeking after him; until, like Enoch, the brother of Jared, Moses, Joseph Smith, and Oliver Cowdery, they shall obtain faith in God, and power to behold him face to face.

CHAPTER XV.

FAITH.—THE CHARACTER OF GOD.

ALTHOUGH belief in the fact that God exists is of first importance, it is not all that is necessary to an intelligent faith. It is the primary element, perhaps, but there are others in addition to that which are needful to a rational exercise of faith—such an exercise of faith that will lead to eternal salvation in God's Kingdom. Something must be known of the character of

---

* Lecture II, on Faith, verse 55

God, of his attributes; for I hold this truth to be self-evident, that without some knowledge of God's character men cannot intelligently exercise faith in him. Without that knowledge faith will ever be imperfect, unsatisfactory, weak and comparatively unfruitful. Hence, we next proceed to inquire into the character of Deity, as he has revealed it to his children; and as we are dependent upon revelation for the knowledge of God's existence, so are we dependent upon revelation for what knowledge we have of his character.

But before I proceed immediately to inquire into the character of the Deity, I think it necessary to remark that men, who exercise faith in God, must not only believe that he is, but recognize him as the creative power by whom all things are made and sustained; that they recognize him as the Supreme Ruler of the universe. As I understand it, that much is implied in the term God. Indeed, unless God is regarded as the supreme governing power, men could not center their faith in him for life and salvation. For if the idea existed that his power was not supreme, absolute—fear would be engendered in the hearts of men that there existed still other powers who would overturn his purposes, and prevent a fulfillment of his promises; and where such fear exists there faith cannot be perfected. There is abundant testimony in the scriptures, however, which proves God to be the creator and sustainer of all things that exist, and the supreme power of the universe. In proof of this I quote the following: "Before the mountains were brought forth, or ever thou hadst formed the earth and the world, even from everlasting to everlasting, thou art God."* "And thou, Lord, in the beginning hast laid the foundation of the earth; and the heavens are the works of thy hands: they shall perish; but thou remainest; and they shall wax old as doth a garment; and as a vesture shalt thou fold them up, and they shall be changed; but thou art the same, and thy years shall not fail."†

The scriptures, however, are more specific than this as to the works of creation in connection with our earth and the heavens connected with it. It is written: "God * * * hath in these last days spoken unto us by his Son, whom he hath appointed heir of all things, *by whom also he made the worlds.*"‡

From this it appears that God through and by Jesus Christ created the worlds, not only one world, but doubtless many; and this agrees with a number of other scriptures. The apostle John says, in opening his Gospel—in plain allusion to Christ: "All things were made by him; and without him was not any thing made that was made. In him was life; and the life was the light of men."* Paul also says: "But to us

---

*Psalms xc: 2.   †Heb. i: 10-12.   ‡Heb. i: 1, 2.   §John i: 3, 4.

there is but one God, the Father, of whom are all things, and we in him; and one Lord Jesus Christ, by whom are all things, and we by him."* "And hath translated us into the kingdom of his dear Son, * * * who is the image of the invisible God, the firstborn of every creature; for by him were all things created, that are in heaven, and that are in earth, visible and invisible, whether they be thrones, or dominions, or principalities, or powers: All things were created by him, and for him: And he is before all things, and by him all things consist. And he is the head of the body, the church; who is the beginning, the firstborn from the dead, that in all things he might have the pre-eminence. For it pleased the Father that in him should all fullness dwell."†

It was doubtless these considerations which led President Young to say: "Christ is the author of this earth, of men and women, of all the posterity of Adam and Eve, and of every living creature that lives upon the face of the earth, that flies in the heavens, that swims in the waters, or dwells in the field. Christ is the author of salvation to all this creation, to all things pertaining to this terrestrial globe we occupy."‡

Christ being, under the direction of the Father the Creator and Redeemer of the earth, he and

---

*I. Cor. viii: 6. †Col. i: 13-19. ‡Journal of Discourses, Vol. III, p. 80.

his Father have a proprietorship in this earth, and by virtue of that are the Supreme Governing Power in it. The Lord Jesus Christ, under directions from his Father, created it; he then redeemed it by his own suffering; he is now, and has been from the beginning, watching over it; and will yet sanctify it, and present it to the Father a glorious, celestial sphere to be added to the redeemed and glorified kingdoms of God. "Remember the former things of old," saith the Lord through Isaiah, "for I am God and there is none else; I am God and there is none like me, declaring the end from the beginning, and from ancient times the things that are not yet done, saying my counsel shall stand, and I will do all my pleasure."*

From the scriptures, then, we get abundant evidence that God is the creator of, and the power that sustains the heavens and the earth, and the Supreme Ruler of them; so that no fear need exist in the mind of any who put their trust in God, that other powers will or can thwart his purposes, for having all power in heaven and in earth, he is able to fulfill his promises.

I now come to the character of the Deity, as we have it revealed to us in the scriptures. The references I make are brief, though sufficient, I hope, for my purpose. I assure my readers,

---

* Isaiah xlvi, 8-10.

however, that they may be indefinitely extended, as the scriptures are replete with such passages.

Moses says: "And the Lord passed by before him and proclaimed, the Lord, the Lord God, merciful and gracious, long-suffering and abundant in goodness and truth."* "The Lord executeth righteousness and judgment for all that are oppressed. He made known his ways unto Moses, his acts unto the children of Israel. The Lord is merciful and gracious, slow to anger and plenteous in mercy. But the mercy of the Lord is from everlasting to everlasting upon them that fear him, and his righteousness unto children's children; to such as keep his covenants and to those that remember his commandments to do them."†

"Every good gift and every perfect gift is from above, and cometh down from the Father of lights, with whom is no variableness, neither shadow of turning."‡ "For I am the Lord, I change not; therefore ye sons of Jacob are not consumed."§ "For God doth not walk in crooked paths, neither does he turn to the right hand nor to the left, or vary from that which he has said, therefore his paths are straight, and his course is one eternal round."‖ "Listen to the voice of the Lord your God, even Alpha and Omega, the beginning and the end, whose

---

*Exodus xxxiv: 6.   †Psalms ciii: 6, 7, 8, 17, 18.   ‡James i: 17.
§ Mal. iii: 6.   ‖ Doc. and Cov., sec, iii: 2.

course is one eternal round, the same today as yesterday and forever."*

"God is not a man that he should lie, neither the son of man that he should repent."† "Into thy hand I commit my spirit; thou hast redeemed me, O Lord God of Truth."‡ "He is the rock, his work is perfect; for all his ways are judgment; a God of truth and without iniquity, just and right is he."§

Of a truth I perceive that God is no respecter of persons, but in every nation he that feareth God and worketh righteousness is accepted with him."‖

"He that loveth not, knoweth not God; for God is love: * * * and he that dwelleth in love dwelleth in God, and God in him."¶ "For God so loved the world that he gave his only begotten Son, that whosoever believeth on him should not perish but have everlasting life."**

I can think of no greater evidence of God's love than that exhibited in the act of permitting his Son, Jesus Christ, to come to the earth and suffer as he did for the sins of the world, that they might not suffer if they would but conform to his laws and thus accept the terms of salvation. It would seem, too, that the same attribute of love exists in the breast of the Son, for the sacrifice he made for the redemption of the

---

*Doc. and Cov., sec. xxxv: 1. † Numbers xxiii: 19 ‡ Psalms xxxi: 5. § Deut. xxxii: 4. ‖ Acts x: 34, 35. ¶ I. John iv: 8-16.
** John iii: 16.

world was a voluntary act. He was not compelled to make the atonement, but of his own free will he volunteered to become our ransom.*

He himself testified: "Therefore doth my Father love me, because I lay down my life, that I might take it again. No man taketh it from me, but I lay it down of myself. I have power to lay it down, and I have power to take it again. This commandment have I received of my Father."†

Thus, the atonement of Jesus, for the children of men, was a voluntary act; and his death and suffering for the world, was the strongest expression of his love it is possible to conceive—"Greater love hath no man than this, that a man lay down his life for his friends."

From the foregoing testimonies we learn the following things respecting the character of God.

"First, that he is merciful and gracious, slow to anger, abundant in goodness, and that he was so from everlasting, and will be so to everlasting.

"Secondly, that he changes not, neither is there variableness with him; but that he is the same from everlasting to everlasting, being the same yesterday, today, and forever, and that his course is one eternal round, without variation.

"Thirdly, that he is a God of truth and cannot lie.

"Fourthly, that he is no respecter of persons,

---

*Pearl of Great Price, p. 41.   † John x: 17, 18.

but in every nation he who fears God and works righteousness is accepted of him.

"Fifthly, that he is love."*

I conclude this chapter with the remarks made upon these attributes of Deity, to be found in one of the lectures on faith in the Doctrine and Covenants:

"An acquaintance with these attributes in the divine character, is essentially necessary, in order that the faith of any rational being can center in him for life and salvation. For unless he was merciful and gracious, slow to anger, long suffering and full of goodness, such is the weakness of human nature, and so great the frailties and imperfections of men, that unless they believed that these excellencies existed in the divine character, the faith necessary to salvation could not exist; for doubt would take the place of faith, and those who know their weakness and liability to sin, would be in constant doubt of salvation, if it were not for the idea which they have of the excellency of the character of God, that he is slow to anger and long suffering, and of a forgiving disposition, and does forgive iniquity, transgression and sin. An idea of these facts does away doubt, and makes faith exceedingly strong.

"But it is equally as necessary that men should have the idea that he is a God who changes not,

---

*I quote the above paragraphs from the III. Lecture on Faith, Doc. and Cov.

in order to have faith in him, as it is to have the idea that he is gracious and long suffering; for without the idea of unchangeableness in the character of the Deity, doubt would take the place of faith. But with the idea that he changes not, faith lays hold upon the excellencies in his character with unshaken confidence, believing he is the same yesterday, today and forever, and that his course is one eternal round.

"And again, the idea that he is a God of truth and cannot lie, is equally as necessary to the exercise of faith in him as the idea of his unchangeableness. For without the idea that he was a God of truth and could not lie, the confidence necessary to be placed in his word, in order to the exercise of faith in him could not exist. But having the idea that he is not man, that he cannot lie, it gives power to the minds of men to exercise faith in him.

"But it is also necessary that men should have an idea that he is no respecter of persons, for with the idea of all the other excellencies in his character, and this one wanting, men could not exercise faith in him; because if he were a respecter of persons, they could not tell what their privileges were, nor how far they were authorized to exercise faith in him, or whether they were authorized to do it at all, but all must be confusion; but no sooner are the minds of men made acquainted with the truth on this point, that he is no respecter of persons, than they see that they have authority by faith to lay hold on eternal life, the richest boon of heaven, because God is no respecter of persons, and that every man in every nation has an equal privilege.

"And lastly, but not less important to the exercise of faith in God, is the idea that he is love; for with all the other excellencies in his character, without this one to influence them, they could not have such powerful dominion over the minds of men; but when the idea is planted in the mind that he is love, who cannot see the just ground that men of every nation, kindred, and tongue, have to exercise faith in God so as to obtain eternal life!

"From the above description of the character of the Deity, which is given him in the revelations to men, there is a sure foundation for the exercise of faith in him among every people, nation, and kindred, from age to age, and from generation to generation."*

CHAPTER XVI.

FAITH.—COURSE OF LIFE.

I HAVE now considered two elements which enter into the principle of faith, and which are essential to its existence; *viz.*, a belief in the being of God; and, secondly, the nature of his

---

* Doc and Cov., Lectures on Faith, No. III.

character. There is still one more thing that must be considered, one more element that must enter into this principle of faith, before it can become a living, active power in the life of man —and that is, herein the worth of faith exists. I may say of faith as Guizot does of science, that it may be a beautiful thing of itself, but it becomes a thousand times grander and more beautiful when it becomes a power; when it becomes the parent of virtue. Indeed if it does not become a power in the life of man, an incentive to noble deeds, it is a dead faith, and is as the body without the spirit, or as salt without its savor—it is good for nothing.

The third element which is essential to faith as a power in the life of man, centers in and depends upon man rather than God. A belief in the fact that God exists, with a correct idea of his character is sufficient for man to exercise faith in him, but man must know something about himself also; that is, he must know that the course of life he is pursuing is in accordance with the will of heaven—is approved of God, before faith can become perfect, or have any marked influence with the heavens. This truth is self-evident. For what confidence can one have that his petition will be heard and answered by the Lord, if all the time he is conscious that he habitually, perhaps wantonly, violates the law of God—if he blasphemes the name of Deity, or speaks lightly, and may be slightingly, of sacred things, or walks contrary to the expressed will of the Lord in the matter of truthfulness, sobriety, chastity, honesty and brotherly kindness? What confidence, I ask, can such a person have that his petitions will be sufficiently respected either to be heard or granted? The understanding answers, none. It stands to reason that such persons must repent, and that earnestly, with real intent, with a fixed determination to respect God and his laws, before they can hope for the powers of heaven to be influenced by them. It is the prayer of the righteous man that availeth much.

On the other hand, if one walk in all honesty of heart before God; if to the best of his ability and knowledge, making due allowance for human frailty—and I do not under-estimate its influence in hindering that perfect walk with God, that is desirable—he keeps the laws of his God, sacrificing his good name among men, if need be, or leaving father or mother, houses or lands, wives and children, counting all things but dross, when compared with the excellence of the knowledge of God—being faithful through good and through evil report—resulting, as it must do, in a consciousness of the approval of heaven—how strong will his confidence become in the presence of the Lord, and what blessings can the heavens withhold from him?

It was this consciousness of having walked truly before his God, which, when the word of the

Lord came to him, that he should surely die, enabled king Hezekiah to turn to the Lord, in confidence, and say: "Remember, now, O Lord, I beseech thee, how I have walked before thee in truth, and with a perfect heart, and have done good in thy sight."* And before Isaiah had left the house of the king, the word of the Lord came again to him, bidding him to return to the king with the glad message that his prayer had been heard, and fifteen years had been added to his life.

It was this consciousness, coupled with a belief in God's existence and a knowledge of his character, that enabled the ancient saints to endure their sore afflictions, taking joyfully the spoiling of their goods. By combining these elements of faith they produced a power by which they "subdued kingdoms, wrought righteousness, obtained promises, stopped the mouths of lions, quenched the violence of fire, escaped the edge of the sword, out of weakness were made strong, waxed valiant in fight, turned to flight the armies of the aliens. Women received their dead raised to life again: and others were tortured, not accepting deliverance; that they might obtain a better resurrection: and others had trial of cruel mockings and scourgings, yea, moreover of bonds and imprisonment: they were stoned, they were sawn asunder, were tempted, were slain with the

---

Isaiah xxxviii.

sword: they wandered about in sheepskins and goatskins; being destitute, afflicted, tormented. Of whom the world was not worthy, they wandered in deserts, and in mountains, and in dens and caves of the earth."*

Such is Paul's testimony respecting the faith and the power thereof among the saints on the Eastern hemisphere; and if we turn to the sacred pages of the Book of Mormon, a like record of sacrifice and heroism could be drawn up to the credit of the saints living on the Western hemisphere.

And so also with the Saints in this present dispensation. It was through faith that the Prophet Joseph Smith had the heavens opened to him and received a glorious vision of God the Father and his Son Jesus Christ; it was through faith that he received the gold plates on which were engraven the history and scriptures of the Nephites, and translated them into the English language; it was by the power of faith that he organized the church and the quorums of the priesthood. It was by the power of faith, too, that the Saints endured the persecutions heaped upon them in Missouri, the land of Zion, taking joyfully the spoiling of their goods, being whipped, imprisoned and murdered. It was by faith they gathered at Nauvoo and converted its

---

* Heb. xi : 33-38.

swamps into a beautiful city, its wilderness into fruitful fields and erected the beautiful temple in the days of their poverty. By faith they restrained their anger when their prophet and patriarch were murdered while under the plighted faith of the State of Illinois, and committed no depredations on the ungodly within their power in retaliation for the cowardly assassination of their leaders.

By faith they followed the prophet Brigham into the desert, going a thousand miles beyond the borders of civilization among savage Indian tribes, their only hope of protection being in the God of Israel. By faith they subdued the sterile soil and made it yield them the bounties of life, and filled the once barren wastes of the Rocky Mountain valleys with towns and villages; farms, gardens, orchards and happy homes for an extent of more than five hundred miles; and by faith they have calmly endured fines, confiscations, exile and imprisonment—persecution under the forms of law—at the hands of the United States government, rather than be untrue to their God.

Such experiences as these I have referred to in the history of the Saints, both of ancient and modern times, demonstrates to the heavens the strength or quality of faith possessed by the Saints, and also exhibits faith as a principle of power, for such it is; who can doubt it when we are told that through faith the worlds were framed by the Word of God;* and through faith the saints in all ages of the world have been able to perform the works already set down to their credit.

Another result flows from these experiences—these sufferings, trials and sacrifices of the saints. They bring to the faithful who endure them the assurance—nay, the knowledge of their acceptance with God. This knowledge occupies an important place in religion, for it is through that knowledge and through that alone, that men will be able to endure the trials that ever have and ever will, in a state of probation, beset the pathway of candidates for the celestial kingdom of God. "Such was and ever will be the situation of the saints of God, that unless they have an actual knowledge that the course they are pursuing is according to the will of God, they will grow weary in their minds, and faint; for such has been, and always will be the opposition in the hearts of unbelievers and those that know not God, against the pure and unadulterated religion of heaven (the only thing which insures eternal life), that they will persecute to the uttermost all that worship God according to his revelations, receive the truth in the love of it, and submit themselves to be guided and directed by his will; and drive them to such extremities, that nothing short of an actual knowledge of their being the

---
* Heb xi: 3.

favorites of heaven, and of their having embraced that order of things which God has established for the redemption of man, will enable them to exercise that confidence in him, necessary for them to overcome the world, and obtain that crown of glory which is laid up for them that fear God." * * * * * * *

"For unless a person does know that he is walking according to the will of God, it would be offering an insult to the dignity of the Creator, were he to say, that he would be a partaker of his glory when he should be done with the things of this life. But when he has this knowledge, and most assuredly knows that he is doing the will of God, his confidence can be equally strong that he will be a partaker of the glory of God."

"Let us here observe, that a religion that does not require the sacrifice of all things, never has power sufficient to produce the faith necessary unto life and salvation; for, from the first existence of man, the faith necessary unto the enjoyment of life and salvation never could be obtained without the sacrifice of all earthly things. It was through this sacrifice, and this only, that God has ordained that men should enjoy eternal life; and it is through the medium of the sacrifice of all earthly things, that men do actually know that they are doing the things that are well pleasing in the sight of God. When a man has offered in sacrifice all that he has for the truth's sake, not even withholding his life, and believing before

God that he has been called to make this sacrifice because he seeks to do his will, he does know, most assuredly, that God does and will accept his sacrifice and offering, and that he has not, nor will not, seek his face in vain. Under these circumstances, then, he can obtain the faith necessary for him to lay hold on eternal life."

"It is in vain for persons to fancy to themselves that they are heirs with those, or can be heirs with them, who have offered their all in sacrifice, and by this means obtained faith in God and favor with him, so as to obtain eternal life, unless they, in like manner, offer unto him the same sacrifice, and through that offering, obtain the knowledge that they are accepted of him. * * * From the days of righteous Abel to the present time, the knowledge that men have that they are accepted in the sight of God, is obtained by offering sacrifice. And in the last days, before the Lord comes, he is to gather together his saints who have made a covenant with him, by sacrifice: 'Our God shall come, and shall not keep silence: a fire shall devour before him, and it shall be very tempestuous round about him. He shall call to the heavens from above, and to the earth, that he may judge his people. Gather my saints together unto me; those that have made a covenant with me by sacrifice.'"*

"Those, then, who make the sacrifice, will have

---

* Psalms i: 3-5.

the testimony that their course is pleasing in the sight of God; and those who have this testimony will have faith to lay hold on eternal life, and will be enabled, through faith, to endure unto the end, and receive the crown that is laid up for them that love the appearing of our Lord Jesus Christ. But those who do not make the sacrifice cannot enjoy this faith, because men are dependent upon this sacrifice in order to obtain this faith; therefore they cannot lay hold upon eternal life, because the revelations of God do not guarantee unto them the authority so to do, and without this guarantee faith could not exist."

"All the saints of whom we have any account, in all the revelations of God which are extant, obtained the knowledge which they had of their acceptance in his sight through the sacrifice which they offered unto him; and through the knowledge thus obtained their faith became sufficiently strong to lay hold upon the promise of eternal life, and to endure as seeing him who is invisible; and were enabled, through faith, to combat the powers of darkness, contend against the wiles of the adversary, overcome the world, and obtain the end of their faith, even the salvation of their souls."*

This, then, is my exposition of the grand principle of faith: It is an assurance of the mind of the existence or reality of things not seen, or

---

* Doc. and Cov., Lecture on Faith, No. VI.

that have not been demonstrated to any other of the senses. It takes root in evidence, more or less convincing to the understanding; and the strength of the faith depends largely upon the quality and quantity of the evidence. The more unquestionable, the more overwhelming the evidence, the more strong and immovable will be the faith.

As a principle of religion, faith centers in God, and bids man hope for salvation and eternal life. I have endeavored to show in the foregoing pages that in order that faith may be intelligently exercised in God, it is essential that there should be a belief in his existence, and correct ideas as to his character. I trust that the evidences pointed out as to the fact that he exists have been sufficient to produce that belief; and that the testimonies adduced have been of a character to fix in the mind of the reader a just estimate of his character. If that has been accomplished, then I feel assured that a faith has been established in the mind that will lead to *repentance*, to an effort to yield obedience to the laws of heaven. That effort persevered in will, in time, bring the consciousness that the course of life being pursued is in accordance with the will of heaven, and by a union of these three elements, that is, a belief in the existence of God, a correct conception of his character, and a knowledge that the course of life pursued is approved of him—will render faith perfect, will constitute it a principle of power, the incentive to all action—as really it is, whether in temporal or spiritual things—leading from one degree of knowledge or excellence to another, from righteousness to righteousness, until the heavens will be opened to them and they will hold communion with the Church of the First Born, with Jesus Christ, and with God the Father, and thus will they make their calling and election sure—through faith ripening into knowledge.

CHAPTER XVII.

REPENTANCE.

IN saying that the first result of belief in God, and in the revelations which he has given is *repentance*, I shall raise no controversy, for it is a truth generally accepted; indeed it follows faith in logical sequence. No sooner does conviction of God's existence, and of the truth of the revelations which he has given of himself, and of his laws, dawn upon the mind, than man becomes conscious of his being a violator of the holy and just laws of heaven. In the days of his unbelief and spiritual darkness he sinned recklessly and wantonly, without regard to God and often in defiance of him; but when belief takes hold of the mind, and when mere belief begins to ripen into intelligent faith through becoming acquainted with the character of the Deity—when it becomes clear to the understanding that he is the creative and sustaining power of all things; when it is understood that from him man derives his existence and that in him he lives, and moves and has his being; and when it is further known that his laws are beneficent and good, shaped for the purpose of ennobling man and exalting him; when some revelation of the great love of God and his Son Jesus Christ rushes in upon the mind like a flood of heavenly light into darkness—how the haughty, rebellious spirit is humbled, the heart softened, and the whole demeanor changed! With what contrition does the man, truly convinced of all these things we have enumerated respecting the Deity, seek the throne of grace and cry aloud: "O God! Have mercy upon me a sinner!" For almost at the same moment that faith took hold of him, he began to understand how great his sins were before God. And that realization grows upon him as conviction, becomes more certain, until the spirit is bowed down with sorrow because of his many violations of the laws of righteousness.

Nor do these remarks apply only to those who have been enormously wicked. Take those of a naturally good disposition, and who have followed the light of reason, and even they, in taking a retrospective view of their lives, will find that they have fallen far short of coming up to what they conceived to be their duty. Even the light they possessed—I mean aside from the revelations of God—revealed to them a higher moral excellence than they have attained. They have not done as well as they could have done. This fact is evident—one of which all may give witness. This being true, that is, man seeing that he has come short of doing his whole duty according to his natural conceptions of what that duty is, how much more distant from the goal of desired excellence will he esteem himself when the light of revelation breaks in upon his life, bringing into bolder relief his mistakes, and revealing to him a purer moral and spiritual life than it was possible for his mind, unaided by revelation, to conceive? I venture the assertion that even the best men—by that I mean those who have best conformed their lives to the rules of conduct dictated by reason—will be ready to say with the apostle, "All have sinned and come short of the glory of God."

Hence they, as well as those guilty of more flagrant sins, will, as faith takes possession of their minds, be brought to repentance through its influence, and be led to seek forgiveness of their sins, and reconciliation with God.

That repentance is the first result growing out of faith in God and the Gospel, is abundantly proven from the scriptures. The multitude that assembled on the day of Pentecost, and listened to the remarks of the apostles, and even heard them speak in tongues, by the power of the Holy Ghost, were ready to scoff at those things, and even went so far as to say that these men were drunken with new wine; but when Peter arose and reasoned with them from the scriptures, proving from the law and the prophets that Jesus, whom the Jews had slain, was both Lord and Christ, his words and testimony were accompanied by so much of the power of God, that conviction took hold of the people, and, as with one voice, they cried, "Men and brethren, what shall we do?" In this instance, then, the first fruits of that faith which had been created in the minds of this people, was a desire to know what they were to do; and the first words that the inspired apostle said in reply were, "Repent, every one of you."*

Paul, of Tarsus, afterwards the great apostle to the Gentiles, at first persecuted the disciples of Jesus, casting both men and women into prison for what he considered their blasphemous faith. And when Stephen was martyred, Paul stood by and held the clothes of those who did the ghastly, cruel deed. He appears to have been proud of and zealous in the prosecution of this work of opposition; but when the Lord appeared to him on the way to Damascus, and announced himself as Jesus whom he persecuted, the ambitious, arrogant Paul was immediately humbled to the dust, and in tremulous accents he inquired, "Lord, what wouldst thou have me

---

* Acts ii.

to do?"* How deep the sorrow, how sincere the repentance was which began in the very moment of his learning the fact that Jesus was the Lord, is witnessed by his life of zealous labors and his suffering in the interest of the kingdom of Messiah.

The Book of Mormon also furnishes a number of examples of like character. When a church was established among the Nephites, in the reign of good King Mosiah, about 100 B. C., the work of God was bitterly opposed, derided and persecuted by the sons of King Mosiah, and especially by Alma, one of the sons of the first Alma, and a man of great influence and consummate eloquence. Paul-like, these men went about doing all the mischief to the people of God within their power; but at last an angel of the Lord appeared to them, to bring them to a knowledge of the truth, and this occurred in answer to the fervent prayers of their parents. The glory of God shone about the angel, and his voice shook the earth. Alma was smitten dumb for a season, and had to be carried to the presence of his father; and when his speech returned to him, the eloquent scoffer of a few days before, was as humble as a child, and as penitent and submissive as it is possible for man to be. He repented of all his former sins, and throughout the remainder of his event-

---

* Acts ix.

ful life, was a zealous missionary and a faithful witness for God.*

Similar in point, too, is the case of Zeezrom, the lawyer, who withstood, for a time, the teachings of Alma and Amulek, but was brought to faith and repentance through the manifestation of the power of God.† Enough, however, has been said in relation to a fact that in the very nature of things is largely self-evident; and surely after the illustration it has received, will not now be questioned; that is, that repentance is the first result growing out of faith in God and in revelation; and therefore it is the subject that, according to the natural order of things, must now receive our attention.

CHAPTER XVIII.

REPENTANCE.

SOMETHING of the importance of the subject of repentance, as connected with the Gospel, may be learned from the stress laid upon it by those who have been sent of God to instruct the people in the ways of life. The burden of John the Baptist's teaching was, "Repent ye, for the kingdom of heaven is at hand."‡ Jesus also told the people of Jerusalem, that except they

---

* The history of this case is in the Book of Mosiah, Book of Mormon, ch. xxvii.   † See Book of Alma, xi-xvi.   ‡ Matt. iii: 2.

repented, they should perish.* When upon the Western hemisphere, among the Nephites, he also taught repentance as one of the conditions of salvation, saying to them, "Whosoever will hearken to my words, and repenteth and is baptized, the same shall be saved."† And of course it follows that those who repented not, and were not baptized, could not be saved.

When the apostles, that were chosen in Judea, began the execution of the commission given them, *viz.*, to go and teach all nations, the very first thing they required the people who received their words to do was that the should repent.‡ Paul bears witness, that though in the days of ignorance God winked at sins, when the Gospel was declared unto the people, he commanded men everywhere to repent. And in this last dispensation, the Lord inspired his servant Joseph Smith to say, "We know that all men must repent, and believe on the name of Jesus Christ, * * * or they cannot be saved in the kingdom of God."§

From these scriptures it is evident that repentance is one of the conditions of salvation, and, indeed, reason, no less forcibly than revelation, would teach us that it is one of the conditions on which salvation is predicated. It must forever precede a forgiveness of sins. He who is impenitent is in no condition to receive a for-

---

* Luke xiii: 1-5. † III. Nephi xxiii: 5. ‡ Luke xiii: 1-5. § Doc. and Cov., sec. xx: 29.

giveness of sins; he does not desire it; he would not receive it; he refuses to surrender, and however much men and angels may deplore his state of mind, one cannot conceive how God would forgive anyone in open rebellion to him and his laws, and who persists in that rebellion. Not until the spirit is humbled, not until the heart throbs with genuine sorrow for repeated violation of God's holy laws, not until the citadel of sin is surrendered, can man hope for forgiveness, or expect salvation.

But what is repentance? I shall venture as a definition this, Repentance is a deep and heartfelt sorrow for sin, producing a reformation of life. That is the significance of the word to my mind as associated with the Gospel; and I think such a definition arises from the spirit, and, I may say, the letter of the scriptures.

"Repent, and turn yourselves from your transgressions; so iniquity shall not be your ruin. Cast away from you all your transgressions, whereby you have transgressed; and make you a new heart and a new spirit, for why will ye die, O house of Israel?"*

Such was the word of the Lord to Israel through the prophet Ezekiel. I call the attention of the reader to the fact, that the idea of turning away from transgressions, and making a new heart and a new spirit, or in other word, a reformation

---

*Ezek. xviii: 30, 31.

of life, is associated with the commandment to repent, and forms part of it.

Paul wrote an epistle to the Corinthian saints, reproving them for their sins, and his sharp reproofs filled them with sorrow. In a subsequent epistle to the same people, and alluding to the effect of his former epistle, he said: "Though I made you sorry with a letter, I do not repent. * * * I rejoice, not that ye were made sorry, but that you sorrowed unto repentance; for ye were made sorry after a godly manner, that ye might receive damage by us in nothing. For godly sorrow worketh repentance unto salvation not to be repented of: but the sorrow of the world worketh death."*

From this passage it appears that Paul recognized two kinds of sorrow, or repentance, one of which has need to be repented of, because unfruitful of reformation, and therefore not profitable in the way of salvation—the sorrow of the world which worketh death. On the other hand is godly sorrow, or repentance which bringeth salvation, known to both men and angels, aye, and likewise to God, by the fruit it bears— good works—forsaking evil, producing a reformation of life. It leads one who stole to steal no more; one in the habit of getting drunk, to get drunk no more; one who blasphemed the name of God to do so no more; and so on as to all things

---

* II. Cor. vii: 8-10.

in which man violates the sacred principles of righteousness. It is written in James: "Submit yourselves, therefore, to God. Resist the devil and he will flee from you. Draw nigh to God and he will draw nigh to you. Cleanse your hands, ye sinners; and purify your hearts, ye double minded. Be afflicted and mourn, and weep: let your laughter be turned to mourning, and your joy to heaviness. Humble yourselves in the sight of the Lord, and he shall lift you up."*

Because of the stress here laid upon the necessity of humility, and the people being commanded to mourn and weep, to let their laughter be turned to mourning, and their joy to heaviness, some religious teachers (like the Pharisees and scribes of old who tithed mint and anise and cummin, but omitted the weightier matters of the law, judgment, mercy and faith) give so much attention to weeping, mourning and crying aloud, in order to appear to be afflicted, that they have overlooked the weightier matters—cleansing their hands, purifying their hearts, resisting the devil and drawing nigh unto God. These ought they to do, and not leave the other—the weeping and mourning, inasmuch as it arises from a deep and heartfelt conviction of sinfulness—undone.

But at present there is too much of what Paul would call "worldly sorrow" mixed up with the

---

*James iv: 7-10.

idea of repentance. Too much mourning over sin, yet running into temptation; an excess of lamentation and not enough of turning away from evil; in a word, the sorrow of the world, which worketh death, is too prevalent. How weary must be the old, old story to God and angels, as well as to men—"we have done those things we ought not to have done, and have left undone those things we ought to have done!"

Then again, the sorrow of the world, the sorrow which worketh death, is too generally accepted for genuine repentance; the latter may be known and distinguished from the former by its being accompanied by a reformation of life, a turning away from that which is evil—the kind of repentance required in the Gospel, the only kind that will be accepted of God, or that savors of salvation. God, whom we esteem as a being in whom all the fullness of perfection dwells, must ever be more pleased with the substance of worship, or religion, or repentance than with the forms pertaining to it, and this is abundantly proven by instances recorded in holy writ.

In the days of Israel's captivity in Babylon, certain messengers from those who were captive, Sherezer and Regem-melech and their men, went up to Jerusalem to inquire of the prophets and priests of the Lord if Israel while in captivity should keep the fast of the fifth month, and weep, separating themselves as they had hitherto done. In answer to these inquiries the word of the Lord came through the prophet Zechariah, and he asks: "When ye fasted and mourned in the fifth and seventh month, even those seventy years, did ye at all fast unto me, even to me? And when ye did eat, and when ye did drink, did not ye eat for yourselves and drink for yourselves? Should ye not hear the words which the Lord hath cried by the former prophets, when Jerusalem was inhabited and in prosperity, and the cities thereof round about her, when men inhabited the south and the plain?"

He reminds them that through the former prophets he had commanded Israel to execute true judgment, to show mercy and compassion every man to his brother; to oppress not the widow and the fatherless, the stranger nor the poor; to let none imagine evil in his heart against his brother. But these things they neglected to do, and the Lord permitted their enemies to scatter them among strange nations.

As a final answer to those messengers, however, the Lord said: "These are the things which ye shall do: speak ye every man the truth to his neighbor, execute the judgment of truth and peace in your gates: and let none of you imagine evil in your heart against his neighbor: and love no false oath: for all these are things which I hate, saith the Lord." And then the Lord, on condition of their doing this, promised them that "The fast of the fourth month, and the fast of the fifth, and the fast of the seventh, and the fast of the tenth, shall be to the house of Judah joy and gladness and cheerful feasts; therefore love the truth and peace."*

Surely, after the spirit of this circumstance is carefully considered, it will be admitted that I am right in my statement, that God is more pleased with the substance of repentance, than with the weeping and mourning attendant upon it; more satisfied with the reformation of the sinner, than with his affliction.

Then, how reasonable and righteous is this law of repentance! When one guilty of violating the laws of heaven desires forgiveness, the very least thing that can be expected of him is that he will refrain from doing again those things which constituted his offense, and form an honest resolution to refrain from evil.

Moreover, repentance is chiefly beneficial to the person who practices it. The commandment from God to repent—always given in connection with the declaration of the Gospel—is really nothing more than an invitation to do one's self a kindness. It can only be an abomination to fools to depart from evil. It is written, also, that "Righteousness exalteth a nation; but sin is a reproach to any people."† And as it is with a nation, so it is with individuals.

Again, the voice of inspiration says: "As righteousness tendeth to life, so he that pursueth

---

* Zech., chapters vii and viii.   † Proverbs of Solomon.

evil, pursueth it to his own death." To repent, then, means to turn aside from the path which leads to death, and choose that which leads to life—to life eternal. And while the angels in heaven may rejoice over one who turns from the error of his way; yet, the chief good arising from the reformation of the sinner, is reaped by himself.

Since God, then, in this matter of repentance seeks only the good of those of whom the requirement is made, "Let the wicked forsake his wicked way, and the unrighteous man his thoughts; and let him turn unto the Lord, and he will have mercy upon him; and to our God for he will abundantly pardon."*

CHAPTER XIX.

REPENTANCE.—HISTORICAL ILLUSTRATION.

HISTORICAL illustration of the truth of the statement made by Isaiah, with which our last chapter closed, and which in effect says that the Lord will have mercy on the penitent sinner and abundantly pardon him—would be easy, whether in the experience of individuals or of peoples and nations.

When Cain was crest-fallen because the offerings of his more righteous brother were accepted,

---

* Isaiah lv: 7.

while his own half-hearted and begrudgingly-tendered offerings were rejected, the Lord said to him, "Cain, why art thou wroth? and why is thy countenance fallen? If thou doest well, shalt thou not be accepted?"* So it would seem that the Lord was just as ready to receive Cain as he was Abel, if the former would only repent.

In my first chapter on repentance (chapter xvii), I referred to the case of Paul's conversion, and I only name it again in order to call the reader's attention to the readiness with which the Lord forgave him fully, and made him an honored servant in his church on his turning away from his sins. In the same chapter reference is also made to the case of Zeezrom, the lawyer, to Alma, the son of the first Alma, and to the sons of Mosiah his companions, all of whom, like Paul, were among the chief of sinners, because they persecuted the Church of God; but on their sincere repentance, as in Paul's case, the Lord freely and abundantly pardoned them. Among the remarkable characters of old, perhaps none are more interesting than the person known in the Book of Ether as the brother of Jared.† He is the prophet whom God chose to lead away a colony from the great tower, built shortly after the flood, to the choice land of America. After this colony had been led from the tower into the wilderness, they pitched their

---

* Gen. iv: 6, 7. † See Book of Mormon.

tents in a land they called Moriancumer, by the sea-side; and here they dwelt for four years.

During this season of rest and peace they forgot their God, and neglected to call upon him. It seems, too, that the brother of Jared was guilty of this thing, as well as his brethren. At last the Lord appeared to the brother of Jared in a cloud, and reproved him for his neglect, and for the space of about three hours he chastened him for his sins. "And the brother of Jared repented of the evil which he had done, and did call upon the name of the Lord for his brethren who were with him. And the Lord said unto him, I forgive thee and thy brethren of their sins; but thou shalt not sin any more, for ye shall remember that my spirit will not always strive with man; wherefore, if ye will sin until ye are fully ripe, ye shall be cut off from the presence of the Lord."* Note how readily the Lord forgave as soon as the transgressors repented!

Time would fail me to tell of Laman and Lemuel, the elder brothers of Nephi, who so frequently were in rebellion against God, and their younger brother, whom the Lord had chosen to be a leader and a prophet unto them. How often they assaulted his person, bound him with cords, scorned his teachings, rejected his warnings and trampled the message of God under their feet! Yet as often as they repented both

---

* Book of Ether, in Book of Mormon, ch. ii.

Nephi and the Lord forgave them, and that freely.

The experience of these persons, and that of many others related in holy writ, is surely sufficient to prove the willingness of God to forgive. Yet, take one more evidence of it, not from personal experience, however, but from the spirit of the teachings of the Son of God. On a certain occasion the apostle Peter came to Jesus and said: "Lord, how oft shall my brother sin against me, and I forgive him; till seven times? Jesus saith unto him, I say not unto thee until seven times: but until seventy times seven.'*

Since the Lord requires so much mercy, such a generous spirit of forgiveness in his children, may it not be reasonably concluded—inasmuch as every noble quality that man possesses, is, in Deity, enlarged and perfected—that God is infinitely more forgiving than he has commanded his children to be? Such a conclusion, it seems to me, is but reasonable; and, indeed, it is needful that such an idea respecting the character of God, should exist in the minds of men; for, as I have remarked elsewhere, such is the weakness of man, and the frequency of his transgressions of God's law, that unless he knows that the Lord is merciful, slow to anger, long-suffering, and always ready to forgive, he would become disheartened; gloomy despair would drive hope

---

*Matt. xviii: 21, 22.

from the soul; and, hope once destroyed, leaves man a prey to all the fiends of hell. He will then give a loose rein to every passion, and under the whip and spur of his desperation, ride recklessly to certain and everlasting destruction. He would have no good, he would know no evil. Lucifer-like, he would exclaim:

> * * * "Whither shall I fly?
> Which way I fly is hell—myself am hell!
> And in the lowest deep, a lower deep
> Still opening wider, threatens to devour me!"

But man is rescued from this gloomy prospect by the assurance of God's longsuffering and willingness to forgive; by knowing that while man may drive compassion from his heart, God never will. Yet stay! there is something more. Because of the loving kindness of our Father in heaven, as abundantly manifested in his willingness to pardon our transgressions, let us not lay the flattering unction to our souls that we can go on sinning, carelessly and recklessly, without making any effort to resist evil, relying, nay, rather, presuming upon the kindness of God to forgive. Such a course would be doing despite to the grace of God; it would be an unmitigated insult to the Most High; a most presumptuous sin, deserving the severest condemnation.

The Lord is faithful to forgive us our sins, and to cleanse us from our transgressions,* but it is

---

* I. John i: 9.

on condition of our repentance, that we confess our sins, and make a manly, determined effort to forsake them. Therefore, while the tender mercies of our God, and his readiness to forgive should encourage men "to pray and not faint," and by that means seek forgiveness of sins, they should also remember that it is decreed that the Spirit of the Lord will not always strive with man,* and that there are some sins that may not be forgiven either in this life, or in that which is to come.†

CHAPTER XX.

REPENTANCE.—HISTORICAL ILLUSTRATION.

IF we turn to the history of peoples and nations in order to learn the lessons which their experiences teach, we shall find that the hand-dealings of God with them as collected bodies, as well as the experiences of individuals, demonstrate the same great facts of God's long-suffering and abundant mercy, and of his willingness to pardon on the first manifestation of sincere repentance.

It was not until the antediluvians had become thoroughly corrupt, not until every imagination of the thoughts of their hearts was evil continually,‡

---

* Gen. vi: 3.   † Matt. xii: 31, 32.   ‡ Gen. vi.

and they rejected the teachings of Noah, and were beyond the hope of reformation, that the Lord sent the flood upon them and cut them off that they might not perpetuate in their posterity their corruption.

Next in chronological order to the antediluvians stands the people of Jared; and from the brief history we have of them in the Book of Mormon, consisting of an abridgement of the twenty-four plates of the prophet Ether, we learn that they were frequently in rebellion against God, and continually straying from his precepts and ordinances. Yet as often as they repented he forgave them; and not only that, but supplemented that forgiveness by such periods of prosperity, that one would think that even if they knew no more than the dumb ass that merely knows his master's crib, they must have been aware that it was to their present as well as to their eternal interests to live in obedience to the will of heaven. Yet sin, individual and national, was added to sin, transgressions followed close upon the heels of each other, and secret combinations were formed for robbery and to obtain political power, spreading rapine, murder and terror throughout the land, and menacing always the security of the political fabric.

In the midst of all this the Lord labored patiently for their reformation, sending his servants, the prophets, to them, to teach them the way of life and encourage them to observe the statutes and judgments of the Lord. When persuasion failed, then warning was given of calamities and judgments, followed by the chastening hand of God; but all to no purpose; reform they would not. They killed the prophets, and persecuted those who attempted to follow their counsels until they filled up the cup of their iniquity, and the Spirit of the Lord entirely withdrew from them, and then began that series of wars in the sixth century B. C., which finally ended in the extermination of the entire people.*

The history of ancient Israel, as recorded in the Bible, is very similar to this. The Lord took them from the bondage of Egypt, to sanctify them a people unto himself. He gave them Moses and Aaron and other wise, faithful men to be their teachers, and led them from the dominion of Egypt towards a choice land, their journey being attended by such displays of God's glory and power as are seldom witnessed by the inhabitants of the earth. The Gospel of the Son of God was first presented to them, but when they would not abide its requirements, the law of Moses, a less excellent law, was given to be their school-master to bring them to Christ.† And when they complained against the free constitution that had been given them, and would no longer sustain the judges whom the Lord raised up to be their leaders, he gave them a kingdom

---

*See the Book of Ether, Book of Mormon, for their history. †Gal. iii; Heb. iv.

according to their desires,* but warned them of the bondage to which it was liable to lead.

The consequences of obedience to the laws which the Lord gave them through Moses, even before the death of that great leader, were plainly set before them; and surely the advantages that are there set forth, leave nothing to be desired, no matter how ambitious of place, power, honor, wealth, glory and dominion a nation might be. And, on the other hand, in case of their forsaking their God and his laws, the judgments, calamities, distress, wars, famines, pestilences, dishonor and destruction that follow, as a consequence of their apostasy from God, are drawn with such vividness, even down to the minutest detail, that had these things been written after they came to pass—after the threatened judgments were visited upon Israel, and especially upon Judah—in a word, if they had been written as history instead of prophecy—they could scarcely be more circumstantial than the prophetic words of Moses.†

But notwithstanding all these promises of favor and blessing on the one hand, and the forewarnings of calamity on the other, Israel rebelled against God, wholly rejected him, and trampled upon his counsels. The generous instructions of the teachers whom the Lord raised up to instruct them in the things of righteousness and

---

* I. Sam. viii. † See Deuteronomy xxviii.

true government, were unheeded. They killed the force and spirit of the law of Moses by their vain traditions. The warnings of the prophets were unheeded, and the prophets themselves were stoned and murdered. The earnest appeals of Lehi, the sharp reproofs of Ezekiel, the prophetic pleadings of Jeremiah as well as the poetic fire and more splendid prophecies of Isaiah could do no more than to bring them to a partial repentance.

These means of correction failing, there was occasional chastisement administered in wars, partial famines and seasons of captivity, to remind them that justice was not dead, though at times it appeared to sleep, and as a foretaste of the terrible wrath which would overtake them if they persisted in their rebellion and wickedness. But all this was of no avail. Neither the instructions of wise teachers, nor reproofs of special messengers from God were sufficient to bring them to repentance: Neither moving eloquence, nor prophetic warnings, nor inspired portrayals of certain calamities could soften their obdurate hearts. Even chastisement failed to produce any permanent reformation.

Finally, the Son of God came among them; but him they rejected, accused and condemned of blasphemy, before their senate, and sentenced him who did no sin to death; led him before Pontius Pilate, the Roman judge, and, under the pressure of popular clamor, compelled that functionary of the Roman government, against the sense of his better judgment, to sign the warrant for his death; and then, amid the cry of "Let his blood be upon us and our children," led him away to his crucifixion.

The climax of their apostasy and rebellion had now been reached. Nothing more to their damnation could they add. They had sowed the wind, they must now reap the whirlwind. So they have. The full fury of outraged justice and righteousness broke upon them with a force that was irresistible. The Romans under Titus besieged their city, Jerusalem, and successfully cut off all supplies of food or assistance from the surrounding country. To the horrors of war waged by the Romans was added that of civil conflict within the walls of the city, more fruitful in calamity and cruelty than the actual conflict with the Roman soldiery. As if of distress there was not already enough, famine preyed upon them, and a million people perished from lingering starvation. If men were brutal, women became fiendish, and fed upon the flesh of their own offspring.*

---

* An incident of this kind is thus related by Josephus: "There was a certain woman who dwelt beyond Jordan; her name was Mary, her father was Eleazar, of the village of Bethezob, which signifies the house of Hyssop. She was eminent for her family and her wealth, and had fled away to Jerusalem with the rest of the multitude, and was with them besieged therein at this time. The

other effects of this woman, had been already seized upon, such, I mean, as she had brought with her out of Persia, and removed to the city. What she had treasured up besides, as also what food she contrived to save, had also been carried off by the rapacious guards, who came every day, running into her house for that purpose. This put the poor woman into a very great passion, and, by the frequent reproaches and imprecations, she cast at these rapacious villains, she had provoked them to anger against her; but none of them—either out of the indignation she had raised against herself, or out of consideration for her case—would take away her life: and, if she found any food, she perceived her labors were for others, and not for herself, and it was now become impossible for her anyway, to find any more food, while the famine pierced through her very bowels and marrow, when also her passions were fired to a degree beyond the famine itself; nor did she consult with anything, but with her passions and the necessity she was in. She then attempted a most unnatural thing—and snatching up her son, who was a child, sucking at her breast, she said, ' O, thou miserable infant! for whom shall I preserve thee in this war, this famine, and this sedition? As to the war with the Romans, if they preserve our lives, we must be slaves. This famine also will destroy us even before that slavery comes upon us. Yet are these seditious rogues more terrible than the other. Come on; be thou my food, and be thou a fury to these seditious varlets, and a by-word to the world, which is all that is now wanting to complete the calamities of the Jews.' As soon as she had said this, she slew her son, and then roasted him, and ate the one-half of him, and kept the other half by her, concealed. Upon this the seditious came in, presently; and, smelling the horrid scent of this food, they threatened her, that they would cut her throat immediately if she did not show them what food she had gotten ready. She replied that she had ' saved a very fine portion for them;' and, withal, uncovered what was left of her son. Hereupon they were seized with a horror and amazement of mind, and stood astonished at the sight, when she said to them: ' Come eat of this food for I have eaten of it myself. Do not you pretend to be either more tender than a woman, or more compassionate than a mother; but if you be so scrupulous and do abominate this my sacrifice, as I have eaten the one half, let the rest be preserved for me also.' After which those men went out trembling, being never so much

At last the Romans forced an entrance into the city, and they with sword and flame were permitted to complete the ruin so well nigh accomplished by the Jews themselves. The beautiful temple was thrown down so that not one stone was left upon another which had not been thrown down. This was done by the Roman soldiery in their mad search for gold. Jerusalem was laid waste and desolate. Hundreds of thousands of her people were put to death, and the remainder of them taken into captivity, or driven into exile.

From that time until now, for more than eighteen centuries, they have remained a broken, scattered people; despised, hated, distrusted, unfriended, oppressed; a hiss and a by-word in every land where they have sought a home. They have learned by a sad experience that it is a terrible thing to reject the tender mercies of God, and fall under his displeasure.

Turning again to the Western hemisphere, we

---

affrighted at anything as they had been at this, and with some difficulty they left the rest of that meat to the mother. Upon which the whole city was full of this horrid action immediately; and while everybody laid this miserable case before their own eyes, they trembled, as if this unheard of action had been done by themselves. So, that those that were thus distressed by the famine, were very desirous to die: and those who were already dead were esteemed happy, because they had not lived long enough, either to hear or to see such miseries." (Wars of the Jews; Josephus, Book VI: chapter iii.)

I advise my readers to compare this incident and other calamities —described by Josephus in these "Wars of the Jews"—with the prophecies which foretold these evils, found in Deuteronomy, xxviii.

have the experience of Israel in the East duplicated in that of the Nephites and Lamanites; the same lesson is taught by their experience, viz., that it is a fearful thing to rebel against God, and reject and fight against his truth. The half-naked American savage, with the desolation that surround him in a splendid land (I mean at the time it was discovered by the Europeans) and filled as it is with the ruins that testify to the grandeur of his departed glory, is a warning of deep significance to the nations now in the zenith of their power, not to follow in his footsteps and reject the counsels of God against themselves.

What shall I say of the cities of Tyre and Sidon, of Nineveh with her hundred gates; of Babylon, "the glory of kingdoms, the beauty of the Chaldees excellence," with her mighty walls, her strong gates and towers, her palatial residences, her magnificent temples, her hanging gardens, the wonder and admiration of all who beheld them! Where are all these? Crumbled into shapeless heaps of ruins that are scarcely sufficient to show where they once stood—nothing left of them but their names. Where, too, are the grand empires of Assyria and Babylon, of Egypt and Persia, of Macedonia and Greece? and, lastly, where is Rome, the most stupendous political fabric yet constructed by the wit of man—where are all these? Where is their strength, their glory, their pride—nay, I ask more, where are the principles that formed the basis of their constitutions, the ideas by which they were governed—principles which they expected would forever perpetuate their institutions—where are all these things, as well as the empires themselves? Like the gorgeous temples, and cloud-capped towers of the cities we have named, they have dissolved into thin air, like the baseless fabric of an empty vision. Look at your maps of today, and you shall find no line or trace of them, not even of the boundaries which once marked the extent of their dominion. All is lost except their names and their history. As in the sight of God the mountains are as unstable and transient as the clouds, so nations rise and pass away. But seek out the causes of their dissolution, look well into it, and you will find that these nations no less than the children of Israel, both Jews and Nephites, were guilty of violating righteous principles, as they understood them, of refusing to repent, and of rejecting the counsels of God, and fighting against his truth. They were guilty of oppression, pride, licentiousness; they tyrannized over the meek and lowly; they wrung from the hands of the poor the wealth their labor created, that they might consume it upon their lusts. These abominations were the causes of their overthrow, and as one reviews the rise and fall of great kingdoms, republics, and splendid empires, he concludes that Byron might well say—

> There is the moral of all human tales;
>   'Tis but the same rehearsal of the past;
> First freedom, and then glory—when that fails,
>   Wealth, vice, corruption—barbarism at last :
> And history with all her volumes vast
>   Hath but one page!

What lessons are here spread out for the reading of the nations today! True, they might be offended if one should tell them that there was danger threatening them for their wickedness, for they esteem themselves righteous; so did the people of the ancient cities and kingdoms I have named. It might be held treasonable, to say that the present governments, which encumber the earth, will pass away like the others have—like the chaff of the summer's threshing floor—for they think they have laid the foundation of their respective political fabrics on so sure a basis, that they will be perpetuated forever. So thought the Babylonians, the Greeks, and especially the Romans; but they have passed away, and have left nothing behind them, but their names and the lessons which their follies and crimes teach.

But I fear you have forgotten in this long digression the subject in hand—repentance. Of the things I would have you remember, this is the sum: True repentance is sincere sorrow for sin, accompanied by a firm resolution to forsake that which is evil. The legitimate fruits of such sorrow—repentance, is a reformation of life. And if, peradventure, through weakness of human nature one should fall into transgression, even after setting his heart to work righteousness, let him not be discouraged, but repeat his repentance, and I believe the experiences I have pointed out in these pages, both individual and national, demonstrate that God is good, and "goodness still delighteth to forgive." He is merciful and willing to pardon abundantly those who are sorry for their offenses, and will make a manly effort to reform. But on the other hand, those who mock him, and presumptuously sin, thinking to impose upon his long-suffering, have need to fear, both persons and nations, for all history teaches that it is a fearful thing to fall under the displeasure of the Most High.

CHAPTER XXI.

BAPTISM.

"EXCEPT a man be born again he cannot see the kingdom of God."* Such was the statement of Jesus to Nicodemus, a Pharisee, and a ruler of the Jews, who came to Jesus by night to be taught of him. The statement of the Son of God created no little astonishment in the mind of Nicodemus, and he inquired if a man could be born again when he was old; could he enter a second time into his mother's womb and be

---
*John iii: 3.

born. Jesus then gave an answer which was explanatory of his first statement: "Except a man be born of water and of the Spirit he cannot enter into the kingdom of God."*

There can be no question about being "born of water," here alluded to, having reference to water baptism administered to those who accept the Gospel, and which, as administered for the first three centuries of the Christian era, represented, most completely, a birth. The candidate for baptism being led down into the water, had his whole person immersed in it, then he was brought forth from that element, and gasped again the breath of life. In order that the resemblance of a birth in this may be clearly seen, I would remind my readers that the infant, previous to its birth, and while in its mother's womb, lives in the element of water, and is nourished by the generous tide of life which courses through her veins and visits her heart. At birth, that life which was connected with the mother is severed, the offspring comes forth from the womb, from the element of water, and breathes the air, which then becomes essential to its existence—it is born into this world. The likeness, in a general way, between this natural birth and Christian baptism, as described above, is sufficiently obvious. In both instances the persons are brought from one element into

---

*John iii: 5.

another, from the water in which they existed into the atmosphere.

Many and various have been the views held respecting this ordinance, as to its necessity, its object, to whom it should be administered, and the manner in which it should be performed. Differences of opinion on this subject have led to schisms in the Christian world, and new sects have been formed, and that because of peculiar views held in respect to baptism. But with those who are willing to take as authority absolute, the teachings of revelation as contained in the Bible, and more especially the revelations of the Lord in these days, there need be no confusion in relation to any of these questions that have perplexed men in regard to this ordinance.

The necessity of water baptism may be maintained upon the broad grounds that it is a commandment from God; for, as I have already shown in preceding chapters, the conditions of man's salvation may be summed up, in general terms, thus—the implicit and complete obedience to the commandments of God; and, as it can be proven that baptism is a general commandment to all who would be saved, therefore it follows that baptism must be one of the things necessary to salvation.

That baptism is a general commandment all may learn who will take the trouble to make inquiry in respect to it. John the Baptist informs us that God sent him to baptize with water and to testify of him who was to come after him, and who was to baptize with the Holy Ghost;* and those who refused to hearken to his teachings and to be baptized of him "rejected the counsels of God against themselves."†

Jesus, himself, also, had those baptized who accepted his teachings; and, indeed, soon after he began his public ministry, it was commonly reported that he made and baptized more disciples than John,‡ and when he gave his last great commission to his apostles, just on the eve of his departure from them, he said:

"Go ye therefore, and teach all nations, baptizing them in the name of the Father, and of the Son and of the Holy Ghost: teaching them to observe all things whatsoever I have commanded you."§

When the apostles began the execution of this commission, which was during the first pentecost after it was given them, Peter commanded those who had been converted through his teachings, to be baptized in the name of Jesus Christ for the remission of their sins, and then he promised them the Holy Ghost.‖ Thus we see there can be no question as to baptism being a general commandment, and one of the conditions of man's salvation, and that being true, how can that condition be neglected and still the blessing of salvation obtained?

---

*John i: 33. †Luke vii: 30. ‡John iv: 1, 2. §Matt. xxviii: 19, 20. ‖Acts ii: 37, 38.

I may say further, by way of argument on the necessity of baptism, that one may reasonably conclude that the Lord does not deal with non-essentials, or require that which is not necessary of his children; therefore from the fact that God has commanded men to be born again, as well of water as of the Spirit; in other words, to be baptized of both water and the Spirit, it may be taken for granted that this baptism is essential to salvation. To question it being necessary, to say nothing of thrusting it aside as non-essential, is to sit in judgment upon the wisdom of God, who has ordained it as a means of salvation to man.

Is it necessary to be born naturally in order to obtain life? All will answer: "Yes, we know of no other way, no other means by which life is obtained." So likewise is it necessary that men should be born into the heavenly kingdom, as well of water as of the Spirit, in order to attain unto spiritual life in the kingdom of God; and without being born of the water and of the Spirit, Jesus himself declares that the kingdom of God cannot be seen, it cannot be entered into—* therefore baptism must be necessary to an entrance into the kingdom of God; and as there is, and can be, no salvation outside of that kingdom, baptism must be necessary to salvation. Not that there is saving virtue in the water itself,

---

* John iii: 3, 5.

but the ordinance derives its virtue from the fact of its being appointed by the Lord as a means of grace to man.

Again, I would ask, is a forgiveness of sins necessary to salvation? I think there can be but one answer to that question, and that in the affirmative. Now, we are informed by both Mark and Luke that John the Baptist "Did baptize in the wilderness, and preach the baptism of repentance for the remission of sins;" and Peter commanded the multitude on Pentecost to "repent and be baptized in the name of Jesus Christ for the remission of sins;"* hence it appears that baptism is the means appointed through which forgiveness of sins is obtained, and since it is evident that men cannot be saved in their sins, and remission of sins comes through baptism, therefore baptism is necessary to salvation.

The necessity of baptism is further demonstrated in the experience of Paul and the devout Gentile, Cornelius, as related in the Acts of the Apostles. It will be remembered that Paul, at first, was a great persecutor of the saints, and that, while on the way to Damascus for the purpose of persecuting them, the Lord Jesus appeared unto him, in a pillar of light, above the brightness of the sun, and demanded of

---

*Acts ii: 38.

Paul, "why persecutest thou me?" To which the trembling Paul said, "who art thou, Lord?"

"I am Jesus whom thou persecutest," was the reply. "Lord," said Paul, "what will thou have me to do?" "And the Lord said unto him, arise and go into the city, and it shall be told thee what thou must do."

Then the Lord sent an angel to his servant, Ananias, living in Damascus, and directed him to go to Paul; and when Ananias came into the presence of Paul, after announcing to him that the Lord had chosen him for a witness for himself, he said: "And now, why tarriest thou? arise and be baptized, and wash away thy sins, calling on the name of the Lord."*

Thus Paul learned what the Lord would have him to do; and is it not a fair inference that it is necessary for all sinners to do likewise, viz., to be baptized, and wash away their sins?

Cornelius, the devout Gentile to whom we have alluded, was a man who prayed much, gave alms to the poor, and indeed was especially loved of the Lord. An angel was at last sent to him, to assure him that his alms and his prayers had come up in remembrance before the Lord, and this messenger also told him to send men to Joppa where he would find one Peter, "And he shall tell thee what thou oughtest to do,"† or,

---

* Acts ix. ch.; also the xxii. and xxvi. chapters same book.
. † Acts x : 6.

as Peter afterwards expressed it, in relating the circumstance to his fellow apostles—"send men to Joppa, and call for one Simon, whose surname is Peter; who shall tell thee words, whereby thou and all thy house shall be saved."*

After Peter went into the house of this devout Gentile and heard of the mercies of God to him, he preached Christ unto him and his household, and as he spake of Jesus and the plan of salvation wrought out for mankind by him, the Holy Ghost was poured out upon them as a witness to Peter that the Gospel was for the Gentiles as well as for the Jews. Then, turning to those that were with him, Peter said: "Can any man forbid water, that these should not be baptized, which have received the Holy Ghost as well as we? And he commanded them to be baptized in the name of the Lord."†

Notwithstanding the general righteousness of Cornelius, and his acceptance with God, it became necessary that he should be instructed in the Gospel, and taught words whereby he and his house should be saved; and, in connection with other things that they were taught as necessary for their salvation, was baptism.

Paul, in writing to the Corinthian saints, uses this expression, which to the world sounds strange and incomprehensible: "Else what shall

---

*Acts xi : 13, 14.   †Acts x : 47, 48.

they do which are baptized for the dead, if the dead rise not at all? Why are they then baptized for the dead?"* And if baptism, as some maintain, is not essential to salvation, I would ask, why then was it considered necessary, by the primitive Christians, that there should be such a thing as baptism for the dead?† Is it not conclusive, that if it was necessary for some one to be baptized for the dead who had not had the privilege of attending to that ordinance for themselves, that baptism is essential to salvation?

But now to come to the most positive of all passages in the New Testament upon this subject: Jesus when he commissioned his apostles used this language: "Go ye into all the world, and preach the Gospel to every creature. He that believeth and is baptized shall be saved; but he that believeth not" [and consequently fails to repent, be baptized or perform any other act of obedience] "shall be damned."‡ Here the matter is before us in the most unequivocal terms; those who believe and are baptized have the sure promise of God that they shall be saved; while those who believe not, and therefore are not baptized, are threatened with condemnation.

I have thus far, confined my illustrations and arguments—upon the necessity of baptism—to

---

* I Cor. xv: 29.

† The subject of salvation for the dead is treated at length in a subsequent chapter, hence I enter into no explanation here.

‡ Mark xvi: 15, 16.

the Jewish scriptures. I have done so, because the young Elders, into whose hands this work will fall, will doubtless be called upon to teach this principle, and support it in the main, upon the authority of what is written in the Bible. But if we turn to the Nephite scriptures, the Book of Mormon, we shall find it sustains the same views in respect to the necessity of baptism, as the Jewish scriptures.

The Lord revealed to the first Nephi, in a vision, very much of the life and labors of the Son of God, although the said Nephi flourished in the fifth century B. C. Among other things, it was revealed to him, that the Son of God would be baptized in water by a prophet who should be raised up for that purpose. Subsequently, when Nephi desired to impress his brethren with the importance and necessity of baptism, he said:

"I would that ye should remember that I have spoken unto you concerning that prophet which the Lord showed unto me, that should baptize the Son of God, which should take away the sins of the world. And now, if the Lamb of God, he being holy, should have need to be baptized by water, to fulfill all righteousness, O then, how much more need have we, being unholy, to be baptized, yea even by water. And now I would ask of you, my beloved brethren, wherein the Lamb of God did fulfill all righteousness in being baptized by water? Know ye not that he was holy. But notwithstanding he being holy, he showeth unto the children of men, that according to the flesh, he humbleth himself before the Father, and witnesseth unto the Father that he would be obedient unto him in keeping his commandments. * * * And again, it showeth unto the children of men the straightness of the path, and the narrowness of the gate, by which they should enter, he having set the example before them. And he said unto the children of men, Follow thou me. Wherefore, my beloved brethren, can we follow Jesus, save we be willing to keep the commandments of the Father? And the Father said, Repent ye, repent ye, and be baptized in the name of my beloved Son. And also, the voice of the Son came unto me, saying, He that is baptized in my name, to him will the Father give the Holy Ghost, like unto me; wherefore follow me, and do the things ye have seen me do."*

The first Alma's teachings are in accord with this: "And now I, Alma, do command you in the language of him who hath commanded me, that ye observe to do the words which I have spoken unto you. I speak by way of commandment unto you who belong to the church; and to those who do not belong to the church, I speak by way of invitation, saying, Come and be

---

* Book of Mormon, II. Nephi, xxxi.

baptized unto repentance, that ye also may be made partakers of the fruit of the tree of life."*

The plain and fair inference from this last clause is, that those who refused to be baptized, would *not* have right to the tree of life.

Further on in his book, he says: "And not many days hence, the Son of God shall come in his glory; * * * And behold he cometh to redeem those who will be baptized unto repentance through faith on his name."†

Here, again, the fair inference is, that those who would reject baptism, could not be redeemed; hence the necessity of baptism.

Turning to the revelations which the Lord has given in this dispensation, in which he commissioned men to preach the Gospel, he said: "Go ye into all the world, preach the Gospel to every creature, acting in the authority which I have given you, baptizing in the name of the Father, and of the Son, and of the Holy Ghost; and he that believeth and is baptized shall be saved, and he that believeth not shall be damned."‡

Still more emphatic, perhaps, because it leaves nothing to implication, is the passage which reads (and this, too, is in connection with sending out men to preach the Gospel): "He that believeth and is baptized shall be

---

*Alma ix: 26, 27. †Alma v: 61, 62. ‡Doc. 'and Cov., sec. lxviii: 8-10.

saved, and he that believeth not, and is not baptized, shall be damned.'*

Thus in the present dispensation, as well as in the former ones, committed to the Jews and Nephites, the necessity of baptism is beyond all question.

CHAPTER XXII.

OBJECT OF BAPTISM.

IN speaking of the necessity of baptism I incidentally referred to the object of the ordinance also; which the reader will doubtless remember, is for the remission of sins. Such was the object for which John the Baptist administered baptism. Mark says: "John did baptize in the wilderness, and preach the baptism of repentance for the remission of sins."† Luke also says: "And he [John] came into all the country about Jordan, preaching the baptism of repentance for the remission of sins."‡

Here it may be a proper time to call attention to the fact that many seek to make nice distinctions between the baptism of John and what they call Christian baptism; that is, baptism in the name of Jesus after the death and resurrection of Messiah, by which members were admitted into the Kingdom of Christ. The controversy on

---

* Doc. and Cov., sec. cxii: 29.   † Mark i: 4.   ‡ Luke iii: 3.

this subject became particularly sharp in the sixteenth century. Zwingle and Calvin, on the one hand, maintained that the two baptisms were identical, and for the same purpose, only that John baptized in the name of the future Messiah, while the apostles baptized in the name of the Messiah already come; on the other hand, Luther, Melancthon and the Catholics maintained there was an essential difference. The latter adopted the views of Tertullian, who lived about the close of the second century and the beginning of the third. To the baptism of John, Tertullian ascribed the negative character of repentance, and to Christian baptism the positive impartation of a new life. This distinction, it is maintained, arises from the words of John himself; *viz.*, "I indeed baptize you with *water* unto repentance; but he that cometh after me is mightier than I, * * * he shall *baptize you with the Holy Ghost* and with fire."* But this reason for any such distinction as that sought to be made is worthless when it is remembered that while Jesus did baptize with the Holy Ghost, and commissioned others to do so, still that baptism of the Spirit did not supplant water baptism for the remission of sins. It was simply an additional principle and ordinance to the doctrines taught by John; and Jesus continued to authorize water baptism before his crucifixion,* and com-

---

* Matt. iii: 11; see also Luke iii: 16, and John i: 25.

missioned his apostles to continue it after he departed from them.* The New Testament is replete with instances of water baptism standing in connection with though, as a rule, preceding the baptism of, the Holy Spirit.† Whereas, to make the words of John quoted a valid reason for supposing a difference between the baptism of John and water baptism after Jesus was resurrected, it would be necessary to prove that the baptism of the Spirit took the place of water baptism as administered by John, which is contrary to the facts in the case, as already noted.

The ordinance of baptism, associated with the proclamation of the Gospel, in any age of the world, is always the same, whether taught by Adam, Enoch, Noah, Abraham, Moses, the Jaredite or Nephite prophets on the Western hemisphere, or by John the Baptist among the Jews. It was administered in the same manner, with the same object in view, and with the same powers and graces attending it before the crucifixion of Messiah as after that event. Only those who administered it before Jesus came in the flesh, performed the ordinance in the name of a future Messiah, while those who have officiated since the death of Jesus, have done so in the

---

* John iii : 22, and iv : 1-3.   † Matt. xxviii : 19, and Mark xvi: 15, 16.

name of the Messiah already come; and that is a difference of little moment.*

One thing which has contributed largely towards creating the impression that a difference existed between the baptism of John and Christian baptism, is the account given in Acts of Paul's finding a number of disciples—twelve in all—at Ephesus, of whom he asked if they had received the Holy Ghost since they believed; to which they replied, they had not so much as heard of the Holy Ghost. "And he said unto them, unto what then, were ye baptized? And they said, unto John's baptism. Then said Paul, John verily baptized with the baptism of repentance, saying unto the people, that they should believe on him who should come after him, that is on Christ Jesus. When they heard this, they were baptized in the name of the Lord Jesus. And when Paul had laid his hands upon them, the Holy Ghost came on them: and they spake with tongues and prophesied."† The fact of Paul rebaptizing those people, who, according to their statement, had been baptized "unto

---

*These views are capable of the strongest proofs from the writings of Moses as revealed to Joseph Smith and now contained in the Pearl of Great Price; from the Book of Mormon, Doctrine and Covenants and also from the Bible. But the reader will find a subsequent chapter on "The History of the Gospel" in which the subject is treated at some length, and to that chapter the reader is here referred if he now wishes to push further his investigation.

†Acts xix: 1-6.

John's baptism," does not necessarily argue a difference between baptism as administered by John and Christian baptism. The circumstance of this rebaptism may be reasonably attributed to other causes.

The preaching of John was always accompanied with a reference to one who should follow after him, mightier than he was, whose shoe latchet he esteemed himself unworthy to unloose: and his baptism was always attended by the declaration: "I, indeed, baptize with water unto repentance, but he that cometh after me is mightier than I; * * * he shall baptize you with the Holy Ghost." So the apostle Paul, when he found these disciples, who claimed to have been baptized unto John's baptism, and yet had not so much as heard of the Holy Ghost, he might well have his suspicions as to the validity of their baptism, and suspect that some person, but partially acquainted with the doctrine of John, and, without authority, had taken it upon himself to baptize these parties. Upon these suspicions, and in order, doubtless, to put the validity of their baptism beyond all question, he re-baptized them with water, and then followed the baptism of the Spirit. This, to my mind, is the most reasonable conclusion to come to respecting this circumstance.

But now to return to the subject of this chapter—the object of baptism:

We have already seen in the first paragraph of

this chapter, that John taught that baptism was for the remission of sins. If we turn to the teachings of the apostles, we shall find that they also taught that baptism was for that purpose. In that memorable discourse which Peter preached at the commencement of the labor of the apostles, after the departure of the Master, when the people, convinced by the power of God which rested upon the apostles, that they were commissioned of God with a message to the world, cried out as with one voice—"Men and brethren, what shall we do?"—he replied: "Repent every one of you, and be baptized in the name of Jesus Christ, *for the remission of sins.*"* Surely nothing in the way of simplicity, plainness or positiveness is left to be desired here. He who runs may read, and the wayfaring man though a fool, need not be in doubt in respect to the object of this ordinance.

Other passages in the New Testament, however, are in harmony with this. When Ananias, in obedience to the commandment from the Lord, went to the afflicted and humbled Paul to tell him what he ought to do, he commanded him to arise and be baptized, and wash away his sins.†

Again it is said: "Know ye not that so many of us as were baptized into Jesus Christ were baptized into his death? Therefore, we are buried with him by baptism into death: that

---

* Acts ii : 38. † Acts xxii : 16.

like as Christ was raised up from the dead by the glory of the Father, even so we also should walk in newness of life * * * knowing this, that our old man is crucified with him, that the body of sin might be destroyed, that henceforth we should not serve sin."* In this passage also, as well as in those previously considered, stands the grand truth that, connected with baptism is the crucifixion of the old man of sin, the destruction of "the body of sin;" and that as Christ arose from the grave by the power of the Father, so those who in baptism have been buried with Christ should also rise from the watery grave to a newness of life. What, I ask, does all this mean, if it does not mean that through baptism it is ordained that men receive a remission of sins, and are made new men in Christ Jesus?

If we turn from the scriptures to the traditions of the early Christians, we shall find that their understanding of the subject is in harmony with the observations and deductions in the foregoing.

Justin Martyr, who wrote about the middle of the second century, in describing the customs observed in receiving new members into the Christian societies, says: "Those who believe and are persuaded that the things we teach and inculcate are true, and who profess ability thus to live, are directed to pray with fasting, and to ask of God the forgiveness of their former sins.

---

* Romans vi : 3-6.

* * * Then we conduct them to a place where there is water; and they are regenerated [baptized] in the manner in which we have been regenerated [baptized]; for they receive a washing with water in the name of the Father of all. * * * This washing is likewise called illumination; because the minds of those who have learned these things are enlightened." He then describes the manner in which the sacrament of the Lord's supper was administered; and thus concludes: "And this food is called by us the Eucharist, which it is unlawful for any one to partake of, unless he believes the things taught by us to be true, and has been washed [baptized] with the washing *for the remission of sins* in regeneration, and lives according to what Christ has taught."*

Of baptism in the third century Dr. Mosheim says: "Baptism was publicly administered twice a year, to such candidates as had gone through a long preparation and trial; and none were present as spectators but such as had been themselves baptized. The effect of baptism was supposed to be the *remission of sins*."†

In Maclaine's translation of Dr. Mosheim's Church History is a passage from *Letter Seventy-third*, of Cyprian, Bishop of Carthage, in which

---

* *Second Apology* of Justin Martyr. Quoted in Murdock's Mosheim, 3d ed., vol. I., p. 137—note.

† Murdock's Mosheim, vol. I (3d edition), p. 189.

that writer says (he wrote in the third century): "It is manifest where and by whom the *remission of sin conferred in baptism is administered:* They who are presented to the rulers of the church obtain by our prayers and imposition of hands, the Holy Ghost."

The following quotation will show what importance is attached to baptism, as to its necessity and object, by the Roman Catholic Church: "Baptism is a sacrament absolutely necessary for all, without which no one can enter into the kingdom of God, for Jesus Christ has said, 'Amen, amen, I say to thee, unless a man be born again of water and of the Holy Ghost, he cannot enter into the kingdom of God.' Hence it was not enough for Saul of Tarsus, converted on the road to Damascus,* to believe; nor for the Chamberlain of Queen Candace, met on the road by Philip, the Deacon;† they had to be baptized in order to obtain remission of their sins, and thus be in the way of salvation; therefore in the Nicene Creed we say: "I acknowledge one baptism for the remission of sins."‡

The Book of Mormon, which we have found so explicit in its treatment of other doctrines, is none the less so in respect to the one now under discussion—the object of baptism. In the

---

* Acts ix: 18.   † Acts viii: 38.   ‡ Catholic Belief (Bruno pp. 56, 57.)

teachings of Alma we have the following: "Now, I say unto you, that ye must repent, and be born again; for the Spirit saith, if ye are not born again, ye cannot inherit the kingdom of heaven; therefore, come and be baptized unto repentance, that ye may be washed from your sins."*

It is written of the third Nephi, that just about the time of Messiah's birth, "he went among the people, and also many others, baptizing unto repentance, in the which there were a great remission of sins."†

This work he continued for more than thirty years after the sign in the heavens of the birth of Messiah had been given. Mormon says of Nephi, that in the thirty and third year after the birth of the Messiah, "he preached unto them repentance, and remission of sins. Now I would have you to remember, also," says Mormon, "that there were none brought unto repentance, who were not baptized with water; therefore there were ordained of Nephi, men unto this ministry, that all such as should come unto them, should be baptized with water, and this as a witness and testimony before God, and unto the people, that they had repented and received a remission of their sins."‡

Lastly, in closing up his abridgment of the writings of the third Nephi, Mormon says: "Hear the words of Jesus Christ, the Son of the

---

* Alma vii: 14.   † III. Nephi, i: 23.   ‡ III. Nephi, vii: 23-25.

living God: * * * Turn, all ye Gentiles, from your wicked ways, and repent of your evil doings, of your lyings and deceivings, and of your whoredoms, and of your secret abominations, and your idolatries, and of your murders, and your priestcrafts, and your envyings, and your strifes, and from all your wickedness and abominations, and come unto me, and be baptized in my name, that ye may receive a remission of your sins, and be filled with the Holy Ghost, that ye may be numbered with my people who are of the house of Israel."*

Turning now to the revelations which the Lord has given on this subject, in the dispensation of the Gospel committed to men in our day, we find the Lord saying to Martin Harris: "And of tenets thou shalt not talk, but thou shalt declare repentance and faith on the Savior, and the remission of sins by baptism and by fire, yea, even the Holy Ghost."†

In a revelation to W. W. Phelps we hear the Lord saying: "And thou shalt be ordained by the hand of my servant Joseph Smith, jun., to be an Elder unto this Church, to preach repentance and remission of sins by way of baptism in the name of Jesus Christ, the Son of the living God."‡

The Lord, subsequently, gave the following as

---

* III. Nephi, xxx.   † Doc. and Cov., sec. xix: 31.   ‡ Doc. and Cov., sec. lv: 21.

a standing law unto the inhabitants of Zion and her organized stakes: "Their children shall be baptized for the remission of their sins, when eight years old, and receive the laying on of hands."*

Clearly, the object of baptism is the remission of sins.

In a revelation given to the Church in September, 1832, in which a number of Elders are directed to go out into the world and preach the Gospel, it is written: "Verily, verily, I say unto you, they who believe not on your words, and are not baptized in water in my name, for the remission of their sins that they may receive the Holy Ghost, shall be damned, and shall not come into my Father's kingdom."†

The teachings of Joseph Smith on this subject may be learned from this one homely but expressive sentence: "You might as well baptize a bag of sand as a man, if not done in view of the remission of sins and getting of the Holy Ghost."

Here, as far as this branch of the subject is concerned, I pause; and surely I may hope that the treatise on the object of baptism has been sufficiently exhaustive, both as considered in the Jewish scriptures and as understood by the early Christians, as well as in the Book of Mormon and the revelations of the Lord in this dispen-

---

* Doc. and Cov. sec. lxviii: 26, 27. † Doc. and Cov., sec. lxxxiv: 74.

sation. From all these sources of information, we learn that baptism is an ordinance through which it is ordained that man shall receive a remission of sins.

CHAPTER XXIII.

THE SUBJECTS FOR BAPTISM.

HAVING shown from all worthy sources of information that baptism is for the remission of sins, and that necessarily repentance and faith precede it, and, moreover, are pre-requisites thereto; it follows as a logical sequence of these facts, that baptism can only be properly administered to those capable of exercising faith in God, and repentance of sin. Therefore the baptism of infants, or of children of such tender years that they are unable to comply with these conditions —is not in accordance with the requirements of the Gospel, and is solemn mockery before God.

The consideration of just two facts, it seems to me, is sufficient to destroy the doctrine of infant baptism; first, the fact that baptism is for the remission of sins; and, second, that infants are incapable of committing sin, cannot repent, and therefore have nothing to be baptized for.

To avoid the irresistible force and right conclusion of this logic, however, those who stand for infant baptism tell us that the baptism of the infant is not for the remission of any actual sins committed by the child, but for original sin. The Roman Catholics teach: "In baptism all infants, without any disposition on their part being required, are cleansed from the stain of original sin, taken into God's favor, made members of Christ's mystical Body, and heirs of the kingdom of heaven. They are thus regenerated, that is, in our Savior's own words, 'born again of water and the Holy Ghost.' As they have contracted the stain of original sin without their knowledge and personal co-operation, so they are freed from sin without their knowledge; and the disposition necessary for grown up persons is not required of them; for infants are incapable of any reasoning act."*

But this position does not help the matter any. The fact remains, that whatever "stain" "original sin" fixes upon the individual, it is done without the exercise of his agency; and, as said above, "without his knowledge." Then how, I ask, can he be held responsible for it, or any requirement, in justice, be made of him to remove the "stain" when it was fixed upon him without the exercise of his will, "without his knowledge," and was a thing which he was powerless to prevent? The system of theology which teaches that God would condemn the child that failed to receive baptism, because of this "stain" fixed upon him by "original sin"—is not

---

Catholic Belief [Bruno] p. 58.

only unreasonable, it is damnable. It represents God as a cruel monster, and drives both justice and mercy from the economy of heaven.

It is true that from the fathers the children may inherit concupiscence; by that I mean a blind inclination to do evil, in one or more directions. Certain passions or mischievous appetites tending to sinfulness is not unfrequently stamped upon the offspring by the parents, or, as figuratively expressed by one of old, the parents eat sour grapes, and the children's teeth are set on edge.* But the children are not responsible for that; and, as the Catholic church teaches this blind, involuntary inclination to evil of our lower nature, is not of itself sinful unless it be consented to by the human will, or rendered strong by bad and not retracted habit.† It is not until the will assents to that which knowledge and experience tell the individual is sinful, that responsibility begins to attach to him. When knowledge instructs the understanding as to that which is good and that which is evil, and the will becomes conscious of its power to assent to the evil or withhold its approval, then the individual becomes accountable before God, and may reasonably be expected to be held answerable for his acts. But it is a noted principle, both in moral philosophy and theology, "that there is no sin where there is no will;"

---

* Jeremiah xxxi: 29.   † Catholic Belief (*Bruno*), ch. iii.

and I would add, there can be no will where there is no knowledge.

I know of no sect or party, however, or individual even, who maintains that infants should be baptized for this concupiscence. Indeed it is most apparent that baptism does not affect this natural tendency to evil, since it is as marked in children who have been baptized in their infancy as those who have not. As before stated, in substance, the admission that baptism is for the remission of sin is fatal to the doctrine of infant baptism, as they are incapable of actual sin; and, "original sin" and concupiscence being fastened upon them without their knowledge, and by circumstances they were powerless to prevent, they cannot be held accountable for them, and should not be required to be baptized for them.

So far I have confined my remarks to that class of people believing in infant baptism who maintain also that baptism is for the remission of sins. There are others, however, who do not so regard baptism; but who look upon it merely as an ordinance by which entrance is gained unto the spiritual kingdom of Christ. But this position does not help out the doctrine of infant baptism. It is only by actual sin, by willful violations of God's holy laws that men become aliens and foreigners to the kingdom of God,*

---

* Col. i: 21, 22.

and, as infants and children not yet arrived at the years of accountability are incapable of such violations of law, they are not aliens to the kingdom of Christ; they are natural heirs to it, and, in the days of their innocence, form part of it, for Jesus himself said: "Suffer little children to come unto me: for of such is the kingdom of heaven." Therefore, being already in the kingdom of Christ, and forming part of it, they have no need of being initiated into it by baptism or any other ceremony; it is only those who have made themselves foreigners and aliens through transgression of the laws of God that have need to repent of their sins, through baptism obtain a remission of them, and thus be brought back to the state of children, without sin, and into the kingdom of Christ.

There is nothing in the scriptures which authorizes the doctrine of infant baptism. It is an invention by man, pure and simple.

It is true that Jesus said, when some of his disciples reproved the people for bringing their children to the Master to be blessed, "Suffer little children, and forbid them not to come unto me; for of such is the kingdom of heaven."* But he did not baptize them. He only laid his hands on them, and blessed them. There is nothing in the passage which warrants the

---

* Matt. xix: 14.

assumption that he commanded them to come unto him by baptism.

Indeed, I believe it is generally conceded that the doctrine of infant baptism was not introduced in the first century at all. The first notice we have of its existence is by Tertullian, appearing against it as a zealous opponent, in the latter years of the second century, "A proof," says Dr. Neander, "that it was not then usually considered as an apostolic ordinance; for, in that case, he would hardly have ventured to speak so strongly against it."*

"As faith and baptism are constantly so closely connected together in the New Testament, an opinion was likely to arise that where there could be no faith there could also be no baptism. It is certain that Christ did not ordain infant baptism. * * * We cannot prove that the apostles ordained infant baptism; from those places where the baptism of a whole family is mentioned† we can draw no such conclusion, because the inquiry is still to be made whether there were any childen in those families of such an age that they were not capable of any intelligent reception of Christianity.‡

The strongest contradiction to this erroneous doctrine, however, comes from the Book of Mormon. It appears that there arose some dis-

---

* Church History (Neander), Vol. I, p. 362. † Acts xvi: 33; I. Cor. i: 16. ‡ Church History (Neander), Vol. I, p. 360.

putations among the Nephites about this matter, and Mormon inquired of the Lord in respect to it, and sent the answer he received, through the inspiration of the Holy Ghost, to his son Moroni, and with it I shall close my remarks on this subject:

"Listen to the words of Christ, your Redeemer, your Lord and your God. Behold, I came into the world not to call the righteous, but sinners to repentance; the whole need no physician, but they that are sick; wherefore little children are whole, for they are not capable of committing sin; wherefore the curse of Adam is taken from them in me, that it hath no power over them; and the law of circumcision is done away in me.

"And after this manner did the Holy Ghost manifest the word of God unto me; wherefore my beloved son, I know that it is solemn mockery before God, that ye should baptize little children.

"Behold I say unto you, that this thing shall ye teach, repentance and baptism unto those who are accountable and capable of committing sin; yea, teach parents that they must repent and be baptized, and humble themselves as their little children; and they shall all be saved with their little children.

"And their little children need no repentance, neither baptism. Behold, baptism is unto repentance to the fulfilling the commandments unto the remission of sins.

"But little children are alive in Christ, even from the foundation of the world; if not so, God is a partial God, and also a changeable God, and a respecter of persons; for how many little children have died without baptism?

"Wherefore, if little children could not be saved without baptism, these must have gone to an endless hell.

"Behold I say unto you, that he that supposeth that little children need baptism, is in the gall of bitterness, and in the bonds of iniquity; for he hath neither faith, hope, nor charity; wherefore, should he be cut off while in the thought, he must go down to hell.

"For awful is the wickedness to suppose that God saveth one child because of baptism, and the other must perish because he hath no baptism. * * * * * * * *

"Little children cannot repent; wherefore it is awful wickedness to deny the pure mercies of God unto them, for they are all alive in him because of his mercy.

"And he that saith, that little children need baptism, denieth the mercies of Christ, and setteth at nought the atonement of him and the power of his redemption.

"Wo unto such, for they are in danger of death, hell, and an endless torment. I speak it boldly, God hath commanded me. Listen unto them and give heed, or they stand against you at the judgment seat of Christ.

"For behold that all little children are alive in Christ, and also all they that are without the law. For the power of redemption cometh on all they that have no law; wherefore, he that is not condemned, or he that is under no condemnation, cannot repent; and unto such baptism availeth nothing.

"But it is mockery before God, denying the mercies of Christ, and the power of his Holy Spirit, and putting trust in dead works.

"Behold, my son, this thing ought not to be; for repentance is unto them that are under condemnation and under the curse of a broken law."*

CHAPTER XXIV.

THE MODE OF BAPTISM.

THERE still remains to be discussed, in connection with baptism, one thing more—the manner of administering it.

In relation to this matter there is much division among professed believers of the Bible. One class maintaining that the immersion of the whole body in water is the only manner in which baptism can be administered; that immersion, in fact, and immersion only, is baptism. Others, however, while they admit that immersion

---

* Moroni, ch. viii.

is baptism, claim that it may be performed in some other manner, by sprinkling or pouring water on the candidates for the ordinance.

Both parties appeal to the original Greek from which baptism and the verb baptize is derived, one insisting that it means immersion, and to immerse only; while the others insist that in some connections the words in the original may mean sprinkling or pouring as well as immersion and to immerse. And as the commandment given to the apostles to baptize all nations* is given without any reference to the manner in which the ordinance is to be administered, they maintain it is immaterial whether it is done by immersion or by sprinkling or pouring.

It cannot be denied that an array of respectable testimony may be drawn up in favor of both theories; but when the meaning of the terms are interpreted in the light of the practice of the early Christians, those who received the doctrine of baptism from the apostles and other servants of Christ—nay, if interpreted by the manner in which these very apostles administered the ordinance—it is evident that immersion alone is the proper method for baptizing for the remission of sins, and initiation into the Church of Christ, whatever other signification may be attached to the words in other connections; for nothing is more evident than that immersion is

---

* Matt. xxviii, 19.

the manner in which baptism was administered by them.

Of John the Baptist it is written: "And there went out unto him all the land of Judea, and they of Jerusalem, and were all baptized of him *in the River Jordan*;"* and to this agrees also the testimony of Matthew.†

Again it is said of him that he baptized "in Ænon near Salim, because there was much water there.‡ And it is said that "Jesus, when he was baptized went up straightway out of the water;"§ from which it is evident that he had been down in the water. From these circumstances, that is, from his baptizing *in* Jordan, and near Salim "where there was much water," and from Jesus going up out of the water after his baptism, there can be no question but John baptized by immersion; and there is nothing to lead us to suppose that he baptized in any other manner.

Take an account of a baptism which took place after the crucifixion of Messiah, and we shall find the same method of administering the ordinance observed. I allude to the baptism of the chamberlain of Queen Candace, by Philip. This person was met by Philip in the highway, and being invited to ride in the chamberlain's carriage he taught him the Gospel. On belief

---

*Mark i: 4.   †Matt. iii: 5, 6.   ‡John iii, 23.   §Matt. iii: 16; Mark i: 10.

taking hold of the chamberlain, as they came to certain water, he inquired of Philip what hindered him from being baptized. To which Philip answered: "If thou believest with all thine heart thou mayest. And he answered and said: I believe that Jesus Christ is the Son of God. And he commanded the chariot to stand still: and they went down both into the water, both Philip and the eunuch; and he baptized him. And when they were come up out of the water, the Spirit caught away Philip that the eunuch saw him no more."*

There can be no two opinions as to the manner in which the eunuch was baptized—it was by immersion. It would seem, too, that had Philip been aware of any other method, that is, had he understood that sprinkling or pouring would answer the purpose, he never would have put himself and the chamberlain to the inconvenience of going down into the water. It is a fair inference, under all the circumstances, that Philip knew of no other method of baptism than by a burial in the water.

We have already referred to baptism being spoken of as being "born of water,"† and to those paragraphs I call the attention of my readers again. It will be seen that immersion best carries out that idea; indeed, it is only by immersion and being brought forth out of the

---

* Acts viii: 36-39. † Chapter xxi.

water, in which a person is brought from one element (water) into another (air), that a birth is represented. Sprinkling or pouring does not represent a birth.

In writing to the saints of Rome, Paul says: "Know ye not, that so many of us as were baptized into Jesus Christ were baptized into his death? Therefore we are *buried* with him by baptism into death; that like as Christ was raised up from the dead by the glory of the Father, even so we also should walk in newness of life. For if we have been *planted* together in the likeness of his death, we shall be also in the likeness of his resurrection."*

In writing to the saints of Colosse, the same apostle reminds them that they had been "*buried* with him [Christ] in baptism, wherein also ye are risen with him through the faith of the operation of God who hath raised him from the dead."†

In these passages the terms "buried" and "planted" are in plain allusion to the manner in which the saints had received the ordinance of baptism, which could not have been by sprinkling or pouring, as there is no burial or planting in the likeness of Christ's death, or being raised in likeness of his resurrection in that; but in immersion there is, and hence we conclude from all these circumstances that baptism among the

---

* Rom. vi : 3-5.   † Col. ii : 12.

saints of God in those days was by immersion, and by immersion alone.

Turning to other sources than the scriptures for information, we shall find that the statement that immersion alone was practiced by the early Christians, say for at least nearly three centuries, is sustained by the most respectable testimony.

Speaking of baptism in the first century, Dr. Mosheim says: "In this century, baptism was administered in convenient places, without the public assemblies; and by immersing the candidates wholly in water."*

Of the second century, the same learned author says: "Twice a year, namely, at Easter and Whitsuntide, * * * baptism was administered by the bishop, or by the presbyters acting by his command and authority. The candidates for it were immersed wholly in water, with invocation of the sacred Trinity, according to the Savior's precept."†

Indeed, the first deviation from baptizing by immersion, occurs in a case recorded by Eusebius, as happening in the third century. He alludes to it in these detracting terms: "He [Novatian] * * * fell into a grievous distemper, and it being supposed that he would die immediately, he received baptism (being sprinkled with water), on the bed where he lay, (if that

---

*Mosheim's Church History (Murdock), third edition, Vol. I, page 87. † Ibid, p. 137.

can be termed baptism): Neither when he had escaped that sickness, did he afterwards receive the other things which the canon of the church enjoineth should be received."*

Even down to the close of the thirteenth century baptism by immersion was the rule and sprinkling and pouring the exception.

Notwithstanding all these arguments, which are in their character so conclusive, many worthy people there are whom they fail to convince. What does this fact argue? That those who fail to understand that baptism must be by immersion are woefully ignorant, or their understanding willfully perverse? No; I would suggest that to them the evidence is simply insufficient and unauthoritative, and that the fact of it being so argues that there is need of some further instruction from the Lord on the subject than is contained in the Bible; that there is need of further revelation from God to settle the question.

In ushering in the Gospel in this dispensation the instruction so much needed was given in April, 1830, and is as follows: "The person who is called of God, and has authority from Jesus Christ to baptize, shall go down into the water with the person who has presented him or herself for baptism, and shall say, calling him or her by name—Having been commissioned of Jesus Christ, I baptize you in the name of the Father,

---

* Eusebius Eccl. Hist. b. vi, ch. 43.

and of the Son, and of the Holy Ghost. Amen. Then shall he immerse him or her in the water, and come forth again out of the water."*

The Book of Mormon is equally plain on this point. When Jesus gave authority to his servants among the Nephites to baptize, he said to them: "Verily I say unto you, that whosoever repenteth of his sins through your words, and desireth to be baptized in my name, on this wise shall ye baptize them: behold, ye shall go down and stand in the water, and in my name shall ye baptize them. And now behold, these are the words which ye shall say, calling them by name, saying, Having authority given me of Jesus Christ, I baptize you in the name of the Father, and of the Son, and of the Holy Ghost. Amen. And then shall ye immerse them in the water and come forth again out of the water. And after this manner shall ye baptize in my name."†

There can be no question as to how baptism should be administered after such instruction as this; while the very pressing need of such a revelation to the Christian world is a great evidence in support of its divine inspiration.

---

* Doc. and Cov., sec. xx: 73, 74 † III. Nephi xi: 23-27.

CHAPTER XXV.

THE HOLY GHOST.

HE who said a man must be born again—born of water, said also that he must be born of the spirit;* and it is to that birth, or baptism of the Spirit that we now direct the attention of the reader.

John the Baptist made reference to this matter when he was preaching repentance and baptism throughout Judea. He told the people that he truly baptized with water, but one should come after him, mightier than he was, who would baptize them with the Holy Ghost.† Afterwards he bore record that Jesus of Nazareth was he of whom he spake. "I saw," said he, "the Spirit descending from heaven like a dove, and it abode upon him [Jesus]. And I knew him not; but he that sent me to baptize with water, the same said unto me, upon whom thou shalt see the Spirit descending and remaining on him, the same is he which baptizeth with the Holy Ghost. And I saw and bear record that this is the Son of God."‡

Jesus frequently alluded to this baptism of the Holy Ghost and the powers that a possession

---

*John iii: 5.   † Mark. 1: 7, 8.   ‡ John i: 32-34, in connection with verse 29-31.

thereof would impart to those who received it; and, finally, after his death and resurrection, and just previous to his departure from among his disciples in Judea, he said to them: "Wait for the promise of the Father, which * * * ye have heard of me. For John truly baptized with water but ye shall be baptized with the Holy Ghost not many days hence."* The reference to the promise made through John the Baptist is obvious; and the disciples who had anxiously looked for its accomplishment, were now informed that its fulfillment was not many days hence.

The promise was fulfilled, for in about seven days† after the Messiah's ascension, on the day of Pentecost, the disciples being assembled with one accord, in one place, "Suddenly there came a sound from heaven as of a rushing mighty wind, and it filled all the house where they were sitting. And there appeared unto them cloven tongues like as of fire, and it sat upon each of them. And they were all filled with the Holy Ghost, and began to speak with other tongues, as the spirit gave them utterance."‡

---

*Acts i: 4, 5.

†Pentecost came fifty days after the Passover, on which day the Lord Jesus was crucified. Allowing that he laid three days in the tomb, and was with his disciples forty days after his resurrection (Acts i: 3), forty-three days of the fifty between Passover and Pentecost was accounted for, leaving but seven between his ascension and the day of Pentecost, when the promise of the baptism of the Spirit was fulfilled.

‡Acts ii: 2-4.

Thus was the promise made by John and repeated by Messiah fulfilled.

I have been particular to call attention to this promise, and its fulfillment, because a similar promise is made to all men of all nations, and in all generations wherever and whenever the Gospel is proclaimed. The promise I allude to was made on this very same day of Pentecost, on which the promise of John and Messiah was fulfilled.

Peter, under the inspiration of the Holy Ghost, so abundantly given to himself and companions on that day, preached a discourse which convinced thousands that Jesus was both Lord and Christ, the Savior of the world; and in answering the question of the multitude as to what they should do, after telling them to repent, and to be baptized in the name of Jesus Christ for the remission of their sins, he added: "And ye shall receive the gift of the Holy Ghost: for the promise is unto you, and to your children, and to all that are afar off, even as many as the Lord our God shall call."*

I call attention to the universality of this promise. It was made to those who were listening to the apostles, but not to them alone, it extended to their children, to them also that were afar off—to those who were a hundred years off, or five hundred, or five or ten thousand

---

* Acts ii: 38.

years off; the promise was to them; and as if this was not sufficiently universal, the apostle adds, "even to as many as the Lord our God shall call"—call, to what? to as many, of course, as are called to yield obedience to the Gospel—to all such the promise extends.

As the promise made by John was repeated and emphasized by the Savior, so, likewise, has this general promise made by the apostle Peter been repeated and emphasized by the Lord, in restoring the Gospel to the earth in this dispensation in which we live. To the first Elders of the Church in our day, he said: "As I said unto mine apostles, even so I say unto you, for ye are mine apostles * * * Therefore * * * I say unto you again, that every soul who believeth on your words, and is baptized by water for the remission of sins, shall receive the Holy Ghost."* So, to those who have faith in the revelations which the Lord has given through the Prophet Joseph Smith, the promise of the Holy Ghost is repeated, and assurance is made doubly sure.

The necessity of this baptism of the Holy Ghost is made apparent, first, by the plain declaration of the Savior himself, wherein he says, except a man is born of the Spirit as well as of the water, he cannot enter into the kingdom of heaven;† and of course outside of the

---

*Doc. and Cov., sec. lxxxiv: 63, 64. †John iii: 5.

kingdom of heaven there can be no salvation, nor perfect happiness; second, its necessity appears from the very nature of things.

Through water baptism is obtained a remission of past sins; but even after the sins of the past are forgiven, the one so pardoned will doubtless feel the force of sinful habits bearing heavily upon him. He who has been guilty of habitual untruthfulness, will at times find himself inclined, perhaps, to yield to that habit. He who has stolen may be sorely tempted, when opportunity airses, to steal again. While he who has indulged in licentious practices may again find himself disposed to give way to the seductive influence of the siren. So with drunkenness, malice, envy, covetousness, hatred, anger, and, in short, all the evil dispositions that flesh is heir to.

There is an absolute necessity for some additional sanctifying grace that will strengthen poor human nature, not only to enable it to resist temptation, but also to root out from the heart concupiscence—the blind tendency or inclination to evil. The heart must be purified, every passion, every propensity made submissive to the will, and the will of man brought into subjection to the will of God.

Man's natural powers are unequal to this task; so, I believe, all will testify who have made the experiment. Mankind stand in some need of a strength superior to any they possess of themselves, to accomplish this work of rendering pure our fallen nature. Such strength, such power, such a sanctifying grace is conferred on man in being born of the Spirit—in receiving the Holy Ghost. Such, in the main, is its office, its work.

I do not draw such a conclusion directly from any one passage of scripture, but from the whole tenor of the teachings of the servants of God, in both ancient and modern times.

We shall see, presently, that it is this spirit which reproves the world of sin, of righteousness and judgment, that it guides into all truth, takes of the things of the Father and reveals them unto the children of men and testifies that Jesus is the Christ These things increase knowledge and faith; and as the foundations of knowledge and faith are broadened and deepened so are the powers to work righteousness increased.

We shall see also that the fruits of this spirit are goodness, righteousness, truth, love, joy, peace and gentleness, and as these things are increased in the soul, viciousness and impurity are rooted out, until the whole man is changed and in very deed becomes a new creature in Christ Jesus—is numbered among the pure in heart, and blessed are the pure in heart, for they shall see and dwell with God.

CHAPTER XXVI.

THE HOLY GHOST.—WHO MAY RECEIVE IT.

THE reader has observed, perchance, that John the Baptist was sent to preach repentance and baptism before the coming of him who was to baptize with the Holy Ghost. We may also have observed in the teachings of Peter on the day of Pentecost, after his arguments and the power of the Spirit by which he spake had aroused belief in the minds of the people, that he required them to repent and to be baptized for the remission of their sins before he gave them the promise of the Holy Ghost.

If we turn to the account given in the Acts of the Apostles of the conversion of the people of Samaria, we shall find the same order observed. Philip went down to that city, taught them the word, which they believed, they repented of their sins, and were baptized; then Peter and John came and conferred upon them the Holy Ghost.*

Then, again, when Paul found a number of men in Ephesus, who claimed to have been baptized unto John's baptism, yet had not so much as heard of the Holy Ghost, Paul was

---

* Acts viii.

careful to rebaptize them—since there seemed to be some doubt as to the validity of their first baptism—before he conferred upon them the Holy Ghost.*

It appears from these circumstances that faith, repentance, and baptism, precede the reception or baptism of the Holy Ghost, and are, in fact, prerequisites to a reception of it. This order, in respect to these principles and ordinances, is further sustained by other passages of scripture.

Just previous to his crucifixion, Jesus said to the apostles: "I will pray to the Father, and he shall give unto you another Comforter, that he may abide with you forever; even the Spirit of truth, *whom the world cannot receive* because it seeth him not, neither knoweth him."† It is evident from this that the world cannot receive the Holy Ghost. And now, who are the world? I answer, those who have not yet put on Christ; or, in other words, those who have not yet entered into the kingdom of God, through faith in God and Christ, repentance and baptism. They are the world; and, according to the word of the Master, they cannot receive the Holy Ghost.

Again: When Peter and other apostles were brought before the senate of the Jews, accused with intent to bring the blood of Messiah upon them, Peter answered: "The God of our fathers

---

* Acts xix. † John xiv: 16, 17.

raised up Jesus whom ye slew and hanged on a tree. Him hath God exalted with his right hand to be a Prince and a Savior, for to give repentance to Israel and forgiveness of sins. And we are his witnesses of these things; and so is also the Holy Ghost *whom God hath given to them that obey him.*"* Not, mark you, to them who have not obeyed him. This is in harmony with the statement that the world cannot receive the Holy Ghost, and also with the other cases we cited where the order in presenting the Gospel to the people was faith in God and Christ, repentance, baptism for the remission of sins, and then the reception of the Holy Ghost.

There is an exception, however, to this rule in the New Testament: the case of Cornelius the devout gentile;† and for this exception there was a special reason. It seems that the apostles applied the narrow and contracted views of the Jews to the Gospel. They thought it was to be confined to the house of Israel—to those of the

---

* Acts v: 24-32.

† Some also note the case of Paul as an exception to the rule, but I think this an error. It is true Ananias, on entering the house where Paul was, put his hands on him and said: "The Lord, even Jesus, that appeared unto thee in the way as thou camest, hath sent me, that thou mightest receive thy sight, and be filled with the Holy Ghost. And immediately," the historian tells us, "there fell from his eyes as it had been scales; and he received sight forthwith, and arose and was baptized." (Acts ix: 17, 18.) But in all this I see nothing to warrant the assumption that he received the Holy Ghost prior to his baptism.

circumcision. They appeared slow to understand that in Jesus Christ all the nations and peoples of the earth were to be blessed, the gentiles as well as the Jews. Consequently, when the time had come to send the Gospel to the gentiles, the Lord opened the way by sending an angel to Cornelius to tell him that his prayers and alms had come up for a memorial before the Lord, and to direct him to send men to Joppa for Peter, who would tell him what he ought to do.*
He at once obeyed the heavenly injunction.

Meantime the Lord prepared Peter to go to the gentiles. In vision he beheld a great net lowered down from heaven, filled with all manner of beasts, and a voice cried unto him, "Rise, Peter, kill and eat. But Peter said, Not so, Lord, for I have never eaten anything that is common or unclean." "What God hath cleansed, that call not thou common," said the voice.† This was done thrice, and before he had wholly concluded what the vision could mean, the messengers from Cornelius were at the gate,—and the Spirit told him to go with them, for the Lord had sent them.

That Peter understood the import of this vision to be that the Gospel was for all mankind, for all races and nations, is evident from the fact that when on the following day he went with the messengers to the house of Cornelius, he said

---

*Acts x: 1-8. †Acts x: 9-17.

to him: "Ye know how that it is an unlawful thing for a man that is a Jew to keep company, or come unto one of another nation; but God hath showed me that I should not call any man common or unclean. Therefore come I unto you without gainsaying, as soon as I was sent for."*

Cornelius related to him his vision and expressed himself as ready to receive the commandments of God. Then Peter preached to him Christ and him crucified and that whosoever believed on him should have remission of sins. And "while Peter yet spake these words, the Holy Ghost fell on all them that heard the word. And they of the circumcision which believed were astonished, as many as came with Peter, because that on the gentiles also was poured out the gift of the Holy Ghost. For they heard them speak with tongues and magnify God. Then answered Peter, can any man forbid water, that these should not be baptized which have received the Holy Ghost as well as we? And he commanded them to be baptized, in the name of the Lord."†

Afterwards, when they of the circumcision complained of Peter going to them who were uncircumcised, he related the whole matter to them, and testified that as he began to speak to Cornelius and his kindred, "the Holy Ghost fell

---

* Acts x: 28.   † Acts x: 44-48.

upon them, as on us at the beginning. * * * Forasmuch, then, as God gave them the like gift as he did unto us, who believed on the Lord Jesus Christ, what was I, that I could withstand God."* When they heard this they held their peace, and the saying went abroad that God had also to the gentiles granted repentance unto life.

The object for deviating from the order in which the principles and ordinances of the Gospel follow each other is obvious—it was that the Jews might have a witness from God that the Gospel was for the gentiles as well as for their own nation. But according to the scriptures, and, I may say, according to the nature and relationship of these several principles and ordinances of the Gospel to each other, the reception of the Holy Ghost comes after repentance and baptism.

In writing to the Corinthian saints who had received the Holy Ghost, Paul says: "What? know ye not that your body is the temple of the Holy Ghost, which is in you, which ye have of God?"†

And again: "Know ye not that ye are the temple of God, and that the Spirit of God dwelleth in you? If any man defile the temple of God, him will God destroy."‡

From these passages this much is learned: that the man who receives the Holy Ghost becomes a

---

* Acts xi: 15-17. † I. Cor. v: 19. ‡ I. Cor. iii: 16, 17.

temple thereof, even the temple of God; and since it is decreed that if a man defiles the temple of God him will God destroy, it may be reasonably inferred that the Holy Ghost dwells not in unholy temples; hence, through faith in God, sincere repentance of all sins, and baptism for the remission of them, man cleanses his temple, his body, that it may be a fit dwelling place for the Holy Ghost.

Thus faith, repentance, water baptism, and then the baptism of the Spirit is the order in which these principles stand, both according to the teachings of the scriptures, and the nature of the things themselves: the one leading up logically to the other, which follows in beautiful and harmonious sequence.

CHAPTER XXVII.

THE HOLY GHOST.—HOW IMPARTED.

THE manner in which the saints under the teachings of the apostles received the baptism of the Holy Ghost was through the laying on of hands. In proof of this I call attention once more to the labors of Philip in the city of Samaria.

It is already known how he taught them the Gospel, how they believed it and were baptized; then we are informed that "when the apostles which were at Jerusalem heard that Samaria had received the word of God, they sent unto them Peter and John: who, when they were come down, prayed for them, that they might receive the Holy Ghost (for as yet he was fallen upon none of them: only they were baptized in the name of the Lord Jesus.) Then laid they their hands on them, and they received the Holy Ghost."*

Previous to the labors of Philip among the Samaritans, one Simon Magus, a magician, had given it out that he himself was some great one, and his influence among the people was considerable. But he, too, became converted to the teachings of Philip, and was astonished at the power which attended his administrations, for the sick were healed, the lame were cured, and unclean spirits cast out of those who were possessed of them. Afterwards when the apostles John and Peter came and conferred the Holy Ghost upon those whom Philip had baptized, Simon was present: "And when Simon saw that through laying on of the apostles' hands the Holy Ghost was given, he offered them money, saying, Give me also this power, that on whomsoever I lay my hands, he may receive the Holy Ghost. But Peter said unto him, Thy money perish with thee, because thou hast thought that the gift of God may be purchased with money."†

Paul, it will be remembered, found a number

---

* Acts viii: 14-17.   † Acts viii: 18-20.

of men at Ephesus who claimed to have been baptized unto John's baptism, but when Paul questioned them as to the Holy Ghost, they had not heard even that there was such a spirit. So doubting the validity of their baptism, he rebaptized them; after which, "when Paul had laid his hands upon them, the Holy Ghost came upon them; and they spake with tongues and prophesied."*

The same apostle, also, in writing to Timothy, exhorts him to "stir up the gift of God which was in him, and which he had received by the putting on of his [Paul's] hands,† alluding, no doubt, to the time that Paul bestowed the Holy Ghost upon him by the laying on of hands.

That this practice of laying on hands for the bestowal or baptism of the Holy Ghost continued in the primitive Christian Church for a long period—at least for three centuries—is evident from the following testimony:

Of the rites and ceremonies of the third century Mosheim says: "The effect of baptism was supposed to be the remission of sins: And it was believed that the bishop, by the imposition of hands and by prayer conferred those gifts of the Holy Spirit which were necessary for living a holy life."‡

In a note on the foregoing question, Murdock,

---

*Acts xix: 1-6. † II. Tim. i: 6. ‡ Mosheim's Church History (Murdock), Vol. I, p. 189.

the most accurate translator of Dr. Mosheim's great work on church history, says: "This may be placed beyond all controversy by many passages from the fathers of this century. And as it will conduce much to an understanding of the theology of the ancients, which differed in many respects from ours, I will adduce a single passage from Cyprian. It is in his Epistle, No. 73, p. 131: 'It is manifest where and by whom the remission of sin conferred in baptism is administered. They who are presented to the rulers of the church, obtain by our prayers and imposition of hands the Holy Ghost.'"*

In another passage Cyprian writes: "Our practice is, that those who have been baptized into the Church should be presented, that by prayer and imposition of hands they may receive the Holy Ghost." While Augustine, in the fourth century, says: "We still do what the apostles did when they laid their hands on the Samaritans and called down the Holy Ghost upon them."†

In subsequent centuries, however, this part of the Gospel was lost, or neglected by some of the

---

* Mosheim's Church Hist., Vol. I, p. 189.

† Laying on hands was employed in the Church for other purposes than imparting the Holy Ghost. It was the manner of administering to the sick (Mark xvi: 18; Acts xxviii, 8); and also of conferring authority or priesthood on men (see Acts vi: 5, 6; viii: 17; xiii: 3); but as we here are only dealing with the ordinance as it relates to a means of imparting the Holy Ghost, I do not stop to discuss the other purposes for which it was employed.

sects of Christendom, and when announced among them today, it is not unfrequently regarded as a new doctrine.* Yet it is not. We have seen that it was a doctrine practiced by the apostles and their immediate successors. Indeed it is named directly as one of the principles of the doctrine of Christ by Paul. The following is the passage: "Therefore not leaving the principles of the doctrine of Christ, let us go on unto perfection; not laying again the foundation of repentance from dead works, and of faith toward God, of the doctrine of baptisms, *and of laying on of hands* and of resurrection of the dead, and of eternal judgment."† And here it may be well

---

* It is a mistake to suppose all Christendom have neglected the practice of this ordinance. The Catholics teach that "Confirmation [by the laying on of hands] is a sacrament instituted by our Lord, by which the faithful, who have already been made children of God by baptism, receive the Holy Ghost by prayer, unction (or anointing with holy oil called *chrism*), and the laying on of the hands of a bishop, the successor of the apostles. It is thus that they are enriched with gifts, graces and virtues, especially with the virtue of fortitude, and made perfect Christians and valiant soldiers of Jesus Christ to stand through life the whole warfare of the world, the flesh and the devil The first recorded instance of confirmation being administered to the faithful is in the eighth chapter of the Acts of the Apostles, where St. Peter and St John confirmed the Samaritans who had been already baptized by St. Philip. 'They prayed for them that they might receive the Holy Ghost. * * * Then laid they their hands on them and they received the Holy Ghost" (Catholic Belief, Bruno pp. 97, 98). The Church of England, and of course the Episcopal churches in the colonies and the United States teach practically the same.

† Heb. vi: 1, 2.

to call attention to the fact, that it is written that "Whosoever transgresseth and abideth not in the doctrine of Christ, hath not God."* And since the religious world has very generally lost sight of this important doctrine of the laying on of hands for imparting the Holy Ghost, it is one evidence, among many others, that they have not God; for the absence of this part of the Gospel proves that they have not continued in the doctrine of Christ.

In restoring the Gospel to the earth in the present dispensation, it seems, from the frequency with which it is mentioned, that particular prominence is given to this doctrine and ordinance through which the Holy Ghost is imparted. Out of the many passages in the Doctrine and Covenants relating to the subject I select the following:

In April, 1830, the same month and year in which the Church of Christ in this dispensation was organized, the Lord in explaining the office and calling of an apostle, said: "An apostle is an elder, and it is his calling to baptize; * * * and to confirm those who are baptized into the Church, by the laying on of hands for the baptism of fire, and the Holy Ghost, according to the scriptures."†

In a revelation to James Covill given in January, 1831, calling him to obedience to the

---

* II. John: 9.   † Doc. and Cov., sec. xx : 38, 41.

Gospel and appointing him to be his servant, even a minister for Christ, the Lord said: "And this is my Gospel: repentance and baptism by water, and then cometh the baptism of fire and the Holy Ghost, even the Comforter, which showeth all things, and teacheth the peaceable things of the Kingdom." After calling him to be his servant the Lord said: "And again it shall come to pass, that on as many as ye shall baptize with water, ye shall lay your hands, and they shall receive the gift of the Holy Ghost."*

Then in a revelation given to Sidney Rigdon, Parley P. Pratt and Lemon Copley, through Joseph the Prophet, on the occasion of these men being sent with the Gospel to the Shakers, the Lord said: "Go among this people and say unto them, like unto mine apostle of old, whose name was Peter; believe on the name of the Lord Jesus. * * * Repent and be baptized in the name of Jesus Christ, according to the holy commandment, for the remission of sins; and whoso doeth this shall receive the gift of the Holy Ghost, by the laying on of the hands of the Elders of this Church."†

As this last is a general law, I do not consider it necessary to cite further passages, though the revelations of the Lord contained in the Doctrine

---

* Doc. and Cov., sec. xxxix: 6, 23 † Ibid., sec. xlix: 11-14.

and Covenants are replete with them. Sufficient has been said to show that the doctrine has been made prominent in this dispensation.

To my mind this ordinance is the most philosophical of any in the Gospel. On one occasion as Jesus passed through a throng of people, a woman who had been troubled with an issue of blood for twelve years, and had spent all her living upon physicians, but received no benefit from them, came up behind him, saying in her heart, if I can but touch the hem of his garment I shall be healed. And it was so, even according to her faith; for pressing through the crowd she laid hold of his garment and was immediately made whole. "And Jesus said, who touched me?" When all denied, Peter and they that were with him said, "Master, the multitude throng thee, and press thee, and sayest thou who touched me? And Jesus said, somebody hath touched me; for I perceive that virtue is gone out of me."*

Now, what had happened. And why the expression—"Somebody hath touched me; for I perceive that virtue is gone out of me." My answer would be that the person of Jesus, aye, and also the very garments he wore, were so charged with that divine influence, known to us as the Holy Spirit, that when the woman with the issue of blood touched his garments, so much

---

* Luke viii : 43, 46.

of that Spirit left him to heal her that it was perceptible to him, and he exclaimed, "Virtue is gone out of me!"

So, when a servant of God, filled with that Spirit, and with authority to act in the name of Jesus Christ, lays his hands upon one who has prepared himself for the reception of the Holy Ghost, through faith, repentance, and baptism, a portion of that Holy Spirit passes from the one who administers, to him upon whom he lays his hands and he is baptized with it. These are the laws by which it is received and conveyed; these are the conditions that must exist, in order that men may obtain this holiest of all influences, and its full and free enjoyment. And its transmission from one person to another by an observance of the ordinances and principles of righteousness we have now considered, is as natural and philosophical in the spiritual things of the universe, as it is for electricity or steam to perform the wonders which these forces are now made to enact in the commercial and mechanical worlds; and which they will not perform, unless the conditions by which their power is made available, are complied with.

I cannot do better in concluding this chapter than to quote a paragraph or two from the works of Apostle Parley P. Pratt:

"To impart a portion of the Holy Spirit by the touch, or by the laying on of hands; or to impart a portion of the element of life, from one animal body to another, by an authorized agent who acts in the name of God, and who is filled therewith, is as much in accordance with the laws of nature as for water to seek its own level; air its equilibrium; or heat and electricity their own mediums of conveyance.

"This law of spiritual fluid, its communicative properties, and the channel by which it is imparted from one person to another, bear some resemblance or analogy to the laws and operations of electricity. Like electricity, it is imparted by the contact of two bodies, through the channel of the nerves.

"But the two fluids differ widely. The one is a property nearly allied to the grosser elements of matter; not extensively endowed with the attributes of intelligence, wisdom, affection or moral discrimination. It can therefore be imparted from one animal body to another, irrespective of the intellectual or moral qualities of the subject or recipient. The other is a substance endowed with the attributes of intelligence, affection, moral discrimination, love, charity and benevolence pure as the emotions which swell the bosom, thrill the nerves, or vibrate the pulse of the Father of all.

"An agent filled with this heavenly fluid cannot impart of the same to another, unless that other is justified, washed, cleansed from all his impurities of heart, affections, habits or practices by the blood of atonement, which is generally applied in connection with the baptism of remission.

"A man who continues in his sins, and who has no living faith in the Son of God, cannot receive the gift of the Holy Spirit through the ministration of any agent, however holy he may be. The impure spirit of such a one will repulse the pure element, upon the natural laws of sympathetic affinity, or of attraction and repulsion."*

In other words, the Spirit of God will not dwell in unholy temples, hence repentance and baptism for the remission of sins go before the baptism of the Spirit that men may be cleansed of their sins, justified before God, and their bodies by these means made fit dwelling-places for the Holy Ghost—the living temples of God.

CHAPTER XXVIII.

THE HOLY GHOST.—CHARACTER AND SOURCE.

CAN the naturalist find out and comprehend the secret of the endless variety of life in the vegetable and animal kingdoms? Can the chemist find out the essences of substances, or make himself master of the secrets of great nature's laboratory where those wonderful combinations are wrought which produce the sub-

---

* Key to Theology, pp. 96, 97, 98.

stances that constitute the material universe? Can the physician or surgeon with scalpel and microscope "trace to its source the lightning of the soul"—trace out the secret springs of life and intelligence in the human organism? Can the astronomer, even with his mightiest telescope, penetrate to the outside curtains of space where worlds and planetary systems do not exist —can he circumscribe the creations of God, within the scope of his vision or knowledge?

To all these questions a negative answer must be given; when man has done his best, when his whole life has been spent in seeking knowledge and finding out wisdom, even then the facts which he has mastered, compared with those beyond the power of his intellect to comprehend, are insignificant; and the fields of knowledge which he has explored, compared with those wherein man has never yet set his foot, are as the few grains of sand compared to the untold millions of such grains that form old ocean's beach.

The great Sir Isaac Newton at the close of his life—a life devoted to the search for knowledge in which pursuit he had been more than ordinarily successful, and most men thought he had accomplished something of which he could boast—said in accents most humble, "I have been like a child playing upon the beach; I have succeeded in finding a few pretty shells, and picking up a few pretty pebbles, but the great ocean lies before me unexplored."

Questions and considerations like these, are calculated to reveal the fact that man, with all his boasted intelligence, is, after all, in this sphere of existence, "cribbed, cabined and confined" to limits extremely narrow, so far as his ability to comprehend facts is concerned.

The naturalist will answer "No," to the question I have set down to him. He will tell us that he can classify the various forms of animal and vegetable life, basing his classification upon certain similarities of structure or habits; but when it comes to accounting for the great variety and forms of life in animated nature; or to telling why it is that one seed produces the mighty, sturdy oak, and another the supple willow; or why each species of animals produces its kind —he cannot inform you. His most careful investigations and patient watching have failed to rob nature of these secrets.

The chemist of a century ago, who thought he had reduced compound substances to their primary elements, and had discovered all the primary elements of substances; could he live today, he would see his "elements" separated and reduced, and a multitude of other elements unknown to him, brought within the compass of chemical science; and yet the existence of the universe itself, remaining as great a mystery as ever. Indeed, the wonder grows rather than diminishes with each succeeding discovery; for these things increase the mystery by revealing the complexity and delicate combinations of substances as they exist in their varied forms.

To the physician, the surgeon, the scientist, the mystery of life remains as much an unsolved problem as it ever did. It is true they claim to have traced it down to its beginning; they say it originates in a substance known to them as protoplasm; that a single cell of this wonderful substance has the peculiar power of producing another cell, and this one still another. This multiplication of protoplasmic cells continuing until it develops in the varied processes of nature into the great variety of animal organisms known to us. Yet after all his work, the scientist, at last, with nervous hand and throbbing brow reaches a point beoynd which he cannot go, and the single cell of protoplasm, with the peculiar power to multiply itself, is as great a mystery as man with his complex organism of bones and nerves and muscles.

To the question I have put to the astronomer, he would doubtless answer, with some impatience, that his best instruments but revealed to him the nearest outposts of the stellar worlds; and that beyond these few street lamps within his vision, with whose positions he has become acquainted and marked down on his chart, are numberless planetary sysems out of the reach of his insruments, but whose existence is revealed by masses of light through which he cannot penetrate. His science is unsatisfied, the little he has learned but reveals to him the vastness and extent of those fields of knowledge beyond his power to enter, much less to reap.

If in relation to these grosser materials or objects, and their relationship to each other, man's knowledge is so limited, and his powers of comprehension so restricted, the reader will not be astonished when I tell him there is very much that is beyond our power to understand in relation to that most subtle, powerful, sensitive and intelligent of all influences, known to us as the Holy Ghost.

What little may be learned of this great spiritual force in the universe, is to be found in the revelations of God, from which we are given to understand that this Holy Spirit which exists throughout the universe and is the medium by which it is governed, emanates from God.

Just previous to his crucifixion, Jesus said to his disciples: "But when the Comforter [which is the Holy Ghost—see John xiv, 26], is come, whom I will send unto you from the Father, even the Spirit of Truth, *which proceedeth from the Father* he will testify of me."*

And this agrees with what the Lord has revealed in this dispensation, in respect to this Spirit. To a number of Elders who had assem-

---

*John xv: 26.

bled together, to learn the will of the Lord concerning them—after telling them that he was well pleased with them, and that their names were written in the book of the names of the sanctified—he said: "Wherefore, I now send upon you another Comforter, even upon you, my friends, that it may abide in your hearts, even the Holy Spirit of promise; which other Comforter is the same I promised unto my disciples, as is recorded in the testimony of John.* This Comforter is the promise which I give unto you of eternal life; even the glory of the celestial kingdom: which glory is that of the church of the first-born; even of God, the holiest of all, through Jesus Christ, his Son: he that ascended up on high, as also he descended below all things, in that he comprehended all things, that he might be in all and through all things [that is, by the power of his Spirit] the light of truth; which truth shineth. This is the light of Christ [or Holy Spirit]. As also he is [that is, by this Spirit—the Holy Ghost], in the sun, and the light of the sun, and the power thereof by which it was made. As also he is in the moon, and is the light of the moon, and the power thereof, by which it was made. As also the light of the stars, and the power thereof by which they were made. And the earth also, and the power thereof; even the earth upon which you stand.

---

* John xiv.

And the light which now shineth, which giveth you light, is through him who enlighteneth your eyes, which is the same light that quickeneth your understandings; *which light proceedeth forth from the presence of God* to fill the immensity of space, the light which is in all things; which giveth life to all things: which is the law by which all things are governed; even the power of God, who sitteth upon his throne, who is in the bosom of eternity, who is in the midst of all things."*

The line in italics represents this "light" which quickened the understanding of the Elders to whom the revelation was addressed, as proceeding from the presence of God, and this is wherein the testimony of this revelation agrees with that of John. Both testify that this Spirit emanates from God, and that this "light" which "proceedeth forth from the presence of God to fill the immensity of space, which giveth life to all things, which is the law by which all things are governed," is identical with that Spirit of which Jesus was speaking, the Holy Ghost, cannot be doubted. Hence, from this revelation we learn not only the source of the Holy Ghost, but that it permeates the universe, and is the power by which the creations of God were brought into existence, by which they subsist, and by

---

* Doc. and Cov., sec. lxxxviii: 1-13.

which they are directed in their respective spheres in such harmony and splendor.

To these ideas respecting the Holy Ghost agree several other authoritative passages. The Prophet Joseph Smith taught that the Holy Ghost has not a body of flesh and bones, "but is a personage of Spirit;" and then adds: "Were it not so, the Holy Ghost could not dwell in us."*

Again it is written: "The elements are the tabernacle of God, yea man is the tabernacle of God, even temples; and whatsoever temple is defiled, God shall destroy that temple."† This cannot allude to God the Father or to God the Son, because each has a tabernacle of flesh and bones, as tangible as man's;‡ but it alludes to God the Holy Ghost, whose tabernacle is in the elements of the universe, giving life and light and intelligence to all things, and is the grand medium of communication between God the Father and his Son Jesus Christ and their vast creations.

So much as to the source and nature of the Holy Ghost; now let us turn our attention to what it does for those who possess it, what gifts and graces it bestows and develops in them.

---

* Doc. and Cov., sec. cxxx.

† Doc. and Cov., sec. xciii; also I. Cor. iii : 16, 17; I. Cor., vi : 19.

‡ The Father has a body of flesh and bones as tangible as man's; the Son also; but the Holy Ghost has not a body of flesh and bones, but is a personage of Spirit. (Doc. and Cov., sec. cxxx : 22; see also Lectures on Faith, v : 2, 3.)

CHAPTER XXIX.

THE HOLY GHOST.—ITS POWER.

AS the time drew near for Jesus to make his great sacrifice, and then depart from the immediate presence of his disciples, he manifested a great desire to comfort them in prospect of this separation, and this he did by promising to send to them from the Father the Holy Ghost, that he might abide with them for ever;* and in explaining to them the powers of this Spirit, he said: "But the Comforter, which is the Holy Ghost, whom the Father will send in my name, he shall teach you all things, and bring all things to your remembrance, whatsoever I have said unto you."

In continuation of his remarks on this subject, he told them he had many things to say unto them, but they could not bear them at that time. "Howbeit," said he, "when he, the Spirit of Truth, is come, he will guide you into all truth: for he shall not speak of himself: but whatsoever he shall hear that shall he speak: and he will show you things to come. He shall glorify me: for he shall receive of mine, and shall show it unto you. All things that the Father hath are

---

* John xiv: 16, 26.

mine: Therefore, said I, that he shall take of mine, and shall show it unto you."*

From these passages four important things are learned respecting the powers of the Holy Ghost:

I. That he will teach all things; and, what is equivalent, "guide into all truth."

II. He will bring all things to remembrance, that is, whatsoever things have been stored in the mind.

III. He will show things to come.

IV. He will take of the things of God and reveal them unto men.

Of the excellence and importance of these several powers it is scarcely needful to speak, since their excellence is evident, upon the mere enumeration of them, yet one cannot refrain from looking at them more in detail. How excellent a thing it is to have a teacher competent to teach all things, and guide into all truth! In view of the fact that the saints possessed the Holy Ghost, and that the Holy Ghost has these powers, one can understand the reasonableness of John's remarks to the saints, in which he says: "But ye have an unction from the Holy One, and ye know all things. * * * The anointing which ye have received of him abideth in you, and ye need not that any man teach you: but as the same anointing teacheth you of all

---

* John xvi: 13 15.

things, and is truth, and is no lie, and even as it hath taught you, ye shall abide in him."*

Moreover, to that extent that a man is guided into all truth, he is preserved from all error. There is no danger of his being deceived, or led astray by every wind of doctrine, or the cunning craftiness of false teachers, so long as he is in possession of that Spirit which guides into all truth. So taught Isaiah, who, in speaking of the time when the house of Israel should possess this Spirit, says: "And though the Lord give you the bread of adversity, and the water of affliction, yet shall not thy teachers be removed into a corner any more, but thine eyes shall see thy teachers: And thine ears shall hear a word behind thee, saying, This is the way, walk ye in it, when ye turn to the right hand and when ye turn to the left."†

As to the second power enumerated, *viz.*: the power to bring all things to the recollection, I maintain that it would be impossible for man to live the law of the gospel without some such grace being conferred upon him by the Lord. The law of the gospel requires men not only to do good to those who do good to them, but to do good to those who despitefully use them; not only to lend to those who lend to them, but to lend to those of whom they can hope to receive nothing in return; to revile not those who may

---

* I. John ii: 20, 27.   † Isaiah xxx: 20, 21.

revile them—in a word, the law of the gospel is summed up in this: "Be ye not overcome of evil; but overcome evil with good."*

However fine this may be in theory, or however beautiful it may look on paper, to carry it practically into the affairs of life is difficult.

When reviled it seems but natural to answer railing with railing, blows with blows, and for injury inflicted, return as much in kind as is within one's power to inflict. And unless in possession of this grace bestowed by the Holy Ghost, *viz.*, having brought to one's recollection the things of Christ's gospel, being reminded in the very moment of temptation of these laws—when smarting under a sense of injustice, or suffering under wrongs heaped upon one—it would be difficult if not impossible to live up to these heavenly precepts. But by having the Holy Spirit as one's prompter in the moments of temptation, and by cultivating the Christian virtue of patience, this law of the gospel, so contrary to the natural disposition, may be complied with, and the follower of Christ, like his Master, may be able to say for those who inflict injury upon him, "Father, forgive them, for they know not what they do."

Thirdly, "He will show you things to come." In other words, the Holy Ghost is the spirit of prophecy, for by it the future has been unfolded

---

* Romans xii: 21. See also Matt. v, vi.

to the minds of the prophets; and by it the scriptures were given. In proof of this I quote the apostle Peter: "The prophecy came not in old time by the will of man: but holy men of God spake as they were moved by the Holy Ghost,"* and that which they spake was written and became scripture.

When an angel visited John on Patmos and that apostle fell at his feet to worship him, the angel said: "See thou do it not: I am thy fellow servant, and of thy brethren that have the testimony of Jesus" [which is the Holy Ghost]: "worship God, for the testimony of Jesus is the Spirit of prophecy."†

These facts will exhibit the inconsistency, nay, I may say, the absolutely erroneous position of those who insist that while the Holy Ghost has continued with men, prophecy and revelation have ceased.

The very fact, as stated in the fourth item taken from these passages under consideration, *viz.*, that the Holy Ghost will take of the things of the Lord and show them unto men, also proves that this Spirit is one of revelation, and is in harmony with the scripture—"The Spirit searcheth all things, yea, the deep things of God. What man knoweth the things of man, but the spirit of a man which is in him? Even

---

* II. Peter i : 21.   † Rev. xix : 10.

so the things of God knoweth no man, but the Spirit of God."*

In addition to these powers there is still another, and it is an important one. The Holy Ghost is a witness for God and Christ: "When the Comforter is come," are the words of the Son of God, "whom I will send unto you from the Father, * * * he will testify of me."† The testimony of Paul is still more emphatic than this: "No man speaking by the Spirit of God calleth Jesus accursed; and no man can say that Jesus is the Lord, but by the Holy Ghost."‡

I have shown in my remarks on the Holy Ghost being "the Spirit of prophecy," that that Spirit and this without which no man can say that Jesus is the Lord—"the testimony of Jesus" —are identical. Several other powers belonging to this Spirit are also enumerated by Paul. He gives us to understand that "There are diversities of gifts, but the same Spirit, and there are differences of administration, but the same Lord. * * * But the manifestation of the Spirit is given to every man to profit withal. For to one is given by the Spirit, the word of wisdom, to another the word of knowledge by the same Spirit: to another faith by the same Spirit; to another the gifts of healing by the same Spirit: To another the working of miracles; to another prophecy; to another discerning of spirits, to

---

*I. Cor. ii: 11. 12.   †John xv: 26.   ‡I Cor. xii: 3.

another divers kinds of tongues; to another interpretation of tongues: But all these worketh that one and the self same Spirit dividing to each one severally as he will."*

In addition to this splendid array of powers and gifts of the Holy Ghost, we are told that its fruit "is love, joy, peace, long-suffering, gentleness, goodness, faith, meekness, and temperance."† Indeed we may say, in the language of Apostle Parley P. Pratt, the Holy Spirit adapts itself to all the organs and attributes of man. "It quickens all the intellectual faculties, increases, enlarges, expands and purifies all the natural passions and affections; and adapts them by the gift of wisdom to their lawful use. It inspires, develops, cultivates and matures all the fine-toned sympathies, joys, tastes, kindred feelings and affections of our nature. It inspires virtue, kindness, goodness, tenderness, gentleness and charity. It develops beauty of person, form and feature. It tends to health, vigor, animation and social feeling. It develops and invigorates all the faculties of the physical and intellectual man. It strengthens, invigorates and gives tone to the nerves. In short, it is, as it were, marrow to the bone, joy to the heart, light to the eyes, music to the ears, and life to the whole being."‡

Such is the Holy Ghost and its sanctifying influence—such is the Spirit given to those who

---

* I. Cor. xii: 4-22. † Gal. vi: 22, 23. ‡ Key to Theology, p. 102.

accept the gospel, who believe in God and Jesus Christ, who repent of their sins and are baptized for the remission of them—then follows the baptism of the Spirit, in other words, the reception of the Holy Ghost through the laying on of hands. Then is developed one or more of its spiritual gifts, and its general purifying influences; enlarging the understanding, ennobling every thought, making pure the heart; in short, it draws man into a nearer relationship with his God, and begins that spiritual education so necessary to prepare him for the glorious presence of his Creator—his Father.

CHAPTER XXX.

AUTHORITY.

I HAVE now considered, at some length, the doctrines and ordinances which constitute the First Principles of the Gospel of Christ. In connection with these principles, however, there is another matter which must claim the reader's attention; *viz.:* the important fact that the gospel must be preached and its ordinances administered by those having authority from God; or the administrations will have no binding force in heaven or on earth, in time or in eternity.

We are informed in the scriptures that the Lord wrought special miracles by the hands of

Paul, whom he had called to be his servant. The sick were healed, aud evil spirits were cast out of those who were possessed. "Then certain of the vagabond Jews, exorcists, took upon them to call over them which had evil spirits, the name of the Lord Jesus, saying, We adjure you, by Jesus whom Paul preacheth. And there were seven sons, of one Sceva, a Jew, and chief of the priests, which did so. And the evil spirit answered and said, Jesus I know, and Paul I know, but who are ye? And the man in whom the evil spirit was, leaped on them, and overcame them, and prevailed against them, so that they fled out of that house, naked and wounded."* These men presumptuously took it upon themselves to act as those who had authority, and the result was that not even the devils would respect their administrations, much less the Lord.

There is a principle of great moment associated with this incident. The question is, if these men, when acting without authority from God could not drive out an evil spirit, would their administration be of force, or have any virtue in it, had they administered in some other ordinance of the Gospel, say baptism for the remission of sins, or laying on hands for imparting the Holy Ghost? Manifestly it would not. And hence we rightly come to the conclusion, so well expressed in one of our articles of faith, that "A

---
* Acts xix : 13-16.

man must be called of God, by prophecy and by the laying on of hands, by those who are in authority to preach the gospel and administer in the ordinances thereof."

Such a conclusion as this could reasonably be drawn also from the words of Paul in Hebrews where he says: "Every high priest taken from among men is ordained for men in things pertaining to God, that he may offer both gifts and sacrifices for sins: * * * And no man taketh this honor unto himself, but he that is called of God as was Aaron."* The manner in which Aaron was called to the priest's office is recorded in the writings of Moses as follows: "Take thou unto thee Aaron thy brother, and his sons with him from among the children of Israel, that he may minister unto me in the priest's office, even Aaron, Nadab and Abihu, Eleazar and Ithamar, Aaron's sons."†

It may be objected that this was the law relating to the calling of high priests alone, but if high priests are to be called in this manner, is it not reasonable to conclude that all who administer in "things pertaining to God" must be called in the same way—that is, of God? So far as the scriptures are concerned, and on subjects of this character their authority is conclusive, wherever we have an account of men administering in the things pertaining to God, and their

---

* Heb v. 1, 5.   † Ex. xxviii, 1.

administrations are accepted of him, they have either been called directly by revelation from him, or through inspiration in those who already had authority from God to act in his name; and to be called by a legitimate, divinely established authority is to be called of God.

On the other hand, whenever men have taken it upon themselves to act in the name of God, so far as any such instance is recorded, it has been followed by some manifestation of displeasure from him.

As an example of this statement, I call attention to the case of Uzza. The Lord appointed Aaron and his sons to take special charge of the ark of the covenant and all the holy things belonging to it. When it became necessary for the camp to move, after all things had been arranged by Aaron and his sons, then the sons of Kohash were to come to bear it; "but," said the Lord, "they shall not touch any holy thing lest they die."* Some generations after this, King David undertook to move the ark from Baalah,—called also Kirjathjearim, where it had remained many years. Uzza and Ahio drove the cart on which the ark and its furniture were placed, and when the company engaged in this pious work reached Chidon, Uzza put forth his hand to steady the ark, for the oxen stumbled, but in doing so he broke the law which had been

---

* Num. iv: 15.

given to Israel*—he acted without authority "And the anger of the Lord was kindled against Uzza, and he smote him because he put his hand to the ark; and there he died before God."†

Take still another case, that of Uzziah. He was one of the kings of Israel; and for a long time he prospered exceedingly because of his righteousness. His enemies were smitten before him, and wisdom was given him to fortify Jerusalem as it never had been fortified before. But in the midst of his glory and the pride of his heart, he undertook to minister in the temple of God in the priest's office; and appeared before the altar to burn incense. " And Azariah the priest went in after him, and with him four score priests of the Lord, that were valiant men: And they withstood Uzziah the king and said unto him, It appertaineth not unto thee, Uzziah, to burn incense unto the Lord, but to the priests, the sons of Aaron, that are consecrated to burn incense: Go out of the sanctuary; for thou hast trespassed; neither shall it be to thine honor from the Lord God. Then Uzziah was wroth, and had a censer in his hand to burn incense: and while he was wroth with the priests, the leprosy even rose in his forehead before the priests in the house of the Lord, from beside the incense altar. And Azariah, the chief priest, and all the priests, looked upon him, and, behold,

---

* Num. iv: 15.   † I. Chron. xiii: 10.

he was leprous in his forehead, and they thrust him out from thence; yea himself hasted also to go out, because the Lord had smitten him. And Uzziah, the king, was a leper unto the day of his death, and dwelt in a several house, being a leper; for he was cut off from the house of the Lord."*

Swift punishment followed upon the presumptuous attempt of this king to exercise the authority of God without having had it conferred upon him: and we have already seen that in New Testament times the Lord would not have respect for the administration of those who spoke in his name without authority, no matter how nearly they conformed to the forms of the ceremony; there was no force in it, and the devil could and did prevail against him.

We have the testimony of Jesus respecting the authority which he had conferred upon his apostles; said he, "Ye have not chosen me, but I have chosen you, and ordained you, that ye should go and bring forth fruit."†

When seven men were chosen to look after the poor and minister to them, they set them before the apostles who, when they had prayed, laid their hands on them and ordained them to their calling.‡

So in the case of Paul. It was not enough that he saw and spoke with the Messiah, not enough

---

* II. Chron. xxvi.   † John xv: 16.   ‡ Acts vi: 1-6.

to have Ananias come and baptize him, and receive the Holy Ghost; for afterwards, when the Lord would have him engage in the work of preaching the gospel and administer in the ordinances thereof, the Holy Ghost said unto certain prophets at Antioch, "Separate me Barnabas and Saul for the work whereunto I have called them. And when they had fasted and prayed, and laid their hands on them, they sent them away."*

Furthermore, as Paul went about confirming the souls of the saints, he ordained elders in every church.† He did not suffer men to take the authority on themselves to minister in the things of God; but warned the saints against such characters. Having assembled the elders of the church of Ephesus, he said to them: "Take heed unto yourselves, and to all the flock, over which the Holy Ghost has made you overseers, to feed the flock of God. * * * For I know this that after my departing, shall grievous wolves enter in, not sparing the flock. And of your own selves, shall men arise, speaking perverse things, to draw away disciples after them."‡

This same thing pressed itself upon his mind when he wrote his Epistle to Timothy; for we find him exhorting that worthy man to "Preach the word; be instant in season, out of season; reprove, rebuke, exhort with all long-suffering,

---

*Acts xiii: 1-3.   †Acts, xiv: 2, 3.   ‡Acts xx: 28, 29.

and doctrine, for the time will come when they will not endure sound doctrine; but after their own lusts shall they heap to themselves teachers, having itching ears; and they shall turn away their ears from the truth, and shall be turned unto fables."*

To this also agrees the testimony of Peter. After speaking of the prophets that were in ancient Israel, he says: "But there were false prophets also among the people [then addressing the saints of his own day], even as there shall be false teachers among you, who privily shall bring in damnable heresies, even denying the Lord that bought them, and shall bring upon themselves swift destruction. And many shall follow their pernicious ways; by reason of whom the way of truth shall be evil spoken of."†

That is just what happened. False teachers arose, damnable heresies crept into the churches, the Gospel was corrupted, and a few generations after the gospel was introduced by the personal ministry of John the Baptist and the Messiah himself, the authority of God was taken from among men.

Hence, when a knowledge of the Gospel was restored to the earth in this last dispensation, it became necessary to restore also the authority to teach it, and administer its ordinances. For this purpose John the Baptist, laboring under the

---

* II. Tim . iv : 2-4.   † II Peter ii : 1, 2.

direction of Peter, James and John, was sent to restore sufficient authority to administer the outward ordinances, to teach faith and repentance, and baptize for the remission of sins.*

Subsequently Peter, James and John were sent of the Lord† some time in the early summer of 1829, and ordained Joseph Smith and Oliver Cowdery to the holy Melchisedek Priesthood—in fact, they were ordained apostles. ‡And as the "Melchisedek priesthood holds the right of presidency, and has power and authority over all the offices in the church in all ages of the world to administer in spiritual things"§—these men, Joseph Smith and Oliver Cowdery, had authority to administer in all the ordinances of salvation, and to organize the Church of Christ; which, under the direction of the Lord, they did. And thus, not only has the Gospel been restored to the earth in this last dispensation, but the authority to administer in all its ordinances, and to build up the Church of Christ and the Kingdom of God on earth has been brought from heaven and bestowed upon men.

---

* Doc. and Cov. sec. xiii. † Doc. and Cov. sec. xxvii: 12.
‡ Doc. and Cov. sec. xx: 2, 3. § Doc. and Cov. sec. cvii:

CHAPTER XXXI.

LAWS OF SPIRITUAL DEVELOPMENT.

IF a man accepts the principles and obeys the ordinances I have now treated upon, and I hope with sufficient clearness, and they are administered by men having authority from God to act in his name, then he is born again, born of the water and of the Spirit—born into the kingdom of God, and hence is a child of God, a citizen of his kingdom.

And since by submitting to these ordinances a man is born into the kingdom, I would remind the reader that his position in that kingdom is closely analogous to the child just born naturally into this world. It possesses all the faculties, all the organs, all the limbs of a man, but they are in embryo, undeveloped. The new born infant has eyes, but it will be some time before it will be able to distinguish objects, or recognize even the kind face of its mother. It has ears, but it cannot distinguish sounds; a tongue but it cannot speak; limbs but it cannot stand or walk or run; nor has it control of the muscles of the hands or arms—it will have to wait for growth and strength before these organs of sense and motion are developed.

Its first attempts at the use of any of these

organs will necessarily be imperfect as to the results. The tongue will speak the first words but brokenly; the first step will be uneven and staggering; the movements of the hands will be erratic and awkward. But by persistent effort the tongue that could only pronounce words brokenly, becomes, at last, eloquent, and crowds listen spellbound by the charm of its music. The uneven, staggering step is changed finally for the elastic step and noble carriage of graceful manhood. The hands so awkward become by practice the hands of the skilled artisan, competent to execute whatever his mind may conceive.

So it is with those just born in the church of Christ. They, at their birth, are not fully developed men and women in the things of God. It is expected that they will have to "grow in grace and in the knowledge of God." Peter exhorted the saints of his day to give all diligence, and add to their faith virtue; "and to virtue knowledge; and to knowledge temperance; and to temperance patience; and to patience godliness; and to godliness brotherly kindness; and to brotherly kindness charity. For if these things be in you and abound," said he, "they make you that ye shall neither be barren nor unfruitful in the knowledge of our Lord Jesus Christ."* Such instructions are applicable to the Saints of this or any other dispensation.

---

*II Peter i: 5 8.

The new born saints will find themselves in a new atmosphere, senitive to new forces operating upon them, new powers developing within them: and as the young child staggers in its first attempts to walk, and has many a fall before it will obtain complete control over its muscles—so the new born member of Christ's church will make many mistakes and perhaps blunders in the days of his infancy.

For this reason, that the child of the kingdom might not grow weary in his efforts at moral and spiritual development, the Lord has revealed his long-suffering and merciful kindness to those who strive to keep his commandments. And such is the weakness of mankind and their frequent violations of the laws of God that had they not the repeated assurances in the revelations respecting God's character that he is slow to anger, abundant in mercy and long-suffering, the heart of man would grow faint, and his effort at spiritual development would be palsied. But with these facts firmly impressed on their minds men struggle on—they pray and faint not*.

If there is one struggle more than another in which the race is not to the swift nor the battle to the strong, but to those who endure to the end, it is in this struggle for eternal life. "He that shall endure to the end the same shall be saved," were the words of Jesus, and I know of

---

* Luke xviii: 1.

no other condition of salvation contemplated in the Gospel of Christ, than this. "Be thou faithful unto death," wrote John to the saints at Smyrna, "and I will give thee a crown of life."* "Blessed are they *who do his commandment*, that they may have right to the tree of life;"† and with such passages the scriptures are replete.

There is no one great thing that man can do and then do no more and obtain salvation. After entering into the kingdom of God, in the manner already pointed out in these pages, it is by learning "precept upon precept; line upon line; here a little and there a little," that salvation will be made secure. It is by resisting a temptation today, overcoming a weakness tomorrow, forsaking evil associations the next day, and thus day by day, month after month, year after year, pruning, restraining and weeding out that which is evil in the disposition, that the character is purged of its imperfections.

Nor is it enough that one gets rid of evil. He must do good. He must surround himself with circumstances congenial to the sensitive nature of the Holy Ghost, that it may not be offended, and withdraw itself from him; for if it does so, amen to his spiritual or moral development. He must cultivate noble sentiments by performing noble deeds—not great

---

* Rev. ii : 10. † Rev. ii : 14.

ones, necessarily, for opportunity to perform what the world esteem great things, comes but seldom to men in the ordinary walks of life; but noble deeds may be done every day; and every such deed performed with an eye single to the glory of God, draws one that much nearer into harmony with the Deity. And "if you wish to go where God is," said the Prophet Joseph, "you must be like God, or possess the principles which God possesses, for if we are not drawing towards God in principle, we are going from him and drawing towards the devil."*

Thus by eschewing the evil inclinations of the disposition on the one hand, and cultivating noble sentiments on the other, a character may be formed that shall be godlike in its attributes and consequently its possessor will be fitted to dwell with God, and if so prepared, there is no question but his calling and election are sure.

CHAPTER XXXII.

HISTORY OF THE GOSPEL.

I THINK it proper in this chapter to give a brief history of the gospel—for this reason: There is a very general idea existing in the Christian world that nothing was known of the

---

* Hist. of Joseph Smith, Apr. 10, 1842.

gospel of Christ—its principles and ordinances, until the personal ministry of the Messiah began; whereas the truth is, the plan of redemption, the gospel, was understood in the eternal heavens before the foundations of the earth were laid; and was revealed to the first patriarchs of the race, and extensively preached many centuries before the coming of Messiah in the flesh.

In proof of the statement that the plan of redemption was understood before even the creation of the earth, I quote the words of the Lord to Abraham: "Now the Lord had shown unto me, Abraham, the intelligences that were organized before the world was; and among all these there were many of the noble and great ones; and God saw these souls that they were good, and he stood in the midst of them; and he said, These I will make my rulers; for he stood among those that were spirits, and he saw they were good. * * * And there stood one among them like unto God, and he said unto those that were with him, We will go down, for there is space there, and we will take of these materials, and we will make an earth whereon these may dwell; and we will prove them herewith, to see if they will do all things whatsoever the Lord their God shall command them; and they who keep their first estate, shall be added upon; and they who keep not their first estate, shall not have glory in the same kingdom with those who keep their first estate; and they who keep their second estate, shall have glory added upon their heads for ever and ever."

"And the Lord said, who shall I send? And one answered like unto the Son of Man, Here am I, send me. And another answered and said, Here am I, send me. And the Lord said, I will send the first. And the second was angry, and kept not his first estate, and, at that day, many followed after him. And then the Lord said, Let us go down: and they went down at the beginning, and they organized and formed (that is the Gods), the heavens and the earth."*

This is a brief account of the controversy there was in heaven, in respect to the plan that should be adopted for the salvation of man, when in his second estate.

In the writings of Moses, as revealed to Joseph Smith, the matter is made still more clear. There we have an account of Satan appearing before Moses, and of his seeking to induce that faithful man to worship him instead of God; but Moses rebuked him in the name of the Lord Jesus, and afterwards the Lord appeared unto him and said: "Satan, whom thou hast commanded in the name of mine Only Begotten, is the same which was from the beginning, and he came before me, saying, Behold I, send me, I will be thy Son, and I will redeem all mankind, that one soul shall not be lost, and surely I will

---

* Pearl of Great Price, p. 41.

do it; wherefore, give me thine honor. But, behold, my beloved Son, which was my beloved and chosen from the beginning, said unto me, Father, thy will be done, and the glory be thine forever. Wherefore, because Satan rebelled against me [his plans being rejected, as we have already seen], and sought to destroy the agency of man, which I, the Lord God, had given him, and also that I should give unto him mine own power, by the power of mine Only Begotten, I caused that he should be cast down, and he became Satan "*

From this we learn the cause of Lucifer's rejection and rebellion—his plan for man's redemption was of such a character that it would have destroyed the agency of man, and robbed God of his honor; and because that plan was rejected, he rebelled against God and was cast out of heaven. This was before the creation of the earth, and this controversy about which the rebellion took place was in relation to the plan of salvation—the gospel.

These things were revealed to the Prophet Joseph, and they throw a perfect flood of light upon the scriptures which refer to Christ as the "Lamb slain from the foundation of the world."† From that expression we see that Jesus was chosen to make the atonement from the foundation of the world, and that the gospel was under-

---

* Pearl of Great Price, p. 9.   † Rev. xiii: 8.

stood from the beginning. The Prophet Joseph Smith said that "at the first organization in heaven we were all present, and saw the Savior chosen and appointed and the plan of salvation made, and we sanctioned it."

Coming to the time when the gospel was introduced among men on this earth, we find it began by a commandment to Adam to worship the Lord his God, and to offer the firstlings of his flock for an offering unto the Lord. Many days after this commandment had been given, an angel of the Lord visited Adam and asked him why he offered up sacrifices. To which Adam replied: "I know not, save the Lord commanded me." "And the angel spake, saying: This thing is a similitude of the sacrifice of the Only Begotten of the Father. * * * Wherefore, thou shalt do all that thou doest in the name of the Son, and thou shalt repent and call upon God in the name of the Son forevermore. And in that day the Holy Ghost fell upon Adam, which beareth record of the Father and the Son, saying, I am the Only Begotten of the Father from the beginning, henceforth and forever, that as thou hast fallen thou mayest be redeemed; and all mankind, even as many as will."*

Enoch, several centuries after this, in describing these events that occurred in the early experience of Adam, said: "He [the Lord] called

---

*Pearl of Great Price, p. 12.

upon our father Adam by his own voice, saying, I am God: I made the world, and men before they were in the flesh. * * * If thou wilt turn unto me, and hearken unto my voice, and believe, and repent of all thy transgressions, and be baptized, even in water, in the name of mine Only Begotten Son, * * * which is Jesus Christ, the only name which shall be given under heaven, whereby salvation shall come unto the children of men, ye shall receive the gift of the Holy Ghost." * * * And it came to pass, when the Lord had spoken with Adam, our father, that Adam cried unto the Lord, and he was caught away by the Spirit of the Lord, and was carried down into the water, and was laid under the water, and was brought forth out of the water. And thus he was baptized; and the Spirit of God descended upon him, and thus he was born of the Spirit, and became quickened in the inner man. And he heard a voice out of heaven, saying, Thou art baptized with fire, and with the Holy Ghost. This is the record of the Father, and the Son, from henceforth and forever; and thou art after the order of him who was without the beginning of days or end of years, from all eternity, to all eternity. Behold, thou art one in me, a Son of God; and thus may all become my sons."*

The reader will here observe that the same

---

*Pearl of Great Price, p. 17.

principles and ordinances were taught to Adam, as the means of salvation, as have been set forth in these pages as the First Principles of the Gospel of Christ. They continued on through the generations of the patriarchs to the days of Noah; and from Noah through the fathers to Abraham, and from Abraham to Moses. At least in one of the revelations of the Lord contained in the Doctrine and Covenants, we have the continuance of the Melchisedek Priesthood traced out through the line of the fathers from Moses to Abraham, from Abraham to Noah, and from Noah to Adam,[*] and I see not how this priesthood can exist among men and not the gospel: for that is what this priesthood is for—to administer in the ordinances of the gospel, and it is obtained through obedience to the gospel.

That the gospel was taught to Abraham and to ancient Israel is also evident from the Jewish scriptures. Paul, in writing to the saints in Galatia explained to them that, "The scriptures, foreseeing that God would justify the heathen through faith, preached before the gospel unto Abraham, saying, in thee shall all nations be blessed."[†] From this then it is clear that the Gospel was taught to Abraham.

The question, however, may arise, what gospel was it? Was it the same gospel which we have seen was taught to Adam; the same that was

---

[*] Doc. and Cov. sec. lxxxiv.   [†] Gal. iii : 8.

taught by the Messiah and his apostles? To which I reply there is but one gospel. There never was but one plan ordained by which mankind are to be saved; and that is denominated in the scriptures "The everlasting gospel," to express its sameness in all generations. Such as it was formed in the grand council of heaven, such it has remained in all ages, and in all dispensations. It is sealed by the precious blood of the Son of God, and like the great Lawgiver whose mind conceived it, whose wisdom brought it into existence, it changes not, neither is there a shadow of variableness in it.

So thoroughly imbued with this idea was the apostle Paul that he said—in writing his epistle to the Galatians: "Though we or an angel from heaven, preach any other gospel unto you, than that which we have preached unto you, let him be accursed. As we said before, so say I now again, if any man preach any other gospel unto you than that ye have received, let him be accursed."* The "gospel" preached to Abraham, was the gospel of the Son of God; there is no other.

But I have also stated that the gospel was taught to ancient Israel in the days of Moses; and in proof of this I offer the following:

In the third chapter of Hebrews, Paul alludes to the transgression of ancient Israel, especially

---

*Gal. i: 8, 9.

to those who, by reason of their sins, were destroyed in the wilderness. Then, in opening the fourth chapter, he says: "Let us therefore fear, lest a promise being left us, of entering into his rest, any of you should seem to come short of it. For unto us [the people of his day] was the gospel preached, *as well as unto them* [meaning ancient Israel]; but the word preached did not profit them [ancient Israel], not being mixed with faith in them that heard it."*

Paul makes a further allusion to the gospel being with the children of Israel, in the days of Moses. Writing to the Corinthians he said: "Moreover, brethren, I would not that ye should be ignorant, how that all our fathers were under the cloud, and all passed through the sea; and were all baptized unto Moses in the cloud and in the sea; and did all eat the same spiritual meat; and did all drink the same spiritual drink; for they drank of that spiritual Rock that followed them: and that Rock was Christ."†

But now to return to the epistle to the Galatians, in which we learned the gospel was taught to Abraham. After making that statement, Paul asks the question: "Wherefore then serveth the law?" That is, if the gospel was preached to Abraham, how came the law of Moses into existence, why was it given to ancient Israel and binding on them? To which the

---

*Heb. iv: 1, 2. †I.Cor. x: 1-4.

apostle replies: "It was added because of transgression, till the seed should come to whom the promise was made. * * * Wherefore the law was our schoolmaster to bring us unto Christ, that we might be justified by faith."*

The matter is still more plainly set forth in the Doctrine and Covenants. In speaking of the priesthood and the ordinances belonging thereto—through which ordinances "the power of godliness is manifest; and without the ordinances thereof, and the authority of the priesthood, the power of godliness is not manifest unto men in the flesh; for without this"—that is without the priesthood and its ordinances—"no man can see the face of God even the Father and live."† The Lord says: "Now this Moses plainly taught to the children of Israel in the wilderness, and sought diligently to sanctify his people that they might behold the face of God; but they hardened their hearts, and could not endure his presence, therefore the Lord in his wrath (for his anger was kindled against them) swore that they should not enter into his rest while in the wilderness, which rest is the fullness of his glory. Therefore he took Moses out of their midst, and the holy priesthood also; and the lesser priesthood continued, which priesthood holdeth the key of the ministering of angels and the preparatory gospel; which gospel is the

---

*Gal. iii: 19, 24. † Doc. and Cov., sec. lxxxiv: 21, 22.

gospel of repentance and of baptism, and the remission of sins, and the law of carnal commandments, which the Lord in his wrath caused to continue with the house of Aaron among the children of Israel until John."*

The above is confirmed by the Jewish scriptures also; for it is written in the concluding chapter of Deuteronomy—"There arose not a prophet since in Israel like unto Moses, whom the Lord knew face to face, in all the signs and the wonders which the Lord sent him to do in the land of Egypt."†

Of the things we have spoken respecting the gospel being presented to Israel, this is the sum: The Lord gave them the gospel, but because they would not observe its sacred requirements, he took it, that is in its fullness, from among them, and also the higher or Melchisedek Priesthood; but left them the lesser or Aaronic Priesthood, and to the part of the gospel which remained, *viz.*, repentance and baptism for the remission of sins, was added the law of carnal commandments, which was to educate them for the fullness of the gospel when Messiah should come with it. At the appointed time Messiah came and taught the gospel of the kingdom; and though the Jews as a nation rejected him, and their sanhedrim sentenced him to death, yet a few received his teachings, and among them the

---

* Doc. and Cov., sec. lxxxiv: 19, 27.   † Deut. xxxiv: 10-12.

Lord Jesus organized His church, established his priesthood and gave to his servants a commandment to go and teach all nations.

They were faithful in discharging their commission, and many received their testimony and obeyed the gospel. Satan, however, working in the hearts of the disobedient, stirred them up to anger against the saints of God, and they were persecuted, imprisoned, and slain. All the apostles, save John, sealed their testimony with their blood, and thousands of their followers were put to death. Edicts the most cruel and heartless were formulated against them by the Roman emperors, and executed with relentless vindictiveness, until the saints of God were well nigh destroyed.*

Meantime heresies crept into the churches; false teachers arose teaching perverse doctrines to draw away disciples after them; the Gospel was perverted, the laws thereof were transgressed, the ordinances were changed, the covenant was broken, until scarcely a vestige of the gospel as delivered to men by the Son of God and his authorized servants remained.

After the sword, the prison, the rack, and the flame in the hands of a powerful, pagan government, together with apostate influences and false teachers had done what they could to break down or corrupt the church of Christ, then another

---

*See Outlines of Ecclesiastical History, part II., "The apostasy."

evil, more dangerous than all that had gone before was brought to bear upon it. A Roman Emperor, Constantine, was converted to the "Christian religion"—yet by that time, 313 A. D., no more like the religion of Christ than dim, misty twilight is like the glorious light of the noon-day sun. He soon loaded the bishops with new honors, dignities and powers. The churches were made wealthy, and luxurious living succeeded the simplicity in the manner of life characteristic of earlier times among the followers of Christ. This luxury, ever more dangerous than storms or quicksands, poverty or chains, proved more disastrous to the church, more fruitful in its corruptions of the Gospel than the storms of persecution which had beaten upon it from its inception.

Through these combined evils that I have very briefly enumerated, the gospel was corrupted, the authority of God, the priesthood, was taken from among men; and then followed long ages of spiritual darkness and wickedness. At last, however, the time came to usher in the dispensation of the fullness of times, in which all things in Christ, both things which are in heaven and things which are in earth, are to be gathered in one, and the work of the Father pertaining to the salvation of this creation, the earth, and those who inhabit it, is to be consummated.

To open up this work a prophet was raised up in the person of Joseph Smith, and to him the

Lord revealed his purposes; telling him also that the creeds of men were an abomination in his sight; that men were drawing near to him with their lips but their hearts were far from him; that they taught for doctrine the commandments of men, having a form of godliness but denying the power thereof.*

After this the angel Moroni was sent to reveal the Book of Mormon; and as it contained an account of the gospel as it was taught to the ancient Nephites on the western hemisphere by the Messiah, and the prophets and apostles authorized to teach in his name; and as this record had been preserved for generations from the hands of wicked men, and has never been corrupted, it contains the fullness of the gospel in its plainness.

While this Nephite record was in course of translation the Lord sent John the Baptist, as already stated in the chapter on authority, to restore the Aaronic Priesthood; afterwards Peter, James and John came and restored the Melchisedek Priesthood, and by the authority which these priesthoods conferred upon him, and under the direction of the Almighty, the Prophet Joseph Smith organized the church, and ordained men and sent them out to preach the gospel in all the world, as a witness that the end was near.

---

* Pearl of Great Price, p 57.

For more than fifty years has this proclamation been sounded among the nations, and thousands have been gathered to the place appointed for the saints to assemble and prepare for the glorious coming of the Messiah. The work has met storms of opposition from the press, pulpit and Congress. Ridicule and the violence of mobs have assailed it; drivings, confiscations of property, imprisonment, and banishment have at various times conspired to dishearten those who have accepted it. But in spite of pulpit, press and Congress; in spite of ridicule, the violence of mobs, unjust imprisonment, schemes of confiscation and drivings, the church of Christ moves steadily on to the fulfillment of its high destiny, and the gospel is being preached in all the world.

CHAPTER XXXIII.

SALVATION FOR THE DEAD.

THE reader will have observed, doubtless, that according to the history of the gospel, as given in the last chapter, there have been long periods of time when it has not been upon the earth.

One of these periods was from the time that Moses and the Holy Priesthood, together with the fullness of the gospel, were taken from among the children of Israel, until the restoration of the gospel in the days of Messiah's ministry in the flesh. Another such period was from the time the gospel was corrupted, in the first two or three centuries of the Christian era, and its restoration in the present dispensation, through the Prophet Joseph Smith.

What became of those who lived in those long periods of time—those untold millions, who never so much as heard the gospel?—I might push the inquiry still further, by calling attention to the fact that even when the gospel has been upon the earth, there are countless millions who lived and died without having an opportunity of obeying it. What is their fate?

In order that the force of these remarks may appear more clearly, I will refer to the present state of the religious world, that is, to the strength of the respective religions, as represented by numbers:

According to the latest and best information on the subject, there are throughout the world:

Roman Catholics	206,588,206
Protestants	89,825,348
Greek and Russian Churches	75,691,382
Oriental Churches	6,770,000
Making the total of all Christians	378,874,936

The other religions stand as follows:

Brahminical Hindoos	120,000,000
Followers of Buddha, Shinto and Confucius	482,600,000
Mohammedans	169,054,789
Jews	7,612,784
Parsees (fire worshipers in Persia)	1,000,000
Pagans, not otherwise enumerated	227,000,000
Making a total of	1,007,267,573*

From this showing it is seen that only a little more than one-third of the world's population are even professing Christians; the other two-thirds know nothing of Christ or of salvation through his Gospel. No one, however, will contend that all professing Christianity will be entitled to salvation, for the very good reason that they do not adopt its precepts in the practices of their lives; so that the one-third that are enumerated as Christians would be reduced to much less than that fraction of the world's population if this consideration is taken into account.

Even if you grant that the gospel of Christ has been upon the earth for the past eighteen centuries, as the Christian world claim, here is a serious question confronting them, *viz.*: What is to be the fate of this greater part of the children of God who have never heard of Christ, and know nothing of the Christian religion?

---

*These statements are taken from a recent work published by Gay Bros. & Co., New York, entitled, "What the World Believes,"

This is a question which confronted those who declared that the gospel and authority to administer in its ordinances had not been upon the earth for a number of centuries. It is a question which confronts them today; but it also may be asked of Christians generally, for even if you allow that they and their fathers before them have had and still have the gospel, here is the great majority of the human race—the children of God—who have not had it in the past generations, and do not have it even now. What becomes of the neglected ones?

To this question the Saints used to reply, in one of their hymns—

> "God is just is all we say,
> Seek no crop where 'twas not planted,
> Nor the day where reigns the night;
> Now the sunshine bright is beaming.
> Let all creatures see aright."

Since those days, however, further light has been revealed from heaven, which gives enlarged views in respect to the plan of human redemption, and brings out in strong relief the justice and mercy of God; enlarges the hope, and dispels the gloom of wretchedness that man-made systems of theology have cast over religion.

The principle which has performed all this, a principle which is permeating all religious thought and shattering to their foundations the old schools of theology, was first revealed by the prophet Elijah, in the Kirtland Temple, in 1836.

It is written in Malachi: "Behold I will send you Elijah the prophet before the coming of the great and dreadful day of the Lord: And he shall turn the heart of the fathers to the children, and the heart of the children to their fathers, lest I come and smite the earth with a curse."*

This prophecy, for so long before the people in the Jewish scriptures, yet no one knowing the meaning thereof, was fulfilled by the aforesaid coming of Elijah to the Kirtland Temple, on the 3rd of April, 1836.

This appearance of Elijah is described as follows—by the way, however, his appearance was preceded by a vision of the Lord Jesus, then of Moses, then of Elias, who committed the keys of the dispensation of the gospel of Abraham—"After this vision had closed," says the prophet, "another great and glorious vision burst upon us, for Elijah the prophet, who was taken to heaven without tasting death, stood before us and said, Behold, the time has fully come, which was spoken of by the mouth of Malachi, testifying that he (Elijah) should be sent before the great and dreadful day of the

---

* Mal. iv: 5, 6. The manner in which Moroni quoted this scripture to the prophet Joseph Smith was, " Behold I will reveal unto you the priesthood by the hand of Elijah the prophet, before the coming of the great and terrible day of the Lord. And he shall plant in the hearts of the children the promises made to the fathers, and the hearts of the children shall turn to the fathers. If it were not so, the whole earth would be utterly wasted at His coming. (Pearl of Great Price.)

Lord come, to turn the hearts of the fathers to the children, and the children to the fathers, lest the whole earth be smitten with a curse. Therefore the keys of this dispensation are committed into your hands, and by this ye may know that the great and dreadful day of the Lord is near, even at the door."*

The key of knowledge this prophet revealed was in relation to salvation for the dead; the means by which the principles and ordinances of salvation could be applied to those who had lived in those periods of time when the gospel was not upon the earth; and also to those who had lived when the gospel was on the earth, but who had not the privilege of hearing it; aye, and even to those who had heard and rejected it; though the spirits of this last class of persons must go to the prison house where they will be required to pay the utmost farthing for their wickedness in rejecting the mercies of God; and will, through their disobedience, have shut themselves out from the heights of glory and exaltation they might have attained unto had they but accepted the truth in the love of it, and walked in harmony with its teachings.

This key of knowledge, I say, gives enlarged views of the mercies of God, and reveals the fact that every man, both in time and eternity, will always have the privilege of doing right, and

---

* Doc. and Cov. sec. cx.

reaping the reward of his righteousness. It brought to light the grand truth that this earth was not the only place where men could hear the gospel and give assent to its doctrines. On the contrary it gives us to understand that in the spirit world the gospel is preached to the departed spirits of men, that is, to those who have departed from this life and that there they are instructed in the way of salvation.

These facts give life and meaning to the scripture which says: "Christ also hath once suffered for sins, the just for the unjust, that he might bring us to God, being put to death in the flesh, but quickened by the Spirit; by which also he went and preached unto the spirits in prison; which sometimes were disobedient, when the long-suffering of God waited in the days of Noah while the ark was a preparing, wherein few, that is eight souls, were saved by water."*

In the chapter following the one I have quoted, the apostle remarks: "For this cause was the gospel preached also to them that are dead, that they might be judged according to men in the flesh, but live according to God in the spirit."† This last quotation proves as plainly as plain statement of holy writ can prove anything, that the gospel is preached also to the dead, as well as to the living; and not only that, but likewise assigns the reason why it is preached

---

* I. Peter iii: 18–20. † Verse 6.

to them, *viz.:* that those to whom it is thus preached might live according to God in the spirit—that is, live in harmony with the precepts of the gospel taught to them, that they may be judged as men will be who have the gospel preached to them in the flesh.

The first passage quoted gives us to understand that the spirit of Jesus went to those spirits that were in prison—to those who had rejected the gospel in the days of Noah, and who from the time of the flood until Jesus visited them, had been paying the penalty of their disobedience in the prison-house prepared for such characters.

In the light of these facts several other scriptures are made plain. We can understand now more clearly the words of Jesus to his apostles, when he said: "Verily, verily, I say unto you, the hour is coming and now is, when the dead shall hear the voice of the Son of God, and they that hear shall live."* And also the words of Isaiah, when speaking of the mission of the Son of God, wherein he tells us that not only is Jesus to be a covenant unto the people, and a light unto the gentiles, but he is also to bring out the prisoners from the prison house. This is the passage: "I the Lord have called thee in righteousness, and will hold thine hand, and will keep thee, and give thee for a covenant of the people, for a light of the gentiles; to open the blind

---

*John v: 25.

eyes, to bring out the prisoners from the prison, and them that sit in darkness, out of the prison house.*

And, as it was with those who rejected the gospel in the days of Noah, so will it be with those who reject the gospel in the days of the coming of the Son of Man. Such is the prediction of the prophet Isaiah. After describing the judgments that will attend the glorious coming of the Son of God, and the punishment that shall overtake the ungodly, he says: "And it shall come to pass, in that day, that the Lord shall punish the hosts of the high ones that are on high, and the kings of the earth, upon the earth. And they shall be gathered together, as prisoners are in the pit, and shall be shut up in the prison; *and after many days they shall be visited.*"†

But while the gospel is preached in the spirit world, it appears from all that can be learned upon the subject, that all the outward ordinances, as baptisms, confirmations, ordinations, anointings, sealings, etc., etc., must be performed vicariously here upon earth for those who accept the gospel in the world of spirits. This is the work that children may do for their progenitors, and upon learning this, the hearts of the children are turned to their fathers; and the fathers in the spirit world, learning that they are dependent upon the action of their posterity for the per-

---

* Isaiah xlii: 6, 7. † Isaiah xxiv: 21, 22.

formance of the ordinances of salvation, their hearts are turned to the children; and thus the work that was predicted should be performed by Elijah—turning the hearts of the children to the fathers, and the hearts of the fathers to the children, was accomplished in restoring the key of knowledge respecting the salvation for the dead.

This, however, is no new doctrine. We have already seen that Peter understood that the Messiah went and preached to the spirits who had rejected the gospel in the days of Noah; and also that the gospel was preached to the dead—without confining it to those who lived in the days of Noah or any other period.

Nor is this all, for Paul says to the saints at Corinth: "Else what shall they do which are baptized for the dead, if the dead rise not at all? Why are they then baptized for the dead?"* And why, I ask, does Paul make this very plain allusion to baptism for the dead, if there is no such ordinance connected with the gospel? No other passage of scripture perplexes the theologians more than this one, and they have exhausted their ingenuity in trying to explain away the evident meaning of it, because it is destructive of some of their horrible dogmas in respect to the eternal damnation of those who

---

* I. Cor. xv: 29.

do not have the good fortune to become acquainted with the truth in this probation.

"From the wording of the sentence"—else what shall they do which are baptized for the dead, if the dead rise not at all? Why are they then baptized for the dead?—"the most simple impression certainly is, that Paul speaks of a baptism which a living man receives in the place of a dead one. This interpretation is particularly adopted by those expounders with whom grammatical construction is of paramount importance, and the first thing to be considered."* To this rendering of the passage could be drawn up a long list of respectable authorities, among them Erasmus, Scaliger, Grotius, Calixtus, Meyer and De Wette.

Epiphanius, a writer of the fourth century, in speaking of the Marcionites, a sect of Christians to whom he was opposed, says: "In this country —I mean Asia—and even in Galatia, their school flourished eminently; and a traditional fact concerning them has reached us, that when any of them had died without baptism, they used to baptize others in their name, lest in the resurrection they should suffer punishment as unbaptized."† This proves beyond controversy the fact that vicarious baptism for the dead was practiced among some sects of the early Christians.

Another fact proves it still more emphatically

---

* Biblical Literature (Kitto) Art. Baptism. † Heresies, xxiii: 7.

than this statement of Epiphanius. The Council of Carthage, held A. D. 397, in its sixth canon, forbids the administration of baptism and the holy communion for the dead; and why would this canon be formed against these practices if they had no existence among the Christians of those days?

We have now seen, not only that baptism for the dead is a principle known to and doubtless practiced by the Corinthian saints, in the days of Paul—and evidently with his approval—and by some of the Christian sects for two or three centuries after his time; but we have also seen that it was forbidden by the council of an apostate church in the fourth century.

In the dispensation in which we now live, however, the knowledge of the ordinance, with a commandment to practice it, and with instructions necessary to its practice, has been restored; and the erection of costly temples, in which this and other ordinances for the dead may be administered, testifies to the zeal with which the Latter-day Saints enter into this work; and is a living testimony to the world that there was virtue in the mission of Elijah. He succeeded in turning the hearts of the children to the fathers; and we may reasonably conclude that the hearts of the fathers have been turned to the children, for they without us cannot be made perfect.

This doctrine of salvation for the dead strikes a deadly blow to the horrible dogmas formulated by uninspired men in the dark ages of apostasy, in relation to the eternal punishment of those who die unconverted and in an impenitent condition. According to the aforesaid dogmas such persons are damned to all eternity, without the least hope for redemption; and ingenuity has exhausted itself to present to the mind the duration of their sufferings.

In the month of March, 1830—six years before the coming of Elijah—the Lord explained, through the Prophet Joseph Smith, the meaning of the terms eternal punishment and endless punishment, in regard to which men have gone astray. In that explanation it is said: "Behold the mystery of godliness, how great is it? For, behold, I am Endless, and the punishment which is given from my hand, is endless punishment, for Endless is my name; wherefore

"Eternal punishment is God's punishment.

"Endless punishment is God's punishment."*

The punishment takes its name from him who administers it; and, since God is Endless, the punishment he inflicts is called endless or eternal.

And, indeed, the punishment exists eternally, and stands ready to be applied to those who violate the laws of righteousness. But because the penalty stands ever ready to vindicate any law which may be broken, it does not necessarily follow that persons violating the law will for ever

---

* Doc. and Cov., sec. xix: 10-12.

have to endure punishment. Mercy, though not allowed to rob justice, somewhere, and at some time, will step forward and claim her own; permitting the violator of law to endure punishment no longer than is necessary to vindicate the law, and satisfy the reasonable claims of justice. Hence we may conclude, that while the actions of men in this probation will greatly affect their standing in the life that is to come, those actions do not, in every case, fix the status of men for eternity.

This doctrine of salvation for the dead not only enlarges the hope of man, but it gives him nobler conceptions of the character of the Deity, and increases his admiration for him. In fact, to my thinking, this doctrine strips the character of God in the inhuman and vindictive cruelty which men, in the past, have delighted to represent him as possessing; and gives new force, and, perhaps, new meaning to the expression, "If in this life only we have hope in Christ, we are of all men the most miserable."

It also vindicates the wisdom of Deity; for it must be a very imperfect wisdom that would construct a plan for the redemption of mankind so imperfect in its operations, so limited in its application as to miss the great majority of mankind, and leave them without redemption throughout the countless ages of eternity. But when one is given to understand, and surely such an understanding is given one in the revelations of God to which the reader's attention has been directed—when one learns that sometime in the eternities, somewhere in the numberless creations of God, the proclamation of the gospel will overtake all the children of our Father, and they have the privilege of accepting it, and will be saved by it, and permitted to enjoy all the happiness and glory their nature and degree of development enables them to encompass—the wisdom, mercy, justice and love of God all stand out in bold relief; and man's heart is warmed with increased admiration and devotion to him: for it teaches him that he worships not a tyrant who delights in the miseries and damnation of his children, but one whose great pleasure and design it is to bring to pass the eternal happiness of man.

CONCLUSION.

MY task now draws to a close. I have completed the exposition of the First Principles of the Gospel of Christ, contemplated in this work. I have endeavored to explain what the Gospel is—its two-fold powers of redeeming mankind from the consequences of Adam's transgression; and also from the consequences of their own personal violations of the principles of righteousness, on the condition of their repentance and obedience.

The various principles and ordinances constituting the gospel have been analyzed and the nature and object of each considered in detail, and then in their relationship to each other—how one principle or ordinance prepares the way and leads up to another: and lastly, their application to mankind, not only in this probation, but how they follow them into the spirit world and throughout the eternities, forever inviting him to peace and eternal felicity.

In all this I see a most perfect system of moral and spiritual philosophy—the perfection of beauty and goodness—a harmonious blending of justice and mercy, of truth and love. How far these pages exhibit those powers and beauties of the gospel, it will be for the reader to judge. But in passing that judgment I ask him to remember this:

>Our whitest pearls we never find,
>   Our ripest fruit we never reach;
>The flowering moments of the mind,
>   Drop half their petals in our speech

And in this probation I do not believe it is given to man to comprehend all the force, the excellence, beauty and power of the gospel. These things will be revealed in their fullness only in eternity.

SUPPLEMENT.

MAN'S RELATIONSHIP TO DEITY.

MAN'S RELATIONSHIP TO DEITY.

WHAT IS MAN THAT THOU ART MINDFUL OF HIM? AND THE SON OF MAN THAT THOU VISITEST HIM.*

I.

IN order to a clear understanding of man's redemption through the atonement of Jesus Christ—the grand central truth of the gospel—it is necessary to know something of the relationship between God and man. The very fact that such a sacrifice was made for his redemption—being no less than the immolation of him, who in heaven bore the second name—argues at once some special relationship between man and Deity. In view of the greatness and importance of that sacrifice, we may well ask, with the Psalmist, "What is man, that thou art mindful of him? and the son of man that thou visitest him?" These questions lead to the investigation of man's origin; for upon his origin his relationship to God depends.

A discussion of this subject must be very imperfect, not to say partial, that does not give some attention to the various theories—at least to the most prominent ones—of man's origin. It is scarcely necessary to say that theories on

---
* Psalms viii: 4.

the subject are quite numerous and widely different; and that in each school of philosophers are men eminent for their learning and intelligence. All existing theories, however, may be arranged under three headings: First, the monogenists, who hold that mankind have descended from a single human pair, created by Deity; and their descendants, modified by climatic influences, food, habits of life and thought constitute the various races of men—this is the theory of those who accept the Bible as authority on the subject; second, the polygenists, who insist not only on one act of creation, but upon a number of independent creations, "each giving birth to essential, unchangeable peculiarities of a separate race, thus constituting a diversity of species with primal adaptation to their geographical distribution;" third, the evolutionists, who believe all existing species are but developments of pre-existing and lower forms of life; which, in their turn, were but developments of still lower forms, and so on back, back until you reach the spontaneous generation of the lowest types of vegetable and animal life, "as the accumulation of mold upon food, the swarming of maggots in meat, * * * the generation of insect life in decaying vegetable substances, the birth of one form arising out of the decay of another; the slow and gradual unfolding from a lower to a higher sphere, acting through a long succession of ages, culminating in the grandeur of intellectual manhood."

Of these theories the first and last only need detain us; and since the theory of evolution is the one more generally accepted by scientific men, and is making rapid progress among the masses, I think it proper to state the basis of this theory more in detail.

The absurdities which theologians have associated with the first named hypothesis of the origin of man and the universe is largely responsible for the existence of the theory of evolution. Finding so much that was contrary to well known facts, not so much in the theory itself, as in the explanations of it by its advocates, induced men of intelligence to look for some other explanation of the genesis of things.

It was doubtless observed that many remarkable resemblances exist between man and the inferior animals. In embryonic development, in physical structure, in material composition and the functions of organs, man and the superior animals are strikingly alike. The skeleton of man when examined minutely and compared with the skeletons of the higher order of animals, seems only a modification of them, and in some instances the modifications appear extremely slight. This resemblance also exists among the inferior animals, and it was this, doubtless, which gave birth to the idea of a common origin for all existing species.

Side by side with the above mentioned facts are others that sustain, it is claimed, the idea of common origin; and suggest an explanation of how the varieties of animal and vegetable forms were brought into existence. The great law of nature is for like to beget like; the tendency of offspring is always to reproduce the parent forms, as every seed produces its kind; that is the general law of nature, and to it a special name is given—it is called *atavism*. But notwithstanding this general law, there is a modification of it, a tendency to variation, slight in some cases and more marked in others. This is a matter of common observation. The male does not follow the precise type of the male parent, nor does the female always inherit the precise characteristics of the mother. "There are all sorts of intermixtures and intermediate conditions between the two, where complexion, or beauty, or fifty other different peculiarities belonging to either side of the house, are reproduced in other members of the same family." This kind of variation in cases where offspring are produced by sexual propagation is attributed to the fact that the thing propagated proceeds from two organisms of different sexes and temperaments. Breeders of our domestic animals take advantage of this tendency to variation, to produce such varieties as are most desirable; and, indeed, for that matter, to obtain new varieties by crossing breeds. Sometimes this tendency to variation acts in the most remarkable and unaccountable manner, and because naturalists can assign no reason for it, they have called it "spontaneous variation." That it may be understood I quote instances of such variation from Professor Huxley:

Reaumur, a famous French naturalist, in an essay on variation, relates a remarkable case of spontaneous variation which came under his observation in the person of a Maltese, of the name of Gratio Kelleia, who was born with six fingers upon each hand, and the like number of toes upon each of his feet. His parents, of course, were ordinary five-fingered persons. This was a case then of "spontaneous generation;" and subsequent circumstanes in connection with this case prove there is a tendency in nature to perpetuate these variations. Gratio Kelleia married, when he was twenty-two years of age, an ordinary five-fingered lady. The result of that marriage was four children. The first, Salvator, had six fingers and six toes, like the father; the second, George, had five fingers and toes; but one of them was deformed, showing a tendency to variation; the third, Andre, had five fingers and five toes perfect; the fourth, a girl, Marie, had five fingers and five toes, but her thumbs were deformed, showing a tendency towards the sixth. These children grew up and when they came to adult years married, and of course it happened that they all married five-fingered and five-toed persons. Now let us see what happened. Salvator had four children, they were two boys, a girl and another boy: the first two boys and the girl were six-fingered and six-toed, like their grandfather; the fourth child had only five fingers and five toes. George had four children. There were two girls with six fingers and six toes; there was one girl with six fingers and five toes on the right side, and five fingers and five toes on the other; the fourth, a boy, had five fingers and five toes. The third son of Gratio Kelleia, Andre, it will be remembered, was perfectly well formed, and he had many children whose hands and feet were regularly developed. Marie, the last, whose thumbs were deformed, married a man with five fingers and toes: they had four children; the first was born with six toes, but the other children were normal.

In this case of Gratio Kelleia and his children is seen the tendency to reproduce the parent stock, and also to perpetuate the variation which so unaccountably appeared. That tendency to perpetuate the variation was very strong, even though these persons with the six fingers and toes, or who only inherited the deformity in part, intermarried with persons ordinarily formed. What would have been the result had the two eldest boys of Salvator taken it into their heads to marry their first cousins, the two first girls of George? It will be remembered that these were all of the abnormal type of their grandfather. Is it not most likely that had these people married and their descendants continued to intermarry with each other, that a new variety of men having six fingers and six toes would have been the result? The second case I quote from Huxley gives us every reason to believe that such would have been the result:

In the year 1791 there was a farmer of the name of Seth Wright, in Massachusetts, who had a flock of sheep, consisting of a ram and some twelve or fifteen ewes. Of the flock of ewes, one at the breeding-time bore a lamb which was singularly formed; it had a very long body, very short legs, and those legs were bowed. In the part of Massachusetts where Seth Wright lived, the fields were separated by fences, and his sheep, which were active and robust, would roam abroad, and without much difficulty would jump over the fences into other people's farms. As a matter of course this gave rise to all sorts of quarrels, bickerings and contention among the farmers of the neighborhood; so it occurred to Seth Wright, if he could obtain a breed of sheep with bandy legs like the one which had so strangely appeared in his flock, it would be to his advantage, as they would not be able to jump over the fences so readily. He acted upon that idea. He killed his old ram, and as soon as the young one arrived at maturity he bred exclusively from him. The result was that all the offspring were like the male parent or female parent, there was no mixing in the offspring the peculiarities of the parents, they were either pure "Ancons" —the name given to the new variety—or pure, ordinary sheep. In consequence of this the farmer in a very few years was able to get a considerable flock of this short-legged variety of sheep and a large number of them were soon scattered throughout Massachusetts. Here is the case then where the tendency to perpetuate a variation culminated in the production of a new variety. And, indeed, this is what is perpetually going on with our domesticated animals,—by what we may call selective breeding; and it is going on, it is claimed by evolutionists, in a natural state, that is, where man's interference does not effect it; in other words, variations are perpetuated by means of what Mr. Darwin has called "natural selection."

Suppose, for instance, that by one of those unaccountable freaks of nature a "spontaneous variation" is produced, as in the case of Seth Wright's sheep; and further suppose that the particular characteristic which distinguished it from the parent stock was favorable to its persistence, by that I mean that the particulars in which it varies from the parent stock will enable the animal, if it be a beast of prey, to secure its food more surely either by an increase of fleetness or stealth, by which it would the more surely run down, or steal upon its victims, and in either case be more sure of its food and hence more secure of existence than the stock from which it came; and if the means of subsistence for these animals were limited, then the variety having the peculiarity of fleetness or stealth would be preserved and perpetuate the peculiarities imparted to it originally by "spontaneous variation," while the original stock would perish. Thus, as evolutionists would say, the fittest would survive in this struggle for existence; and thus the original variation would be preserved and perpetuated and a new variety brought into existence as effectually by this natural means of selection as if man had superintended it for his own benefit. That individuals in organic forms increase in a proportion greater than the provisional means of support is a theory pretty well demonstrated; there is, therefore, a constant struggle for existence in nature, in which the strongest, those best fitted to live and improve their species, prevail. Every variation, therefore, that is favorable to races of plants or animals is seized upon by this principle of natural selection and preserved.

Another way of presrving variations is by what our latter-day naturalists call "sexual selection." "Throughout nature," say they, "the male is the wooer; he it is who is armed for fight, and provided with musical organs and ornamental appendages, with which to charm the fair one. The savage and the wild beast alike secure their mate over the mangled form of a vanquished rival. In this manner the more highly favored of either sex are mated, and natural selections made by which better ever producing better, the species in its constant variation is constantly improved."

It is now time to pause and see what conclusions these facts have led our scientist to draw. I have called attention to the striking resemblance between man and the superior animals; in the development of the embryo, in the material of which they are composed, and in the use of organs they are alike; and especially very much alike in physical structure, the skeleton of man only slightly varying from that of the higher order of animals; and that resemblance in something like gradation exists throughout the organic world. Of course there are marked structural variations even in closely allied species, and we have seen that there is a tendency in species to vary and also to preserve the variation; and where the peculiarity of the variation is favorable to the individual it is almost certain to be preserved by the process of natural selection. New varieties thus produced may be expected to produce still other variations that will remove them further than ever from the stock from which their parents came, until the variation amounts to what our naturalists denominate specific difference. By this process what we now call varieties may eventually become species, as our species, according to the evolutionists, were once nothing more than varieties; and the groups which naturalists classify as genera, families, order, classes, etc., are but the remains of still older species, which have continued their existence side by side with the new species, which have been produced from them by this process of variation; and but for the fact that so many intermediate species have become extinct, they claim that the multifarious forms of organic life could be traced, through all the minute variations that have occurred, back to a common origin; even back to the mysterious substance in which life seems to generate—protoplasm.

Such are the basic principles on which is grounded the theory of evolution, as I understand the subject from the works of its advocates, though my effort to be brief may have rendered my statement of those principles very imperfect.

One thing more should be stated in connection with this theory, and that is that very long periods of time are demanded for the slow work of variation preserved by natural selection to accomplish the wonders attributed to it. To measure the time claimed by evolutionists by the lapse of years is simply out of the question; they ask for a long series of ages, each of which, though doubtless unequal, consists of millions of years. As the Rev. George B. Cheever remarks: "The first postulate of this philosophy is that of countless millions of years to work in, with no Creator, and with no authority that can bring it to book." To prove that such long periods of time have elapsed, during which organic forms have existed on the earth, the evolutionist triumphantly points to the revelations of geology, and there gives proof which there is, perhaps, no denying, of the lapse of time he pleads for; and also proof of organic forms of life in those various ages, fossilized remains of which are found in the strata of the earth's crust.

If you say to the advocate of evolution that it is incredible that variations preserved by natural selection could result in the production of such a wonderful organ as the eye; he replies "that if numerous gradations from a simple and imperfect eye to one complex and perfect can be shown to exist, each grade being useful to its possessor, as is certainly the case; if further, the eye varies and the variations be inherited, as is likewise certainly the case; and if such variations should be useful to any animal under changing conditions of life; then the difficulty of believing that a perfect and complex eye could be formed by natural selection, though insuperable by our imagination, should not be considered as subversive of the theory."* But with this statement and some further observations upon it, Mr. Darwin himself seems not altogether satisfied that he has removed the difficulty which he admits is enough to stagger anyone; "I have

---

* Origin of Species p. 143, (American Edition, 1883.)

felt the difficulty," he says, "far too keenly to be surprised at others hesitating to extend the principle of natural selection to so startling a length."*

If you say that it is incredible that natural selection can account for the production of such a wonderful thing as the mind of man—his "reasonable soul," the reply is that instinct varies among the inferior animals no less than physical structure, and though there may be no perceivable proportion or gradation between structural variation and variation of instinct; still, if the fact is admitted that among animals instinct varies, then it is easy to conceive that some of those variations may be favorable, and if favorable then natural selection would perpetuate them and make them dominant. From this basis they make another step the difference between the mental faculties of man and animal is immense, but the high culture which belongs to man evolutionists maintain has been slowly developed, and the separation between the mental powers of lowest man and the highest ape is no greater than that which exists betwe n the lowest ape and some of the lower forms of life, say the Zoophytes.

If you say that articulate language surely marks a wide gulf between man and the lower animals, the reply is that animals are not devoid

---

* Ibid p. 146

of expedients for expressing emotions, and from those expedients may have been evolved through intermediate species, now extinct, articulate language.

If you ask why, if species have descended from other species by fine gradations, do we not everywhere see innumerable transitional forms? Why is not all nature in confusion, instead of the species being, as we see them, well defined? The answer is that the intermediate species have become extinct, that we must look upon each existing species as having descended from some unknown forms; that natural selection acts slowly by preserving profitable modifications. "Each new form will tend in a fully stocked country to take the place of, and finally exterminate, its own less-improved parent form, and other less favored forms with which it comes in competition; thus both parent and all transitional varieties will generally have been exterminated by the very process of the formation and perfection of the new."*

If you object further, and call attention to the fact that in the great geological record, of which evolutionists boast so much, that not even in that can be found the intermediate transitional forms that should, according to their theory, link together by fine gradations the species†—this ob-

---

* Origin of species, p 134.

† Geology assuredly does not reveal any such finely graduated organic chain; and this, perhaps, is the most obvious and serious

jection, otherwise fatal to the theory of evolution, is avoided rather than answered by putting forth the claim that the geological record is very imperfect, and comparatively only a few of its pages have, as yet, been read by man.

After thus escaping from the difficulty of there being no intermediate transitional forms between the species, we come to other facts not less important, and even, perhaps, more fatal to the hypothesis of evolution—I refer to the phenomena presented by "hybrids," and in order that I may not be charged with over-estimating the value of the objection founded on this class of phenomena, I shall quote the words of Professor Huxley, one of the chief apostles of evolution, and give his estimate of the weight of the objections:

"There is a most singular circumstance," says the professor, "in respect to natural species—at least about some of them—and it would be sufficient for the purposes of this argument, if it were true of only one of them; but there is, in fact, a great number of such cases—and that is, that similar as they may appear to be to mere races or breeds, they present a marked peculiarity in the reproductive process. If you breed from the male and female of the same race, you of course have offspring of the like kind; and if you make the offspring breed together, you

---

objection which can be urged against the theory [of evolution.] The explanation lies, as I believe, in the extreme imperfection of the geological record.—*Darwin*, Origin of Species p. 205.

obtain the same result; and if you breed from these again, you will still have the same kind of offspring; there is no check. But if you take members of two distinct species, however similar they may be to each other, and make them breed together, you will find a check, with some modifications and exceptions— * * * if you cross two such species with each other, then,— although you may get offspring in the case of the first cross, yet if you attempt to breed from the products of that crossing, which are what are called hybrids*—that is, if you couple a male and a female hybrid—then the result is that in ninety-nine cases out of a hundred you will get no offspring at all; there will be no result whatsoever. * * * Thus you see that there is a great difference between 'mongrels,' which are crosses between distinct races [varieties], and 'hybrids,' which are crosses between distinct species. The mongrels are, so far as we know, fertile with one another. But between species, in many cases, you cannot succeed in obtaining the first cross; at any rate it is quite certain that the hybrids are often absolutely infertile one with another. Here is a feature, then, great or small as it may be, which distinguishes natural species of animals."†

Now, by the side of these facts, the sterility

---

* The product of the horse and the ass—the mule—is an example.
† Huxley's Lectures, pp 106, 107.

of species and hybrids, let us place another; that of the fertility of varieties. So long as you breed together descendants from a common stock they continue fruitful to each other, without any check. Now, if naturalists cannot produce by selective breeding varieties from a common parentage that are infertile to each other, then it is quite clear that species did not come from varieties by the process of variation preserved by natural selection, since here is a phenomenon existing in connection with species which cannot, to all appearances, be produced by breeding together varieties. Mr. Huxley remarks on this, that if it could be proven not only that this *has* not been done, but that it *cannot* be done, then Mr. Darwin's hypothesis would be utterly shattered.* Well, up to the present it *has not* been done, the gentleman last quoted admits the fact; he asks, "what is really the state of the case? It is simply that, so far as we have gone yet with our breeding, we have not produced from a common stock two breeds, which are not more or less fertile with one another."†

What do these facts prove, I mean the sterility of species and hybrids on the one hand, and the fertilities of varieties, descendants from a common stock, on the other? Why that the great law of nature is, as announced in holy writ that every seed shall produce after its kind, and

---

* Huxley's Lectures, p. 141. † Lectures, p. 141.

every fish, fowl, creeping-thing, beast, and man shall bring forth after his kind*—that is what it proves. And though man may for a moment by crossing species cause a slight deviation from that great law, it can be but for an instant, the monstrosity cannot be perpetuated, it dies out by being made unfruitful.

How do these facts affect the theory of evolution? Let us remember upon what that theory rests. It rests upon the principle that lower forms producing favorable variations and these being preserved by the process of natural selection amount finally to the production of distinct species; but we have seen that varieties cannot produce what may be called the great characteristic of species—infertility to each other; then also we have seen there is a check to variation in the sterility of species and hybrids. Add these facts to that other fact that neither in living nature nor in the geological records can be found the intermediate transitional forms linking together by fine gradations the species, and the theory of evolution lies stranded upon the shore of idle speculation.

II.

There is one other objection to be urged against the theory of evolution before leaving it; it is contrary to the revelations of God. I

---

*Gen. I: 11, 12, 21, 24, 25.

have not in mind, at present, the revelations respecting the creation of the earth and of vegetable and animal life; but rather the revelations which speak of the Atonement of Jesus Christ. According to the revelations of God contained in the Bible, man was created just and right—"sufficient to have stood, yet free to fall." He transgressed, in some way, the holy commandment given him, and by that transgression became fallen man, subject to sin and death, and entailed the same evils upon his posterity. Both he and they were powerless to extricate themselves from the consequences of that violation of law; but a sacrifice was prepared, a Redeemer was provided, both for Adam and all his posterity. In the meridian of time that Redeemer appeared in the person of Jesus of Nazareth, who eventually was offered up a sacrifice for sinful man—he suffered for sins, the just for the unjust, that he might bring us to God.* That this was the mission of Jesus Christ is evident from the whole tenor of the scriptures.† But if the hypothesis of evolution be true, if man is only a product evolved from the lower forms of life, better still producing better, until the highest type of intellectual manhood crowns with glory this long continued process—then it is evident that there has been

---

* I. Peter iii: 18.

† See the chapters in "The Gospel" on General Salvation, where this idea is treated at some length.

no "fall," such as the revelations of God speak of; and if there was no fall, there was no occasion for a Redeemer to make atonement for man, in order to reconcile him to God; then the mission of Jesus Christ was a myth, the coinage of idle brains, and Jesus himself was either mistaken, or one of the many impostors that have arisen to mock mankind with the hope of eternal life.

Such is the inevitable result of accepting the philosophy of evolution, after which all the world is now running—it is destructive of the grand central truth of all revelation; as well ancient as modern; as well the revelations given to Moses and the prophets, as those given to the apostles of the New Testament; as well those given in Asia, as those given in America; for the central truth of all revelation is the fall of man, and the redemption through the atonement of Jesus Christ. All things else contained in the revelations of God to man are subordinate and dependent for their strength and force upon this leading truth.

I am aware that there is a class of men who profess to be "Christian evolutionists," and who maintain that Christianity can be made to harmonize with the philosophy of evolution. But how are they made to harmonize? We are told that Jesus is still a Redeemer, but in this sense he gave out faultless moral precepts, and practiced them in his life; and inasmuch as people accept his doctrines and follow his example they will be redeemed from evil. But as to the fall of man and the atonement made for him by the Son of God—both ideas are of necessity rejected; which means, of course, denying the great fundamental truths of revelation; it is by destroying the basis on which the Christian religion rests, that the two theories are harmonized—if such a process can be called harmonization. It is on the same principle that the lion and the lamb harmonize, or lie down together—the lion eats the lamb.

It was stated in the first part of this writing that the follies of those who profess a belief in the theory of creation as revealed in the Bible, were largely responsible for the existence of the theory of evolution; that their exegesis of the revelations on the subject were so manifestly absurd, and contradicted so many well known and indisputable facts, that scientific men sought for other explanations of the origin of things. The theologians in the apostate churches of Christendom have maintained that God created the heavens and the earth—the universe—out of nothing, in six days. A statement than which it is impossible to conceive one more absurd, or one which contradicts more completely every fact demonstrated by the experience of man. Every sense, every possible conception of the mind bears witness that from nothing, nothing comes. The idea of creating the universe out of nothing, however, is rapidly passing away from the minds of the present generation; and it is conceded by many theologians that ther is no warrant for such a doctrine in the scriptures; but that it became generally accepted through a misconception of the meaning of the word create. "The meaning of this word," says Rev. Baden Powell, of Oxford University, "has been commonly associated with the idea of 'making out of nothing.' But when we come to inquire more precisely into the subject, we can of course satisfy ourselves as to the meaning only from an examination of the original phrase." The learned professor then proceeds to say that three distinct Hebrew verbs are in different places employed with reference to the same divine act, and may be translated respectively, "*create*," "*make*," "*form* or fashion." "Now," continues the professor, "though each of these has its shade of distinction, yet the best critics understand them as so nearly synonymous that, at least in regard to the idea of making out of nothing, little or no foundation for that doctrine can be obtained from the first of these words." And, of course if no foundation for the doctrine can be obtained from the first of these words—viz., the verb translated create; then the chances are still less for there being any foundation for the doctrine in the verb translated, "made," "formed" or "fashioned."

This is in harmony, too, with the teachings

of the Prophet Joseph Smith. He says "You ask the learned doctors why they say the world was made out of nothing; and they will answer, 'Don't the Bible say he *created* the world? and they infer, from the word *create* that it must have been made out of nothing. Now the word *create* came from the word *baurau*, which does not mean to create out of nothing; it means to organize, the same as man would organize materials and build a ship. Hence we infer that God had materials to organize the world out of chaos—chaotic matter, which is element, and in which dwells all the glory. Element had an existence from the time he [God] had."*

Professor Baden Powell further says, "The idea of 'creation' as meaning absolutely 'making out of nothing,' or calling into existence that which did not exist before, in the strictest sense of the term, is not a doctrine of scripture; but it has been held by many on the grounds of natural theology, as enhancing the ideas we form of the divine power, and more especially since the contrary must imply the belief in the eternity and self existence of matter."† Theologians have held, generally, that to admit the doctrine of the eternity and self existence of matter detracted from the perfection of Deity, though how that can appear is difficult to comprehend.

---

*Journal of Discourses, Vol. vi: p. 6.
†Kitto's Biblical Literature, Art. Creation.

Not only have so-called theologians been compelled to renounce the unphilosophical idea that the universe was created out of nothing; but they also have to admit that there are indisputable evidences of the earth having a greater antiquity than their interpretations of the word of God allow. That is, the earth itself bears in its own bosom the evidence that it is more than six thousand years old. And though it may turn out, on further investigation, that some of the claims of geology are extremely absurd; owing to the fact, perhaps, that the founders of that science have not considered sufficiently the effect of conditions not now existing and forces not now in operation, but which doubtless existed and operated in the earlier ages of our earth's existence—yet when extremely liberal allowances for all these things are made, the indisputable evidence adduced from the science of geology is sufficient to establish the statement that the earth is more than six thousand years old; and it might be added also that from the same source it is evident that the earth was not created or organized from pre-existing element in six days of twenty-four hours duration.

These facts which geology unquestionably demonstrates have thrown sectarian theologians into dismay. The dogmas concerning the creation formulated with so much pomp and circumstance by the apostate churches of Christendom, respectable only for their antiquity, are going to pieces before the facts discovered by geologists and churchmen, or theologians, call them which you will, are filled with alarm lest all confidence be lost in revelation; and many of them are making frantic efforts to harmonize the facts of revelation with the facts of science. Unfortunately, however, some of these proceed on lines which result the same as the efforts of some to harmonize the theory of evolution with the gospel—as the latter efforts end in the destruction of the gospel, so the former end in denying the inspiration of scripture, in relegating it to the realms of poetry, which means kicking it contemptuously out of the domains of fact, of history. "We affirm," say they, "that it cannot be history—it may be poetry."*

There is nothing in the Bible, however, which drives believers in revelation to those straights—straights in which they throw overboard, practically, the word of God; discard it, or, in other words, degrade it to the level of romance—making it nothing better than the idle coinage of the half frenzied brains of day-dreamers. If the dogmas of apostate Christendom respecting the creation were given over as a romance instead of the revelations of God, and those revelations

---

* Kitto's Biblical Literature, Vol. I., p. 486. Such also were the views of the late Henry Ward Beecher, and in fact all of his school, which I am sorry to say is rapidly increasing in numbers, both in the United States and England. For the continental countries I cannot speak.

were re-examined, and especially if re-examined under the inspiration of the Holy Ghost, it would then be found that there is nothing in the scriptures requiring the believer in revelation to accept the idea of recent or instantaneous creation of the earth. There is no more warrant in the Bible for the doctrine that the earth was begun and completed—created—about six thousand years ago, and that instantly, at the word of God, than there is that it was made out of nothing. On the other hand there is very much to lead one to believe the contrary.

Six thousand years ago our earth reached that degree of perfection that it was fitted for the abode of man; and it is interesting to note, in this connection, that geologists have found no evidence of the existence of man on the earth only in the strata of the earth's crust belonging to the latest geological periods, and most probably only in those made within the period of history. But while the Bible may teach that it was only about six thousand years since man was placed upon the earth, how long the period of formation lasted previous to that time, how long it required to prepare this planet with all its wealth of fruits and vegetables and animal life, for the abode of man, is not known. "It is called in the scriptures," says Apostle Orson Pratt,

"Six days; but we do not know the meaning of the scriptural term 'day.' It evidently does not mean such days as we are now acquainted with—days governed by the rotation of the earth on its axis, and by the shining of the great central luminary of our solar system. A day of twenty-four hours is not the kind of day referred to in the scriptural account of the creation; the word 'day' in the scriptures seems often to refer to some indefinite period of time. The Lord, in speaking to Adam in the garden says, 'In the day thou eatest thereof thou shalt surely die;' yet he did not die within twenty-four hours after he had eaten the forbidden fruit; but he lived to be almost a thousand years old, from which we learn that the word 'day' in this paragraph, had no reference to days of the same duration as ours. Again it is written, in the second chapter of Genesis, 'In the *day* that he created the heavens and the earth;'* not six days, but 'in the day' that he did it, incorporating all the six days into one, and calling that period 'the day' that he created the heavens and the earth.†"

As a further evidence that "day" as used in connection with the acts of creation does not mean a period of duration of twenty-four hours, it may be mentioned that it was not until the period called the fourth day that the sun reflected his light upon our earth and ruled the day; and divided the light from the darkness, giving us the day and night regulated by the rotation of

---

* These are the generations of the heaven and of the earth when they were created, in the day that the Lord God made the earth and the heavens. Genesis ii : 4.

† Journal of Discourses, Vol. xiv : p. 234-5.

the earth upon its axis; so that the preceding three days were not of twenty-four hours duration, but certainly referred to some other division of time, which was also, doubtless, employed throughout in speaking of these acts of creation.*

Moreover, it is said in this first chapter of Genesis,

"In the beginning God created the heaven and the earth.

"And the earth was without form and void; and darkness was upon the face of the deep."†

How long it remained in that condition before

---

* Respecting this creation of the sun as referred to in the above, Apostle Orson Pratt has made some remarks at once ingenious and instructive, he says:

" What I understand by the formation [creation] of these celestial luminaries, is that He [God] then caused them to shed forth their light [that is upon the earth.] I cannot suppose that it would take the Lord six days to form such a little speck of a world as ours, and then for Him on the fourth to form a globe fourteen hundred thousand times larger than the earth. This does not look consistent to me. If it took six days to form a small world like ours, we might certainly suppose that it would require more than one day to form the sun, which contains a quantity of matter sufficient to make some three hundred and fifty four thousand worlds like this, and whose actual size or magnitude is fourteen thousand times larger than our globe; consequently I understand by the formation of the sun and moon and stars, and setting them in the firmament of the heavens, that He merely suffered their light to shine on the fourth day, to regulate the evenings and mornings, that were produced prior to that time, probably by some other cause. The Lord wanted by these luminaries to divide the day from the night, and he set them for times and seasons in the firmament of the heavens." *Journal of Discourses*, Vol. xvi : pp. 316-7.

† Genesis i : 1, 2.

the Spirit of God moved upon the face of the waters, or the six great periods of creation began, it would be impossible to say, since we have no data in revelation to go upon; but the duration was doubtless sufficient to allow all the myriads of years claimed by geologists as necessary for the formation of our planet. Then how long those periods of time were which are called "days" in the Bilbe, is uncertain; but enough is known to justify us in the belief that they were great periods of time, in which the successive acts of creation occurred. In which continents were up-raised, and mountains were heaved up by volcanic eruption, exposed to warmth and light and covered with vegetation, and animal life, and then worn away by the combined action of the atmosphere and rains, much of their matter being carried back to old ocean's bed, and settling there as sediment, forming new strata of rocks, occasionally imbedding vegetables and animals which became fossilized; and these strata, being afterwards thrown up from the bottom of the ocean are exposed to view, and from what he there finds, the geologist conjectures at the condition of the earth and forms his judgment as to what animals and vegetation were then upon it—there was time for all this, let it be performed ever so slowly.

While the Bible account of the creation gives sufficient margin to allow all the time claimed by the geologists for that work, let their claims be ever so extravagant, still let geologists have some modesty about them and admit—as perforce they must—that they do not know that the same conditions existed, or the same forces operated in those long ages of the past that now exist and operate. Hence it is not unlikely that changes resulting in the advancement of the earth's formation, and in its preparation for the abode of man were much more rapid then than now. This is not begging the question, there is no need of that; but it is mentioned in passing, as pointing to a condition of things not unlikely to have existed.

III.

WHAT is most perplexing about the Bible narrative of this work of creation is that two accounts are given of it; and apparently there is an irreconcilable difference between them. In the first chapter of Genesis is a statement of the creation in respect to this earth and the heavens connected with it, from the time it was without form and void until it was a fit dwelling place for man: or, to put it in other words, the account seems to reach from highly attenuated nebulæ to the solid earth clothed with its wealth of vegetable and animal life, with man placed upon it as the crowning excellence of the Creator's work. But after this elaborate account of the creation contained in the first chapter of Genesis, we are startled to read in the second chapter—

"These are the generations of the heavens and of the earth when they were created, in the day that the Lord God made the earth and the heavens, and every plant of the field before it was in the earth, and every herb of the field before it grew: for the Lord God had not caused it to rain upon the earth, *and there was not a man to till the ground.*"

One naturally pauses here to ask, what had become of the grasses, herbs, and trees spoken of in the first chapter of Genesis? what of the fishes of the sea, the fowls of the air, the beasts of the field? what of man, male and female, of whose creation we have just read? and of the commandment to multiply and replenish the earth? Is it not strange that after reading of the creation of man in the first chapter that we should be told in the second that there was not a man to till the ground? Proceeding with this second account of creation the Bible says:

"But there went up a mist from the earth, and watered the whole face of the ground. And the Lord God formed man of the dust of the ground, and breathed into his nostrils the breath of life; and man became a living soul. And the Lord God planted a garden eastward in Eden; and there he put the man whom he had formed. And out of the ground made the Lord to grow every tree that is pleasant to the sight, and good for food. * * * And out of the ground the Lord God formed every beast of the field, and every fowl of the air; and brought them unto Adam to see what he would call them: and whatsoever Adam called every living thing that was the name thereof."

What is especially difficult in this second account of creation is that it reverses the order of that work as given in the first. The first account commences with the formation of the earth from chaotic matter and then records the various steps of progress in succinct and natural order—the same order, too, that science insists upon—up to perfection: the second begins with an account of the creation of man, the planting of a garden as the beginning of vegetable existence, and then the creation of the fowls of the air and the beasts of the fields.

The writings of Moses as revealed to Joseph Smith, in December, 1830, and now contained in the Pearl of Great Price, make this matter of the creation of man still more emphatic by saying:

"And I, the Lord God, formed man from the dust of the ground, and breathed into his nostrils the breath of life; and man became a living soul, *the first flesh upon the earth*, the first man also."

But if these writings of Moses make emphatic the apparent contradiction in these two accounts of creation, they also furnish the key by which the whole matter may be understood, and, as I think, explained. After giving an account of the creation, much as it is contained in the first chapter of Genesis, it is then stated—

"And behold I say unto you, these are the

generations of the heaven and of the earth, when they were created, in the day that I, the Lord God, made the heaven and the earth, and every plant of the field before it was in the earth, and every herb of the field before it grew. For I, the Lord God, created all things, of which I have spoken, spiritually, before they were naturally upon the face of the earth. For I, the Lord God, had not caused it to rain upon the face of the earth. And I, the Lord God, had created all the children of men; and not yet a man to till the ground; for in heaven created I them; and there was not yet flesh upon the earth; neither in the water, neither in the air; but I, the Lord God, spake, and there went up a mist from the earth, and watered the whole face of the ground. And I, the Lord God, formed man from the dust of the ground, and breathed into his nostrils the breath of life; and man became a living soul, the first flesh upon the earth, the first man also; nevertheless, all things were before created, but spiritually, were they created and made according to my word."*

As to the character of this spiritual creation nothing is known; nothing, so far as I know, has been revealed in relation to it. Here let me say, by way of caution, that those who accept the revelations of God as truth need not be alarmed or worried if they meet with things in the sacred writings that they cannot explain or understand, as in the case of this spiritual creation of the heavens and the earth which preceded the natural, or what we regard as the actual

---
* Pearl of Great Price, p. 6.

creation of the earth. In this and in all cases of like character we claim for those who accept the revelations of holy writ as facts, what Professor Huxley claims for those who build up theories on their conception of facts in nature, viz—"There is a wide difference between the thing you cannot explain and the thing which upsets your theory altogether." This idea is a pendulum which should swing just as high for the believer in revelation as for the scientist. Not that there is anything wrong with revelation, the difficulty arises from our inability to comprehend it; but when increased intelligence shall give us enlarged views and keener powers of penetration, we shall then find that the revelations of God are in strict accord with the facts in the case, and perfectly simple however incomprehensible they may have seemed to us in the day when we saw as through a glass darkly. But this is a digression.

Though we cannot understand the nature of this spiritual creation, yet to learn that the first account of the creation in the Bible is of a spiritual creation and the second of an actual or natural one, gives some comfort, from the fact that it does away with all charges of inconsistency or contradiction between the two accounts. For since they are descriptions of two different things instead of one thing, there is nothing in the law of consistency requiring the accounts of different events to be alike.

In these articles, however, what turns out to

be an account of the spiritual creation of the earth has been spoken of and treated as the natural or actual creation.* It has been treated so purposely, because I believe the natural in the order of its creation and development corresponds with the creation and development of the spiritual. Furthermore, I believe the account in the first chapter of Genesis could be safely accepted as the announcement of the general plan of creation, not only of our planet but of all worlds; and in it will be found ample scope for the belief that the earth came into existence by the accretion of nubulous matter; that it took thousands of years, yea, millions, perhaps, for the condensation and solidification of that matter; granting as long periods as geologists may demand for the formation of the earth's curst; that then followed the changes which were wrought during the six great periods named in Genesis; beginning with the production of light, and ending with placing man upon the completed planet as its lord and sovereign under God.

The careful reader of this paper will say, however, that the statements in the last paragraph permit all the old difficulties to surge back upon

---

*I do not wish in making this distinction between the spiritual and natural creation, and in using the word "actual" to be understood as implying that the spiritual creation was *not* an actual creation. It may have been just as tangible and actual as the creation on which we walk. I only use the expression to make a distinction between the natural and spiritual crea ions.

us; all the old apparent inconsistencies between the first and second accounts of creation in Genesis remain unreconciled. For if the natural creation of our planet corresponded to the spiritual creation of it, the spiritual standing in the same relationship to the natural as the well devised plan of the architect does to the actual erection of a building—then the account given of the spiritual creation of our earth may as well be regarded as the account of the actual creation of it also. But this leaves all the difficulties between the two accounts of creation in the Bible untouched, and we must look to other facts than those yet considered if we would see them removed.

The Prophet Joseph Smith is credited with having said that our planet was made up of the fragments of a planet which previously existed; some mighty convulsions disrupted that creation and made it desolate. Both its animal and vegetable life forms were destroyed. And when those convulsions ceased, and the rent earth was again consolidated, and it became desirable to replenish it, the work was begun by making a mist to rise that it might descend in gentle rain upon the barren earth, that it might again be fruitful. Then came one of the sons of God* to

---

* Lest any one should doubt that Adam was one of the sons of God, I call attention to the verse of Luke, iii chapter, where in tracing the genealogy of Jesus back to Adam, and coming to Cainan it goes on to say that "he (Cainan) was the son of Enos, which was the son of Seth, which was the son of Adam, which was the son of God."

the earth—Adam. A garden was planted in Eden and the man placed in it, and there the Lord brought to him every beast of the field and every fowl of the air, and Adam gave names to them all. Afterwards was brought to Adam his wife, whom, since she was derived from man, he named wo-man; and she became his help-mate, his companion and the mother of his children. In this nothing is hinted at about man being made from the dust, and woman manufactured from a rib, a story which has been a cause of much perplexity to religious people, and a source of much impious merriment to reckless unbelievers. We are informed that the Lord God made every plant of the field before it was in the earth, and every herb before it grew* on our planet. As vegetation was created or made to grow upon some older earth, and the seeds thereof or the plants themselves were brought to our earth and made to grow, so likewise man and his help-meet were brought from some other world to our own, to people it with their children. And though it is said that the "Lord God formed man of the dust of the ground"—it by no means follows that he was "formed" as one might form a brick, or from the dust of this earth. We are all "formed" of the dust of the ground, though instead of being moulded as a brick we are brought forth by the natural laws of procreation; so also was Adam

---

* Genesis ii: 4, 5.

and his wife in some older world. And as for the story of the rib, under it I believe the mystery of procreation is hidden.

Of the things I have spoken, this is the sum: There was a planet created on the plan of the spiritual creation described in the first chapter of Genesis; beginning with the condensation of nubulous matter to a "fire ball," then the cooling of the surface and thickening of the earth's crust, and the envelopment of it in water; then came light, and by internal eruptions portions of land were thrown above the surface of the water —"the dry land appeared;" then came the simpler forms of vegetation; then the sunlight visited the earth, and doubtless higher forms of vegetation, fruit-trees and flowers and grains were brought forth; then came the creatures that abound in the ocean, that fly in the air, and the beasts of the earth. Not by the process of evolution, but by the various species suitable to the condition of the earth's development being brought from some other and older sphere, with power to propagate their kind, until the changed conditions of the earth became unfavorable to them, when they became extinct and were replaced by other species of a higher type. Then came the mighty convulsions which, for some cause or other, and doubtless for some wise purpose, disrupted that planet; and when from its fragments a new world—our present planet—was brought into existence, it was made the abode of man, as described in the second account of the creation in Genesis, which begins by placing man upon the earth, and then the inferior animals.

Accepting this statement of Joseph Smith relative to our planet in its present state being created or formed from the fragments of a planet which previously existed, one may readily understand how the supposed differences between scientists and believers in revelation have arisen. Scientists have been talking of the earth's strata that were formed in a previously existing planet; they have considered the fossilized flora and fauna imbedded in those strata, and have speculated as to the probable lapse of time since those animal and vegetable forms of life existed; and have generally concluded that the age is so far remote that there is no possible chance of harmonizing it with the account of the creation as given in the Bible. Believers in the Bible, on the other hand, have generally taken it for granted that the account of the creation in the sacred record, would give to the earth no greater antiquity than six thousand years; and have held that within that period the universe was created out of nothing by the volition of Deity—an idea so palpably absurd that intelligence, despite all church authority to the contrary, everywhere rejects it.

The theory set forth in this writing that before Adam was paced upon this earth to people it with his offspring, the matter of which it is composed existed in another panet, which by some mighty convulsions was broken up, and from its ruins was formed our present earth, at once affords a means of harmonizing those facts established by the researches of men and the facts of revelation. If scientists shall claim that myriads of years or of centuries must have been necessary to form the earth's crust, it may be allowed by the believers in revelation, for there is nothing that would contradict that idea in the revelations of God on the subject. If scientists shall claim that the fossilized remains in the different strata of the earth's crust reveal the fact that in the earlier periods of the earth's existence only the simpler forms of vegetation and animal life are to be found, both forms of life becoming more complex and of higher type as the earth becomes older, until it is crowned with the presence of man—all that may be allowed. But that this gradation of animal and vegetable life owes its existence to the processs of evolution is denied. As before explained, the claims of evolution are contrary to all experience so far as man's knowledge extends. The great law of nature is that every plant, herb, fish, fowl, beast and man produces his kind; and though there may be slight variations from that law, those variations soon run out either by reverting to the original stock, or else by becoming incapable of producing offspring, and thus become extinct.*

Furthermore, since we have learned that God made "every plant of the field before it was in the earth, and every herb before it grew" (*i. e.* in our earth), the gradation of life forms which the naturalists discover in the various strata of the earth's crust may reasonably be accounted for

---

* Since beginning this writing I have found some remarks on the subject of evolution by the late President John Taylor, which cannot fail to be of interest to the student of the subject: " The Animal and vegetable creations are governed by certain laws, and are composed of certain elements peculiar to themselves. This applies to man, to beasts, fowls, fish and creeping things, to the insects and to all animated nature; each one possessing its own distinctive features; each requiring a specific sustenance, each having an organism and faculties governed by prescribed laws to perpetuate, its own kind. * * * These principles do not change, as represented by evolutionists of the Darwinian school, but the primitive organisms of all living beings exist in the same form as when they first received their impress from their Maker. There are, indeed, some very slight exceptions, for instance, the ass may mix with the mare and produce the mule; but there it ends; the violation of the laws of procreation receives a check, and its operations can go no further. Similar compounds may possibly be made by experimentalists in the vegetable and mineral kingdoms, but the original elements remain the same. Yet this is not the normal but an abnormal condition with them, as with animals, birds, etc., and if we take man he is said to have been made in the image of God, for the simple reason that he is the son of God; and being His son, he is, of course, his offspring, an emanation from God, in whose likeness we are told he is made. He did not originate from a chaotic mass of matter, moving or inert, but came forth possessing, in an embryotic state, all the faculties and powers of a God. And when he shall be perfected, and have progressed to maturity he will be like his father—a God, being indeed his offspring. As the horse, the ox, the sheep and every living creature, including man, propagates its own species and perpetuates its own kind, so does God perpetuate His.—Mediation and Atonement, pp. 164, 165.

aside from the theory of evolution—viz., by the animal and vegetable life forms of some older earth being brought to our own; different species being transplanted as changed conditions in the soil and atmosphere and temperature of our earth rendered it favorable to their production, the older species becoming extinct as the changed conditions of the earth became unfavorable to them.

Then too, the theory advanced in this writing gives ample room for the reconciliation of another serious difficulty between the scientist and the believer in revelation. To the latter Adam is the first man; the former maintains that there are evidences which prove the earth to have been inhabited before Adam's time. Whether or not the planet which existed previous to our own, and out of the ruins of which our own was organized was inhabited by man as well as by vegetation and animals, I cannot say; all remarks on this subject would be conjecture merely. But if the researches of scientists prove beyond all question that there were pre-Adamic races, then doubtless they were inhabitants of that world which was destroyed, but the evidence of their existence as well as the evidence of the existence of animals and vegetation was preserved in the re-creation of that planet to form this earth. Though, in this connection, I must say that so far as I have examined the works of those who treat on the subject of pre-historic man, or pre-Adamic races, they have hung the heaviest weights on the slenderest of threads; and I am inclined to the opinion that Adam was the progenitor of all races of men whose remain have yet been found.

So much then for the different theories as to the origin of things pertaining to our earth; as to the beginning of the universe, that is beyond the scope of this inquiry, and may be dismissed by saying that it had no beginning. We conclude this part by quoting one of our hymns:*

> If you could hie to Kolob,†
> In the twinkling of an eye,
> And then continue onward,
> With the same speed to fly,
>
> D'ye think that you could ever,
> Through all eternity,
> Find out the generation
> Where Gods began to be?
>
> Or see the grand beginning,
> Where space did not extend?
> Or view the last creation,
> Where Gods and matter end?
>
> Methinks the Spirit whispers—
> No man has found "pure space,"
> Nor seen the outside curtains
> Where nothing has a place.
>
> The works of God continue,
> And worlds and lives abound;
> Improvement and progression
> Have one eternal round.

---

* L. D. S. Hymn Book, 252, 17 ed.

† A planet near the residence of God.—Book of Abraham, Pearl of Great Price, p. 30.

IV.

I think it must be evident to all who have looked upon the dead, that man is a dual being. Who that has stood by the bier of a friend, a parent, child or wife, and looked upon the lifeless form stretched upon it, but has felt that the being he loved has departed, that he is looking upon the casket merely that contained the jewel —the spirit. This truth forced upon man's consciousness in the presence of the dead is also sustained by the word of God, in which it is said —speaking of that mysterious change to which all flesh is subject, and which man calls death— "Then shall the dust return to the earth as it was; and the spirit shall return to God who gave it.*

It is my purpose to show in this writing, that this spirit of man existed before it was united with the body, that it is an emanation from Deity, and hence the relationship of Fatherhood on the part of God, and sonship on the part of man. It is written by the Apostle Paul that, "God who at sundry times and in divers manners spake in times past unto the fathers, by the prophets, hath in these last days spoken unto us by His Son, whom he hath appointed heir of all things, *by whom also he made the worlds.*† The palpable meaning of this passage is that God employed the spirit of Jesus Christ in creating worlds—not one world only, but doubtless many.

---

* Ecclesiastes xii: 7   † Hebrews i: 1, 2.

And if it was the spirit of Jesus which acted as God's agent in the creation of the worlds, there can be no doubt as to the spirit of Jesus having an existence before it was tabernacled in the body born of the virgin Mary.

Nor is the above passage of scripture the only one which sustains the fact of the existence of the spirit of Jesus Christ previous to its union with the body. There are many expressions which fell from the lips of our Lord himself that prove the fact. When some of his disciples murmured at certain doctrines he had been teaching them, he exclaims—"Doth this offend you? what and if ye shall see the Son of Man ascend up where he was before?"*—doubtless referring to the place he occupied in the mansions of his Father before the creation of the earth.

Again, just previous to his betrayal, in his prayer in Gethsemane, he said to his Father, "I have glorified thee on the earth, I have finished the work which thou gavest me to do. And now, O Father, glorify thou me with thine own self, even with the glory which I had with thee before the world was."† No more direct allusion to his pre-existence could be given than this; and from it we learn that such existence extended back to a period previous to the creation of the earth we inhabit.

To all appearances Jesus was as other men in

---

*John vi: 61, 62. †John, xvii.

his physical organism. He was born of woman; nourished in the same manner and with the same food; subject to heat and cold, hunger and thirst and weariness. He was pre-eminently the man of sorrows, and more than other men subject to pain. In short he possessed all the organs, dimensions, passions and attributes of man; but in him the passions were refined and so nicely checked and balanced, and the attributes so developed and made subject to the will divine that he was a perfect man—a God! So nearly did he resemble other men that his countrymen, and especially his neighbors, failed to recognize God in him. And when he began his mission among them they said: "Whence hath this man this wisdom, and these mighty works? Is not this the carpenter's son? is not his mother called Mary? and his brethren, James and Joses, and Simon, and Judas? And his sisters are they not all with us? Whence then hath this man all these things? And he did not many mighty works there because of their unbelief."*

We may now turn our attention to the more immediate object of this writing—the relationship between man and Deity.

An important inference may be reasonably based upon this similarity between the Son of God and other men, viz: that if the spirit which inhabited the body of Jesus had an existence

---

* Matt. xiii, 64-58.

before it dwelt in the flesh, is it not possible, and, rather is it not probable, that the spirits of other men, or of all men, also existed before they were born into the world? Since Jesus was so much like his brethren in the many respects noted, it requires no great effort to believe that they resemble him in this particular matter of the pre-existence of their spirits.

The question, however, rests upon stronger grounds than mere inference. The Lord said to Job:

"Where wast thou when I laid the foundation of the earth? declare if thou hast understanding. * * * Who laid the cornerstone thereof, when the morning stars sang together and all the Sons of God shouted for joy?"*

From this scripture one thing is certainly evident, viz: that before the creation of this earth—before the foundation was laid or the measuring line stretched upon it, there were "Sons of God" in existence; and they shouted for joy; perhaps it was at the prospect of the creation of the earth we inhabit that they shouted. And since it was the spirit of Jesus Christ under the direction of God the Father which created the worlds, it is but reasonable to suppose that he was present on that occasion, and may not they have been where the spirit of Job was also?

This doctrine of the pre-existence of spirits

---

* Job xxxviii, 2-7.

makes another scripture clear: "Before I formed thee in the belly I knew thee," said the Lord to Jeremiah; "and before thou camest forth out of the womb I sanctified thee, and I ordained thee to be a prophet unto the nations."* It was the spirit of Jeremiah which the Lord knew; which, in common with the spirit of Jesus, of Job, of Adam, and, in short, of all men,† dwelt in the presence of God; and as the spirit of Jeremiah possessed those peculiar characteristics which are favorable to the exercise of prophetic powers, the Lord foreordained him to be a prophet unto the nations.

In the revelations which the Lord gave to Abraham it is said:

"Now the Lord had shown unto me, Abraham, the intelligences that were organized before the world was; and among these were many of the noble and great ones; and God saw that these were good; and he said, these I will make my rulers; for he stood among those that were spirits, and he saw that they were good; and he said unto me, Abraham, thou art one of them, thou wast chosen before thou wast born."‡

This scripture not only proves the pre-existence of the spirits of men, but gives us to understand that some were more highly developed than

---

* Jeremiah i, 5.

† At the first organization in heaven we were all present, and saw the Savior chosen and appointed and the plan of salvation made, and we sanctioned it.—*Joseph Smith.*

‡ Pearl of Great Price, p. 32.

others, were more noble, and hence set apart for special labors, some to be rulers; others, as in the case of Jeremiah, to be prophets, each one in the mighty multitude being assigned to the particular sphere, and given to the particular privileges that his state of development and degree of faithfulness entitled him to receive.

From the scriptures we learn that at one time there was war in heaven:

"And there was war in heaven: Michael and his angels fought, and the dragon fought and his angels. * * * And the great dragon was cast out, that old serpent called the Devil and Satan, which deceiveth the whole world; he was cast out into the earth, and his angels were cast out with him."*

To this also agrees the testimony of Jude:

"And the angels who kept not their first estate but left their own habitation, he hath reserved in everlasting chains under darkness unto the judgment of the great day."†

I have called attention to those passages to prove that there were some spirits who dwelt with God, so wicked and rebellious, that they had to be cast out of heaven, and became the devil and his angels; as well as some who had developed such nobility of character, that God had set them apart or ordained them to be his rulers. Between these two extremes of good and bad, obedient and rebellious were, I doubt not,

---

* Rev. xii.   † Jude 6.

all degrees of faithfulness and nobility of conduct; and I hazard the opinion that the amount and kind of development in that pre-existent state influences the character in this life, and brings within reach privileges and blessings commensurate with their faithfulness in the spirit world. Yet, I would not be understood as holding the opinion that those born to wealth and ease, whose lives appear to be an unbroken round of pleasure and happiness, must therefore have been spirits in their first estate that were very highly developed in refinement, and very valiant for God and his Christ. Regarding this present state of existence, where as a sphere man is sent to obtain an experience and further develop the intelligence within him, and obtain a knowledge of good and evil, from seeing them in contrast and contact with each other—I hold that that condition in life which is calculated to give the widest experience to man, is the one most to be desired, and he who obtains it is the most favored of God.

One step more in this digression in order that I may state further that I believe it consistent with right reason to say that some of the lowliest walks in life, the paths which lead into the deepest valleys of sorrow and up the most rugged steeps of adversity, are the ones which, if a man travel in, will best accomplish the object of his existence in this world. The stream that leaps over cliffs of rocks, thence goes tumbling down through some canyon's rugged defile, then divides into babbling brooks, now coquetting with the sunbeams or dancing in the sheen of the moon, then stealing into the shade as it meanders through the meadows, and then quickening its speed makes a final rush down a rocky declivity into the ocean—keeps its waters pure; while the stagnant pool is overgrown with sedges; is a place for toads to knot and gender in; breeds miasmata and infests the air with disease germs; its water is impure and it is altogether unlovely and undesirable. So it is with the life of man. The conditions which place men where they may always walk on the unbroken plain of prosperity and seek for nothing but their own pleasure, are not the best within the gift of God. For in such circumstances men soon drop into a position analogous to the stagnant pool; while those who have to contend with difficulties, brave dangers, endure disappointments, struggle with sorrows, eat the bread of adversity and drink the water of affliction, develop a moral and spiritual strength, together with a purity of life and character, unknown to the heirs of ease, and wealth, and pleasure. With the English bard, therefore, I believe

> Sweet are the uses of adversity!

And with the Scotch poet I would say that those events, usually regarded as misfortunes,

> Give the wit of age to youth;
>   They let us ken oursel';
> They make us see the naked truth,
>   The real guid and ill.
>
> Thou losses and crosses
>   Be lessons right severe,
> There's wit there, ye'll get there,
>   Ye'll find nae other where.

What the mountain gorge, the beatling crags, and steep declivities are to the stream—enabling it to dash on in its course and by its very motion purify itself—so are what we usually denominate adverse circumstances to the life of man—they are the means of development and of purification only—the pathway of fiery trials is the one ordained of God for his favored sons.

In proof of this I direct you to the lives of the saints and the prophets; but above all to the life of the Son of God himself! The life of the Prophet Joseph Smith is an illustration second only to that of Messiah. He was wont to say:

"I have waded in tribulation lip-deep; but every wave of adversity which has struck me, has only wafted me that much nearer to Deity."

"Envy and the wrath of man have been my common lot all the days of my life; and for what cause it seems mysterious, unless I was ordained from before the foundation of the world for some good end, or bad, as you may choose to call it. * * * It all has become as second nature to me, and I feel like Paul, to glory in tribulation, for to this day has the God of my fathers delivered me out of them all."

The Lord, while the prophet was a prisoner in Liberty Jail, said to him:

"If thou art called to pass through tribulation; if thou art in perils among false brethren; if thou art in perils among robbers; if thou art in perils by land or by sea; if thou art accused with all manner of false accusations; if thine enemies fall upon thee; if they tear thee from the society of thy father and thy mother, and brethren and sisters; and if with a drawn sword thine eneimes tear thee from the bosom of thy wife and of thine offspring * * * And if thou shouldst be cast into the pit, or into the hands of murderers, and sentence of death be passed upon thee; if thou be cast into the deep; if the billowing surge conspire against thee; if fierce winds become thine enemy; if the heavens gather blackness, and all the elements combine to hedge up the way; and above all, if the very jaws of hell shall gape open the mouth wide after thee, know thou, my son, that all these things shall give thee experience, *and shall be for thy good*. The Son of Man hath descended below them all; art thou greater than he? Therefore hold on thy way, and the priesthood shall remain with thee, for their [the wicked] bounds are set, they cannot pass. Thy days are known, and thy years shall not be numbered less; therefore, fear not what man can do, for God shall be with you for ever and ever."*

If all this affliction was for the "good" of one of the most favored of God's sons, is it not a

---

Doc. and Cov., Sec cxxii.

fair conclusion that the trials and adversities of the other sons of God are for their "good?"

Let us now consider the relationship existing between the spirits of men and God. Zechariah speaks of God as not only laying the foundation of the earth, but also as forming the spirit of man within him,* while the writer of the book of Hebrews alludes to Jesus as the *first* begotten† of God. The same writer also saith:

"We have had fathers of our flesh which corrected us, and we gave them reverence; shall we not much rather be in subjection to the Father of spirits and live?"‡

We now begin to see why Jesus taught his disciples to pray, "Our Father which art in heaven." The words "Our Father" are not meaningless, but express the relationship between God and man. And not in any mystical way either, but in reality, the relationship being as much a fact as that existing between any father and son on earth.

This relationship accounts for the interest of God in man; it explains why he is "mindful of him;" why all created things are made but for his use, to supply his necessities, to furnish him with comforts, or afford him the means of experience and education. It makes us understand why such a gulf exists between man and the rest of the animal creation—man is the offspring of

---
*Zech. xii: 1.   †Heb. i: 6   ‡Heb. xii

Deity and inherits his Father's attributes. It is true those attributes are undeveloped; and often distorted even from that degree of perfection it is possible for them to arrive at in this state of existence; but that they exist in man is beyond all question.

The relationship between God and man also enables us to understand how it is that God permitted such an atonement as the crucifixion of Jesus Christ to be made for his redemption. Among men may be seen how strong are the paternal feelings; but how much stronger and perfect they are in God than in man is manifest in this, that "God so loved the world that he gave his only begotten Son, that whosoever believeth in him should not perish but have everlasting life."*

Following as a consequence of the fatherhood of God is the brotherhood of man. And since Jesus Christ is the first begotten in the spirit world (and the "only begotten" of the Father in the flesh) it follows that he is our elder brother; a relationship which accounts for his willingness to make the great atonement which brings life and immortality within the reach of his brethren.

God and Christ, then, are by no means beings afar off that man may not know. Nor does God look upon mankind as worms or worthless things. On the contrary they are his offspring.

---

*John iii: 16.

He regards them with all the affection of a loving father—

> He sees their hopes he knows their fear,
> And looks and loves his image there!

He delights not in their destruction, but would have all men to be saved; and for that purpose has established the gospel.

I point out this noble relationship of man to Deity, not to flatter the former, but because I believe it to be a fact. It is a theme I love to contemplate, not because it debases Deity, but because it elevates man, and must inspire him with noble aspirations, and to the performance of virtuous deeds. If but once understood and realized by mankind, I believe the conception would be a strong incentive to the reformation of the world; as it at once explains many things which have been regarded as mysterious, and explodes many of the absurdities which have crept into the men-invented systems of theology. Furthermore it brings man so near to Deity that like their Elder Brother—being in the form of God—being the children of God—they may think as Christ did, that it is no robbery to be equal with God,* and may labor with worthy ambition to that end. Heirs of God they are, even joint heirs with Jesus Christ, if they obey the gospel of the Son of God; and they have the assurance of holy writ that when he shall appear they shall be like him.†

---

* Phil. ii: 1-8.   † I. John iii: 2

www.ingramcontent.com/pod-product-compliance
Lightning Source LLC
Chambersburg PA
CBHW021943240426
43668CB00037B/490